CLASSIC CRIME SERIES

THE ROYAL BACCARAT SCANDAL

by

The Rt. Hon. Michael Havers
Edward Grayson and Peter Shankland

SOUVENIR PRESS

Contents

List of Illustrations

Authors' Note to the First Edition

In this book there are many passages of biographical material about King Edward VII when he was the Prince of Wales, because without him the developments of the Tranby Croft house party would not have occurred. But it is important for the reader to appreciate that this material is highly selective. It is concerned only with those episodes in his life that, in our view, influenced, consciously or sub-consciously, the behaviour of those connected with him in the Baccarat case. The material is therefore not to be interpreted as offering a thumb-nail biography, but only as a summary of those scandals with which the Prince's name, justifiably or unjustifiably, was linked. For example, the Lord Beresford incident of 1891 is outlined because it is, within months, contemporaneous with Tranby Croft and it discloses the attitude of mind of Sir Edward Clarke, Solicitor-General and Gordon-Cumming's leading counsel, towards the Prince's involvement in private scandals. It should not be inferred that such episodes constituted the main elements of the Prince's life, and for an all-round view there are many biographies to which the reader should refer. In particular we whole-heartedly recommend Sir Philip Magnus's excellent *King Edward the Seventh* (although, incidentally, our researches have led us to dissent from his conclusions about the Tranby Croft affair).

Authors' Note to the Second Edition

Since this book was published in 1977 the law has remained the same.

On reflection, we feel we did not place sufficient emphasis upon the fact that the alleged slander was an allegation of a criminal offence and that the Lord Chief Justice Lord Coleridge failed even to mention to the jury that this required the burden of proof to be discharged on the basis of beyond reasonable doubt (now a very successful play).

What has happened since 1977 is the *Archer v Star* libel action.

We are now satisfied that if the Baccarat case had been heard in 1987 Gordon-Cumming would have won.

It only remains for us to express our great gratitude to Peter Carter-Ruck and Ernest Hecht without whom this second round of the Baccarat case would not have happened.

Acknowledgements

We wish to offer our thanks to Her Majesty the Queen for so graciously permitting us to consult the files in the archives at Windsor so that no shred of evidence which might help in establishing the truth about the Baccarat Case should be overlooked. We have also to thank the Royal Librarian, Sir Robin Mackworth-Young, KCVO, for his interest and useful suggestions, and two members of his staff, the Assistant Registrar Miss Elizabeth Cuthbert, and Miss Dimond.

The staffs of the British Newspaper Library and the London Library have been of the greatest assistance to us. Of individuals who have helped us we wish to mention Mr David Shankland of Messrs. Lovell White and King, and Mr C.G. Maby, CBE, of Penningtons who provided information about Sir George Lewis, and also Miss H.W. Thompson, formerly principal of the Hull High School for girls for taking us round Tranby Croft. Thanks are also due to Councillor A.H. Cammidge, JP, Mr Donald A.H. Cox, Mr Peter Collinson, Miss Jill Crowther, Miss Margaret Simpson, Mr Tim Thompson, Mr D.W. Warran, Mr Maurice Webster and Mrs Hazel Willard.

We acknowledge our indebtedness to the following publishers and agents for allowing us to quote from published works: Constable & Co. Ltd., *(Notable Cross-examinations* by E.W. Fordham); W.H. Allen & Co. Ltd., *(My Life and Loves* by Frank Harris); The Bodley Head *(Reminiscences and Reflections* by Heber L. Hart); Evans Brothers Ltd., *(My Memories of Six Reigns* by Her Highness Princess Marie Louise); Hutchinson's Publishing Group Ltd., *(Life's Ebb and Flow* and *Afterthoughts* by Frances, Countess of Warwick, and *Edwardians in Love* by Anita Leslie); Jonathan Cape Ltd., *(Youth is a Blunder* and *Winter is in July* by Elma Napier); Curtis Brown Ltd., *(Their Good Names* by H. Montgomery Hyde); Routledge & Kegan Paul, *(Hoyle's Games Modernised* (1742), 20th edition revised by Lawrence H. Dawson); William Hill (Football) Ltd., *(The Hill Story* by the William Hill Organisation).

CHAPTER ONE

The Wilsons of Hull

The rise to fame and fortune of an obscure family, proverbially achieved in two generations and declining in the third, was a phenomenon of the industrial revolution, but no family rose more spectacularly than the Wilsons of Hull. The founder of their fortune, Thomas Wilson, was a small keelowner who lived in a time of change and was quick to take advantage of it : he built steamers while others still believed in the future of sail, and was thus admirably placed to handle the rapidly expanding exports from the industrial north, and also the imports of wheat, timber and general cargoes required by a population crowding in from the agricultural areas to the towns and factories.

When his two sons joined him, Charles and Arthur, the firm prospered exceedingly : it soon grew large enough to offer through rates to traders who had formerly been accustomed to consign their goods to be trans-shipped, perhaps several times, before they reached their destinations. Competitors were bought up, or run out of business, dock companies and railways competed eagerly for their custom.By the 1880's, after their father's death, the brothers owned over fifty vessels, all having green hulls and red and black funnels : Messrs Thomas Wilson Sons & Co, had become the world's largest private ship-owners. Their motto was 'Business first and everything else afterwards.' Two million pounds, it was rumoured, they divided between them in a single year.

As employers the brothers were respected : even Samuel Plimsoll in his violent campaign against shipowners who risked the lives of their crews by neglecting safety precautions, had a good word for them. They had few labour troubles. They took an interest in local government, they made munificent gifts to local institutions, they looked after their employees. Great deference was shown to them because of their wealth : when Arthur Wilson's term of office as Sheriff expired, the Mayor of Hull, so it is reported, burst into tears while making a speech detailing the benefits the brothers had showered upon the town. But they were unmoved by flattery : if anyone opposed their plans, or if they were involved in an industrial dispute, they would say, 'We'll take our ships away, and where will Hull be then?' No one took this seriously. Their interests were too closely interwoven with those of the town for them ever to separate, though some would have liked to see the monopoly broken and business more evenly distributed. The only change they made was to form themselves into a public company, keeping most of the shares in the family.[1]

In medieval times, when business was controlled by the guilds, successful merchants would build fine houses within the town, live in them, and so remain part of the community; but during the industrial revolution when the towns grew larger, more overcrowded and pestilential, and when women began to have a say in where the family should live, it was only natural that the merchants who could afford it should move out and build houses in the unspoiled countryside which could easily be reached by horse or carriage from their places of business.

Country house life was already well established in England as in the rest of Europe – it was the ideal of the Roman Villa, the Renaissance Garden, the chateaux on the Loire : it was certainly a pleasant way of life and had many advantages for those who could afford it. The merchants with their newly acquired wealth came into contact with the old landed aristocracy with their great estates, their sports, their agricultural interests, their stud farms, their old gardens, their collections of *objets d'art*. It was a very exclusive aristocracy at times, but the balance of the underlying economy was being disturbed because profits from agriculture were declining whereas profits from commercial enterprise were frequently very large indeed.

The owners of the country houses spent a great deal of time visiting and entertaining each other. Sometimes the gatherings had a political bias, and women were able to exercise their influence through friendships with leading statesmen, sometimes they reflected the artistic tastes of the host and hostess. Nothing was expected of guests except that the women should behave with modesty and decorum, and be perfectly virtuous – at least in the eyes of the world – and that the men should behave as gentlemen : whatever they did must not only be correct but done gracefully.

Sometimes, particularly in Scotland, the household was run on more religious lines. Every morning the staff trooped in to the dining-room, or morning-room, neatly dressed and each carrying a hymn book. Then the master of the house would read a chapter from the Bible to the staff and the assembled family, and recite a long improvised prayer, and then lead a hymn or a psalm, before the guests were permitted to enjoy the succulent breakfast dishes already sizzling on a long row of hot-plates. Then, if it was a Sunday, guests and family would depart in a long parade of carriages to the local church for an interminable sermon, to be followed again by evening prayers – but for the rest of the week, pleasant, though seemly, recreation was permitted.

Charles Wilson established himself in a country house near Warter Priory, and went into Parliament as Liberal member for West Hull. Arthur Wilson called himself a Unionist, but he had no great interest in party politics, and there was no perceptible difference between his views and those of his brother : the style of his oratory when he spoke at meetings has been likened to that of a gentleman presiding at a farmers' dinner.

He married the daughter of a postmaster of Leeds and built a mansion for her, well away from the town in the district of Tranby. He called it Tranby Croft. Because she knew how to entertain and loved society, he also bought a house in London, 17 Grosvenor Square, where, a journalist reported, you could sit on a sofa that had cost £1,000 and look at cut flowers that had cost £1,500 – possibly a slight exaggeration, about the flowers anyway ![2]

The pattern of life in the West End of London was as delightful as in the great country houses, so long as you could forget the condition of the great toiling masses in the East End who had made it possible : most of the highly privileged people in the upper classes managed fairly successfully to do this. The daily routine in the London Season – May, June and July – was a ride or a drive in Hyde Park in the morning where ladies in the daintiest of feminine attire and top-hatted gentlemen gathered to watch the seemingly endless parade of the smartest carriages and the best horses and horsemen in the kingdom.

Here one might see the famous *demi-mondaine*, Catherine Walters, 'the pretty breaker of horses' and of hearts in her close-fitting riding habit, managing her thoroughbred chestnuts with consummate skill under the approving eyes of the men about town; or, a true aristocrat, the fascinating Lady Brooke might come along, driving her phaeton – a light, open, four-wheeled carriage – with high-stepping bays, admiring friends crowding round her on horseback and on foot; followed, perhaps, by a lumbering but well-preserved coach from a forgotten age containing a fantastically dressed disapproving dowager and her attendants.

Then there were luncheon engagements and a further visit to the park : this time the ladies and gentlemen of the inner circle of society would alight near Hyde Park Corner and sit on the little green chairs in rows, for it was not etiquette to handle the reins oneself in the afternoons : sometimes there would be a clatter of faster hooves as the royal carriage drove by with the Prince of Wales and Princess Alexandra, whose simple sweetness had captivated the Londoners, bowing to left and right : the men would stand up and raise their hats, the women would curtsy and then resume their animated conversations, for there were exciting evenings to be discussed – receptions at the great Mayfair houses, and waltzes to be danced to the swaying rhythm of diaphanous ball dresses of white tulle or chiffon with sparkling diamonds in the arms of adoring young men or officers of the Blues or the Lifeguards.

The aristocracy at that time were divided between the Court Set surrounding Queen Victoria, and the Marlborough House Set surrounding the Prince of Wales and Princess Alexandra. The Queen had withdrawn, since the death of her husband the Prince Consort in 1861, from the ceremonial parade of royalty before her loyal subjects, and therefore the Prince of Wales was kept busy presiding at official dinners, laying foundation stones, opening bazaars and welcoming foreign dignitaries : her neglect of this part of her duty infuriated Gladstone and other politicians and alienated a section of the press, but she steadfastly refused to attend ceremonies alone that she had once attended with her husband. In spite of this she retained the affections of the middle classes, whose influence was steadily increasing, and her picture, with or without the Prince Consort, had the place of honour in many a poor working man's house.

She excluded the Prince of Wales from any share in the burden of government; she neither trusted his ability nor relied upon his judgement. He carried out his routine duties punctiliously; but apart from this he seemed to live entirely for pleasure : the great hostesses vied with each other to provide him with sumptuous entertainment, broad acres were open to him for hunting and shooting, men were honoured and women were flattered by his attention, his affable manner made him popular with everyone with whom he came into contact.

The Queen's disappointment in her eldest son was perhaps inevitable as she could not help comparing him with his father whom she had adored. She had had every reason to do so. It would be difficult to find in the pages of history an example of a more perfectly virtuous prince than Albert of Saxe-Coburg; he was generous, high-minded, studious and cultured, a wise counsellor to the Queen. He had laboured unceasingly, unobtrusively behind the scenes, throughout his twenty years in England, to make the monarchy respected, to encourage the arts, to make the wealthy more conscious of their obligations to the poor, to set an example of virtuous living.

His further ambition was to educate his eldest son to follow worthily in his footsteps : there were anxious consultations between the parents and eminent men of the time, but in the end nothing seemed more likely to produce the desired result than the plan of the Prince Consort's own education. An old friend, the confidential adviser to the House of

Coburg, Baron Stockmar, was called in to advise on the curriculum, tutors of becoming gravity were engaged who could be relied upon to see that every hour of the young prince's life was usefully employed and that all possible distractions and temptations were removed from his path. A word of warning from the Queen's aging friend, Lord Melbourne, was disregarded : 'Be not over solicitous about education,' he wrote, '. . . it may mould and direct character, but it rarely alters it.'

Precisely for this reason the system, excellent no doubt in theory, had the opposite effect from what his parents had intended – the young man had not the same character as his father. Under the stern regime of constant study he became increasingly stubborn and rebellious, loathing books, detesting tutors, and showing a complete inability to learn anything of an improving nature.

When he was nearly fourteen he was taken for a short visit to Paris with his parents : the glamour of the Empress Eugénie and the fascinating women who surrounded her, the relaxed atmosphere of the court and its brilliance, the great attention that was paid to him personally, all delighted him. He begged, in vain, to be allowed to stay longer. It was a sudden glimpse of paradise.

His early attempts to break away from the rigid system that had been imposed upon him brought such crushing rebukes that he quickly learned his personal affairs would have to be managed with great discretion. When he was seventeen he was sent on an educational tour of Germany : his governor reported to his shocked parents that after dinner one evening he had kissed a pretty girl. Soon it was the talk of the town : 'The Prince's squalid little debauch,' Mr Gladstone called it.

At nineteen he had another glimpse of a different kind of life : he was sent on a good-will visit to Canada and the United States because the Prince Consort foresaw that the crown would be an essential link between the dominions and the mother country, and because he wished to promote Anglo-American friendship. It was a great success. The young prince showed an unexpected talent for getting on with people of all walks of life, and for making impromptu speeches. Except for one place in Ontario where there was an anti-Catholic demonstration because he had previously visited Quebec, he had a rapturous welcome wherever he went, and particularly in New York.

When he got home he was kept in seclusion while he studied for his military examinations. Then, in the summer of 1851, he was sent for a course of infantry training to Curragh Camp in Ireland : his obliging fellow officers smuggled a young actress, Nellie Clifden, into his bed. She felt greatly honoured, and talked too much. In the following November, just after his twentieth birthday, his parents heard about it – they were negotiating at the time for his marriage to Princess Alexandra of Schleswig-Holstein. He was at Cambridge, still pursuing his studies sequestered, of course, from the other students.

The Prince Consort investigated the stories of his son's behaviour at Curragh that were going the rounds of the London clubs, and when he could no longer doubt that they were true he took a special train, on 25th November, to Cambridge. It seems he forgave the contrite youth, who agreed to give up Nellie Clifden – apparently she had followed him to England – and they parted friends.

Immediately after this interview the Prince Consort became seriously ill : he himself put it down to sorrow and worry about his son's wicked ways, but actually he had typhoid though his doctors failed at first to diagnose it. A fortnight later he was dead. The heartbroken queen blamed 'the dreadful affair at Curragh' for his death, and it was long before the poor remorseful Prince of Wales, who was an affectionate son in spite of the divergence of his views, could see that the typhoid had had something to do with it as well.

When he married in 1863 and took up residence in Marlborough House, governors and tutors disappeared as if by magic and he could live exactly as he pleased, provided he didn't cause a scandal. With the revenues of the Duchy of Cornwall, accumulated during his minority, his parents had bought Sandringham for him, in Norfolk, with 7,000 acres because every gentleman in those days had to have a country estate. He established there the best partridge shooting in England. Life became an endless round of dinners, receptions, balls and country house parties with romantic interludes. In Princess Alexandra he had a beautiful and loving wife to look after his home and children : although he went his own way, he always admired and respected her, and she added grace to the ceremonies at which they appeared together.

Queen Victoria meanwhile continued to live in seclusion at Windsor, Balmoral, or Osborne House in the Isle of Wight. While the ladies of the Prince's fast Marlborough House Set wore immaculate riding-habits, tea-gowns, elaborate ball dresses or *negligée* as the occasion demanded, she sat in profound gloom, always in black with very full skirts, her bodice buttoned down the front, and with a square *décolletage* : her sleeves were wide, reaching to just below the elbow, and she wore a white widow's cap with long streamers. Her bracelets were gold chains from which hung lockets containing wisps of the hair of her children and grandchildren.[3]

She demanded the strictest morality and the most rigid observance of the rules of etiquette from her ladies-in-waiting, who were never allowed to sit down in her presence. Her moral standards imposed themselves on the Court Set, which was composed of her closest friends, and on the middle classes generally.

In spite of her seclusion she played a very active part in the country's political life : she kept in close touch with her cabinet ministers, worked indefatigably reading and commenting on the despatches that were brought to her every morning, corresponded with her many relations in the ruling families of Europe, and found time to send acid notes to her eldest son, chiding him for his behaviour. His requests to be allowed to see the despatches always met with a stern refusal : she said that to delegate any of her authority would be an act of disloyalty to her dead husband. To justify her refusal she exaggerated his supposed incompetence and lack of interest in serious subjects so constantly complained of by his tutors : her ministers encouraged her in this attitude, not wanting another royal personage giving his views and complicating affairs. It was no secret that his views were not identical with those of the Queen. His visits to Osborne House were sometimes painful ordeals, but with great tact he always avoided an open breach while at the same time refusing to discuss his choice of friends, his gambling, and his frequent attendance at race meetings.

For a year or two after his marriage he seems to have been satisfied with Princess Alexandra; then his thoughts began to stray to the many other fascinating women who might be his for the asking. He began rather carefully, first in France where he was accustomed to spend five or six weeks *en garçon* every spring : he was particularly happy among the actresses and *demi-mondaines* of Paris, and he formed a lasting liaison with the Princess de Sagan. At the same time he used his considerable diplomatic talents to work for a closer union between France and England, undeterred by the fact that Queen Victoria wanted friendship with Germany and until the Franco-Prussian War favoured Prussian domination of Europe.

At the end of the grouse shooting season he usually went for a 'cure' to Bad Homburg or Marienbad : these visits to Germany were sometimes marred by minor disagreements with his nephew Wilhelm who became Emperor in 1888 – but Wilhelm did please him on one occasion by appointing him Colonel of the 5th Pomeranian Hussars.

Although his liaisons on the Continent were handled with discretion he made no attempt to hide them. Reports on how he chose to live while abroad soon crossed the Channel, and aspiring ladies laid their plans accordingly : it soon became fashionable in high society to accord the Prince any favours he desired and for husbands to be complacent about it, while planning adventures of their own.

The Marlborough House Set naturally behaved as he did. Many a young matron, having provided her husband with a few children to secure the inheritance, began a new life of adventure and romance : for husbands it was a welcome change to be able to have affairs with women of their own class. There were certain very strict rules : the proprieties had to be observed; liaisons had to be tacitly accepted by all the parties concerned, and nothing was mentioned before the servants or the children. Country house parties favoured these unconventional arrangements where a discerning or conniving hostess allocated the bedrooms tactfully to suit the inclinations of her guests : she had to be aware of all that was going on, and invite those couples who wished to be together. The flavour of romance was an added attraction at these parties, and a welcome addition to a life of ease and comfort in which everything necessary was done by servants and in which everything was planned for amusement – shooting birds not required for food but as a test of skill, and riding to hounds instead of riding to work.

The Prince took pleasure in discussing his friends' affairs but the one unforgivable sin in his eyes was for anyone to cause a scandal, not only because of the painful experiences of his youth, but because sections of the community and of the press were always on the watch for an opportunity to criticise. The spicy stories that appeared from time to time, however, intrigued rather than offended the public, and when he took a beautiful woman of humble birth, Lillie Langtry, as his acknowledged mistress, it rather added to his popularity. Whatever Princess Alexandra may have felt, she added to her other graces the image of a faithful, patient, all-forgiving wife and mother : this pleased the public, both men and women, and assured for her the respect and friendship of the Prince.

As year after year passed he devoted himself more whole-heartedly to the pursuit of pleasure. He ruled his world of high society as autocratically as Queen Victoria ruled her establishment at Windsor or Osborne House. He never forgot that he was the Prince. Dress had to be correct and appropriate to the occasion, and every point of etiquette was punctiliously observed : no one who had been divorced, and no separated couples even if not divorced, could be invited to court. A host who absentmindedly asked him to ring for the butler, a gentleman who chaffed him when he missed a shot at billiards, a lady who tripped over her long train and fell on her face before him at a reception, were banished from his presence.

He broadened the basis of society by receiving into his circle of friends wealthy merchants, self-made businessmen, American heiresses, Jewish financiers and leading politicians, even those who opposed him in principle. Wealth was important to him, but charm and ability counted also. He loved the theatre, constantly attended performances and began the movement to make actors and actresses socially acceptable : but there were whole sections of the community that he practically ignored : he knew of the dreadful poverty in London and other cities, and he could be spontaneously generous when face to face with it, but, unlike his father, he was hardly aware of it as a vast human problem although Carlyle and Ruskin were crying out that it was a shameful blot on English life, and the works of the leading novelists, Dickens and Thackeray, were charged with social comment – but the Prince disliked authors and scarcely ever read a book. He studied the Radical newspapers but tended to look on their protests as potential threats to the constitution rather than as the expression of legitimate grievances. He had little time for lawyers : he understood that they were necessary in an ordered society, but he saw no reason why he should notice them : his close friend, Lady Brooke, wrote :

> The Prince had a horror of highbrows. As a class we did not like brains. . . .
> We acknowledged that it was necessary that pictures should be painted,
> books written, the law administered; we even acknowledged that there
> was a certain stratum whose job it might be to do these things. But we
> did not see why their achievements entitled them to our recognition. . . .[4]

There were very strong currents of republicanism, fostered by the theory that because France and the United States had become republics this was the modern trend and that Britain would inevitably follow : the theory was largely disproved when the Prince fell dangerously ill in 1871, the tenth anniversary of his father's death : the whole country showed its sympathy with the royal family and its solidarity behind the throne. Republicanism was still a potential threat, however, and the Prince was keenly aware of how important it was not to bring the monarchy into disrepute. An even greater threat was the powerful non-conformist religious movement whose adherents professed a harsh puritanical way of life and were extremely censorious of their neighbours.

It was really extraordinary that there were so few scandals. The first to affect him personally came upon him out of the blue at the beginning of 1870. It was caused by the total ignorance at the time about mental afflictions, and by the unwholesome avidness shown by the public to be shocked by revelations of how life was lived in high society. The plight of the beautiful young Harriett Mordaunt, aged only twenty-one, which today arouses only pity, provoked in her own time scorn and hatred. After the premature birth of a son she became obsessed by the idea that there was something wrong with it : a few days later the child developed an eye infection; she became hysterical, convinced that it was caused by inherited venereal disease; she sent for her husband and confessed that she had committed adultery with Lord Cole, Sir Frederick Johnstone and the Prince of Wales. The eye infection was quickly cured, and there was no trace of venereal disease either in mother or child, but the harm had been done.

Her husband, Sir Charles Mordaunt, forced her desk and took from it letters written to her by the Prince of Wales and other men. He began proceedings for divorce. The Prince had certainly visited her occasionally and sent her a valentine, but the letters were perfectly innocuous. Her family maintained that she was insane and unfit to plead : her husband's family maintained that she was shamming. Medical experts disagreed, so the judge ordinary, Lord Penzance, ruled that the question would have to be decided in the open court. By the time the case came up she was quite obviously insane, and had deteriorated physically to an extraordinary degree, but the legal point was whether she was insane when the writ was served on her.

The Prince was subpoenaed as a witness. Strenuous efforts were made by his friends to save him from the embarrassment of having to appear. The Queen wrote to the Lord Chancellor saying that the fact of the Prince's intimate acquaintance with a young married woman being publicly proclaimed would show an amount of imprudence that could not but damage him in the eyes of the middle and lower classes.

The Lord Chancellor, however, advised him not to raise any question of privilege, for the law was clear – the heir to the throne could be subpoenaed and forced to appear. Whenever the Prince was in trouble he consulted Mr George Lewis, the most famous solicitor of the day : the advice he gave was, 'Accept the summons. Go boldly into the witness-box – it is the only way to clear your name.'

He did so. He was examined by his own Counsel and denied categorically that he had committed adultery with Lady Mordaunt. The jury decided that she was insane, thus preventing Sir Charles Mordaunt from getting his divorce.

For ten days the case had entertained the London public with salacious stories of life in high places, and everyone was tragically the worse for it. In the eyes of the public the indiscretions of the Prince were magnified into crimes : for some weeks after his appearance in court he was hissed in the streets of London and greeted in the theatre with booing and cat-calls. At Ascot he had a bad reception when he drove up the course, but when a horse in which he was believed to have an interest won the last event, the crowd cheered him in the royal stand.

'You seem to be in a better temper now than you were this morning, damn you !' he told them, and the crowd laughed and cheered again.

It was a lesson not to be forgotten. A few months later, the Franco-Prussian war gave them something else to think about.

The next scandal, six years later in 1876, seemed at first to have little to do with him: in the course of a highly successful tour of India he was enjoying a tiger hunt in Nepal when to his camp in the jungle came a letter to the Earl of Aylesford, 'Sporting Joe Aylesford,' who was there as the Prince's personal guest: it was from his wife announcing that she was about to elope with Lord Blandford. This was precisely the sort of thing that the Prince disliked. He sent Sporting Joe home to deal with the situation. Unfortunately Joe's way of dealing with it was to stamp about London saying what he would do to Lord Blandford, who by this time had agreed with Lady Aylesford that they didn't want to elope and cause a scandal after all.

Then Lord Randolph Churchill took a hand in it – he was Lord Blandford's younger brother. He telegraphed to the Prince asking him to use his influence to prevent Sporting Joe suing for divorce. Receiving no reply, he went to Princess Alexandra and told her he had a bundle of letters written by the Prince to Lady Aylesford, and that if he didn't step in and stop the divorce the letters would be published and there would be such a scandal that he would never sit on the throne of England.

The Prince was at Malta on his way home when heard of this : he still refused to intervene, and he was so angry that he sent Lord Charles Beresford to Lord Randolph bearing a challenge to a duel : the reply was an insolent letter saying that the Prince was well aware that such a duel would be impossible.

In the event there was no divorce because the old Duke of Marlborough intervened – he was the father of Lord Blandford and of Randolph Churchill – to prevent the family name being dragged through the divorce court. This society scandal, therefore, did not become a public scandal. The Prince banned Lord and Lady Randolph Churchill from all court functions and let it be known that they were not to be invited anywhere : only two of their friends disobeyed this injunction.

By 1890 all this had receded into the past. Except for some trouble brewing with Lord Charles Beresford over Lady Brooke, the Prince's social horizon was reasonably clear and he was able to look forward with pleasurable anticipation to the St Leger week at the Doncaster Races, the great sporting event of the north of England.

Usually he stayed with an old friend, Christopher Sykes, at Brantingham Thorpe, but this was no longer possible : Sykes, from excess of loyalty, had spent more than he could afford in entertaining, and his home was now in the hands of creditors. Therefore the Prince graciously accepted an invitation from Mr and Mrs Arthur Wilson of Tranby Croft. He could perhaps have stayed more conveniently with the Duke and Duchess of Portland at Welbeck, but in pursuance of his policy of encouraging successful merchants and businessmen by his patronage and bringing them into society, he chose to accept the Wilsons' invitation although Tranby Croft was at some distance from Doncaster.

Mrs Wilson had been a success in London : she and her charming daughter, Ethel, had even caused a mild sensation by the style and originality of their clothes, so much so that it had become fashionable, for a short time, for ladies of the Marlborough House Set to order gowns from their dressmaker, Madame Clapham, in Hull.[5] But it was not only on account of their wealth, and of her social success, what the Prince wished to honour them : the Wilson brothers' ships and the efficient services they provided were an asset of considerable national importance, and they deserved to be recognised.

CHAPTER TWO

A Game of Baccarat

The most prominent names on Mrs Wilson's list of guests, after the Prince of Wales, were Lord and Lady Brooke: Lady Brooke was the ruling favourite; the Prince was deeply and emotionally attached to her. She was no mere passing fancy. Wherever he went he expected her to be invited also – with Lord Brooke, of course, who had his own diversions. Next on the list came the Earl and Countess of Coventry, then Lieutenant-General Owen Williams who commanded the Blues – the Household Cavalry: he had been the Prince's equerry on the Indian Tour and was the brother of the too romantic Lady Aylesford; then Lord Edward Somerset and his cousin Captain Arthur Somerset, Mr Reuben Sassoon, the sophisticated Jewish banker, Sub-Lieutenant Berkeley Levett, nephew of the Earl of Denbigh – he was a friend of the family – and a few more close friends of the Prince.

The family consisted of Mr and Mrs Arthur Wilson, their son Arthur Stanley Wilson (called Jack), their daughter Ethel with her husband Mr Lycett Green, son of a local manufacturer, an MP and Master of the York and Ainstey Foxhounds: the Greens, like some other successful industrialists, had hunted and shot their way into society.

Not on the original list of guests but included at the last minute at the Prince's request, was Sir William Gordon-Cumming, Lieutenant-Colonel in the Scots Guards. He had the reputation of being a gallant soldier, popular with his men because of his unflagging spirits under all circumstances. He had served with distinction in the Zulu War, having volunteered for this particularly hazardous service after the disaster to a British force at Isandlwana: he was the first man to enter Cetywayo's kraal when it was finally captured after the Battle of Ulundi. He served also in the Egyptian and Sudanese Campaigns and survived the desperate Battle of Abu Klea in the Gordon Relief Expedition when a British Square was broken by the Mahdi's fanatical tribesmen. In peace time he was an intrepid hunter of tigers, not from the comparative safety of an elephant's back, but by stalking them on foot through the jungle.

For the past twenty years His Royal Highness had honoured him with his friendship. He had a London house which he lent on occasion to the

Prince, 40,000 acres of beautiful but not very productive land in Scotland, an income of £60,000 a year, and he traced his descent through Charlemagne. He was also a relentless pursuer of young women and was said to be the handsomest and most arrogant man in London. He once said to Lady Churchill's sister Leonie who broke away from him in a lonely corridor, 'Silly little fool! All the young wives try me!' Whether this was strictly true or not, it reflected his reputation.

He had been once before to Tranby Croft and had known Ethel and her mother in London. His military record and his friendship with the Prince ensured that he was always treated with respect, though not always with affection.

The Marlborough House Set delighted to pass on to each other the latest examples of his arrogance: a gentleman whom he had just met for the first time came up to him and said how delighted he was to have made his acquaintance but might he just mention that his name was Gilette with the G soft as in gentleman? Gordon-Cumming replied, 'I thought it was hard, as in beggar.' It is not even certain that he said beggar. And then it seems that one day, having come off guard duty at Buckingham Palace, a physician who had attained his life's ambition and been summoned to one of the royal bedsides, asked him, 'Did you see my brougham at the palace gates?' 'No, really?' he replied, 'Is one of the servants ill?'

But it was not only the vain and the foolish who suffered from his outspoken comments. On meeting Lord Hartington, Postmaster-General in Gladstone's administration, he said, 'Harty-Tarty! When are you going to make Louisa an honest woman?' Louisa was the Duchess of Manchester, one of the wealthiest and most influential London hostesses. (Hartington eventually did so, when he had become Duke of Devonshire, after parting regretfully with Catherine Walters. He was the famous statesman who once dreamt he was making a speech in the House of Lords, and woke up to find that he was.)

There was another side to Gordon-Cumming's character, better known to the regiment and to his intimates than to society: he could be courteous and sympathetic when he wished to be. No doubt for this reason, and because he had first-hand knowledge of the campaign, he was chosen to convey the respects of the army to the exiled Empress Eugénie and to describe to her how her only son, the young Prince Napoleon who was serving as a volunteer with the British army, had died under the spears of the Zulus while on patrol near Ulundi.

Once Gordon-Cumming's family had owned half Scotland, but it had been on the decline ever since the death of his ancestor, the Red Comyn, by the hand of Robert the Bruce. It was typical of the Prince's policy of integrating the wealthy merchants with the old aristocracy, that he was bringing with him to enjoy the hospitality of the great shipowner, whose family had risen to prominence in two generations, the bearer of one of the oldest and proudest names in the country.

On Monday morning, 8th September, wearing frock-coat and top hat as smartly as if it had been a uniform, Gordon-Cumming waited at Kings Cross Station for the Prince who had honoured him with his friendship and whom he had been trained to serve. He was tall and very strong, his face deeply tanned from service and travel in Africa and India. Beside him stood a thin melancholy stooping figure, the elderly dandy, Christopher Sykes, called Seagull Sykes because he had once tried to introduce a private member's bill for the protection of seabirds; and also a young dandy, Berkeley Levett, reputed to be the best-dressed man in London : he was a subaltern in Gordon-Cumming's regiment, the Scots Guards, and he evidently regarded his senior officer with both respect and admiration. He was a rather nonchalant young man with a nose slightly reminiscent of the Duke of Wellington's.

When the Prince joined them, he told them that unfortunately Lady Brooke would be unable to join them owing to the death of her step-father, Lord Rosslyn, in Scotland. They moved along the platform attended by the station master, and boarded the old royal saloon attached to a special train that left at 12.30. The Prince now in his fiftieth year, had a broad handsome bearded face, and although he was rather short and thick-set he carried himself with dignity.

At about four o'clock they reached Hull where a large crowd had congregated on the platform. Here the royal party changed into another special train which left a quarter of an hour later and reached Hessle at five fifteen. Their host, Mr Arthur Wilson, was at the station to welcome them : he was a short compact figure with a round clean-shaven face and a plentiful crop of curly grey hair. He did not look at all like 'a man of the world'. It was difficult to imagine that he was a millionaire ship-owner entertaining the Prince of Wales. As Master of the Holderness Hunt he seemed more in character : his manner was simple, hearty and direct[1]

Open carriages were waiting for them. They passed under a triple arch garlanded with evergreens and flowers outside the station, and there were two arches farther on : one of these was in the grounds of Tranby Croft. The whole route was gay with flags and bunting.[2]

Whereas Gordon-Cumming's ancestral castle of Gordonstoun seemed to have grown out of the ground in the course of centuries, Tranby Croft looked as if it had been set down bright, new and complete, just as it had appeared on its architect's drawing board. Built in the Italianate style favoured by Queen Victoria and the Prince Consort for Osborne House, it was perhaps not beautiful but it was of convenient size to entertain a fair number of guests without being so large that the feeling of intimacy was destroyed. It was of white brick with stone dressings, and it had a carved stone entrance : it stood on rising ground with a pleasant view and it was approached by a carriage drive nearly a mile long through trees and shrubberies. The stables and a water-tower formed a hollow square to one side of the house and there were extensive gardens and greenhouses.

The staff were devoted to the Wilson family. Everything had been prepared to make the Prince's stay as pleasant as possible : the entrance-hall was adorned with busts of the royal family, and on the panelling of the dining-room there were four hundred carved cupids, each with a different expression. Dinner was served on heavy Georgian silver plates, the choice wines in fine glasses from Murano : large and generous hospitality was provided on the scale to which the Prince was accustomed.[3]

Mr Arthur Wilson was not much in evidence. He left the entertaining of his guests entirely in the hands of his very capable wife : he had what has been called 'the bluff unreadiness of speech of a typical country squire'.

After dinner on the first evening, that of 8th September, there was music in the drawing-room, the charming daughter of the house sang, and then there were recitations. At about eleven o'clock, at the Prince's desire, they began to play baccarat in the library : he had introduced the game from the Continent, and although by a High court ruling it had been declared illegal on the grounds that it was a game of chance rather than of skill, it was frequently played at fashionable house parties. The Prince, rather portly now and tired of dancing, was extremely fond of it : he always travelled with a set of baccarat counters, the gift of Sir Edward Hulse : they were made of leather of different patterns, colours and sizes, representing values of 5/- up to £10 and each one was engraved on the back with the Prince of Wales's feathers in gold. The game was not usually played at Tranby Croft because Mr Arthur Wilson wished to discourage his hot-headed sons, whom he thought did not understand the game, from playing for high stakes. Therefore there was no baccarat table. One had to be improvised by placing three small whist tables together and covering them with a tapestry cloth of variegated colours.

The Prince took the bank. He sat at the centre table which was rather higher than the other two. The guests crowded to the tables, some sitting to the right of the Prince and some to the left, while others stood around to watch. Among the latter was Christopher Sykes : having in his better days royally entertained, he was now a tolerated guest in one country house after another, the butt of the Prince's jokes when the Prince was in joking mood, always uncomplaining, always ready to say, 'as your Royal Highness pleases.'[4] Another onlooker was Ethel's husband, Lycett Green : sport was his main interest – he rarely touched a card. Having spent the day cub-hunting, he was tired and went to bed early.

Mr Reuben Sassoon took charge of the counters and issued to the players as many as they required, keeping an account of what each had received. The Prince and Gordon-Cumming explained to the beginners what they had to do. Drinks were brought, some of the gentlemen lit cigars, and the game began.

Baccarat is very simple. Four packs of cards, that is 208 cards altogether are shuffled and placed in front of the banker. He deals two cards to the player on his right, two to the player on his left, and takes two himself. The object of the players is to make up as nearly as possible the number nine, tens and court cards not counting – perhaps a three and a five, or a four and five : for this purpose they may each ask for another card but by doing so they may spoil the hand by exceeding the number nine, so it is customary to ask for another card only if the first two add up to five or less. Similarly the banker may also take another card, his decision depending partly on the amount of money that has been staked on one side and on the other. The rest of the players hold no cards but simply bet on those held by the players on either side of the banker.

In this case the bank's liability was limited to £100. As a seasoned player, Gordon-Cumming had a sheet of white paper before him upon which he marked by pencil dots each time the bank won and each time the players won, trying to match science against chance. There was some conversation with his neighbour, young Stanley Wilson, about the difficulty of distinguishing the counters against the tablecloth : Gordon-Cumming said, 'Let's put our stakes on the white paper,' and although the others did not, he proceeded to do this so that they could be very clearly seen.

Most of them were putting on small stakes, but he was playing rather a dashing game that attracted attention, usually wagering £5 for a coup, and up to £25 : his system, known as *coup de trois,* or sometimes as *masse en avant*, was to leave his stake on if he won the coup and add another £5 and also his winnings to it for the next coup : when he lost he handed his stake up to the croupier on this paper because the counters could not be raked in owing to the unevenness of the tables.

At the very beginning of the game, Stanley Wilson noticed a single bright red £5 counter on Gordon-Cumming's white sheet of paper : then his attention was distracted, and when he looked again there were three bright red counters on it. The cards were favourable, and Gordon-Cumming was paid £15. This aroused his suspicions.

Some time later he thought he saw Gordon-Cumming drop three red counters from his hands onto the white paper to add to his stake after the cards had been declared favourable : he whispered to his neighbour on the other side, Lieutenant Berkeley Levett, 'This is too hot ! The man next to me is cheating !'

'Impossible,' Levett replied.

'Well, look for yourself !'

Levett looked, and a few minutes later he agreed, 'This is too hot.'

They played for about an hour and a half, and when they had finished the Prince commented to Gordon-Cumming in a pleasant and friendly way that he had been lucky.

'Why, sir,' he replied, 'I could not help winning with such a tableau as this,' showing him the record he had kept on the piece of white paper.

The Prince had asked his hostess for a more convenient table to be provided for the following evening, so after the game was over Stanley Wilson ordered the butler to get a long table from the pantry and cover it with green baize. Then the two young men went to Levett's room.

Levett threw himself down across the bed and said, 'My God ! To think of it ! Lieutenant-Colonel Sir William Gordon-Cumming caught cheating at cards !'

Wilson asked, 'What are we going to do ?'

'For goodness sake, don't ask me,' he replied. 'He is in my regiment and was my own captain for a year and a half. What can I do ?'

Wilson decided, 'I know what I shall do, I shall have a talk with my brother-in-law in the morning.'

When he left Levett he went to his mother's dressing-room and told her what had happened. 'For goodness sake, don't let us have a scandal here,' she said and begged him to say nothing about it.

He consoled her by saying that he had ordered another table from the butler : 'I think, at any rate, that will stop him. He won't be able to cheat to-morrow night.'

On the following morning, Tuesday, 9th September, Stanley Wilson took a walk with his brother-in-law, Mr Lycett Green, along the carriage drive in front of the house and told him he had seen Gordon-Cumming cheating. Lycett Green was as astounded as Levett had been. He could not believe at first that a man whose position in society appeared to be unassailable, should have laid himself open to a charge of this kind, so he too replied, 'It is not possible!' Stanley assured him that he was quite certain and that Berkeley Levett had seen something also.

Later that morning the party set out for the races by special train from Hessle Station: the Prince invited several of them, including Gordon-Cumming, to travel with him in one of the saloon carriages. They alighted at Doncaster Cattle Dock Station and were driven in open landaus drawn by glistening chestnut horses to the Town Moor Course where an ample lunch was provided in the Wilsons' box in the Members' Grandstand.

The St Leger Week at the Doncaster Races was as popular in the North as Epsom Down and the Derby in the south; all classes crowded to see the sport. Fine ladies and gentlemen hobnobbed with jockeys and tipsters and mingled with working men and their families, entertainers and purveyors of refreshment – a cross-section of the community. They had the excitement of seeing the Prince's two-year-old filly 'Pierette' win the Clumber Stakes – a popular win. In the evening they returned to Tranby Croft, no suggestion having been made that reflected on the play of any member of the party.

After dinner the Prince again wished to play baccarat. He was shown a long narrow table covered with green baize that had been set up in the billiard-room between the billiard table and the fireplace: he drew a chalk line right round it, about six inches from the edge, behind which the players were supposed to keep their counters when not in play.

Before the guests passed from the drawing-room to the billiard-room, Stanley reminded his mother, 'It will be all right to-night because we have got a baccarat table with a chalk line on it.'

The Prince again took the bank. General Williams was croupier. When Gordon-Cumming came up to join the players there were only two seats left vacant, and whichever he chose he would be surrounded by the Wilson family. He took the chair next to Ethel Lycett Green – her husband had already told her on the previous night that he had cheated. Immediately opposite Gordon-Cumming, nose to nose, was Berkeley Levett. It was still not a regular baccarat table; it was too narrow – only three feet across – and the chalk line left so little room that it was difficult to keep the counters between it and the edge of the table. Lycett Green had told them he was going to watch Gordon-Cumming's play, and if he cheated again he would denounce him then and there: they were all agog to see what would happen.

After about half an hour Lycett Green thought he saw Gordon-

Cumming push a blue counter over the line : it aroused his suspicions, but none of the other watchers saw anything wrong. Then Gordon-Cumming staked a red £5 counter four inches beyond the line – Stanley Wilson thought he also pushed a £10 brown counter just over the line; just on the line Lycett Green thought.

The bank lost and had to pay. Gordon-Cumming said, 'There's another tenner, sir, to come here,' upon which the Prince said 'Give him another tenner, Owen,' and to Gordon-Cumming, 'I wish you would put your counters so that they can be seen better.' Ethel thought he pushed the counter forward as he was saying the £10 had not been paid. Then she thought he pushed a counter forward under a piece of paper.

Lycett Green felt convinced he had seen an act of cheating : he left the table and went into the adjoining smoking-room, wondering what to do. He sat down and wrote a note to his mother-in-law saying that Gordon-Cumming was a cheat and a scoundrel and that she ought to stop the game. He gave this note to the butler who delieverd it to Mrs Wilson. She glanced at it – and did not stop the game, but she immediately thought that she too saw an act of cheating – that Gordon-Cumming had pushed a counter over the line with the end of his pencil. Lycett Green returned to his place and went on playing for the rest of the evening. While Stanley Wilson was holding the cards he won five successive coups, winning money for himself, and more for Gordon-Cumming who was betting more heavily.

Next morning news came that Mrs Wilson's brother had died unexpectedly in Hull : it was suggested that they should all leave at once, but Mrs Wilson sent a message expressing the hope that the party would not break up. She happened to meet Gordon-Cumming on the stairs : she begged him not to let this news interrupt his plans, that he should go to the races and let the visit end in the way that had been previously arranged. Therefore, except for Mr and Mrs Wilson, they all went to the races again : it was 10th September, the day of the St Leger, the most important event of the meeting.

On the way there, Lycett Green, finding himself in the same railway carriage as Lord Edward Somerset, told him that several of the party had seen Gordon-Cumming cheating, and asked his advice about what course he ought to take. Lord Edward Somerset said he would like to consult his cousin, Captain Arthur Somerset : he did so during the day, and Lycett also talked to his father about it, whom he met at the races.

Captain Somerset was 'dumbfounded', he says, 'but at once realised what this might mean with His Royal Highness in the house and actually taking part in the game.' He replied that the matter was so delicate that he couldn't give an opinion, and suggested consulting Lord Coventry who was 'a thorough man of the world of considerable ability and the soul of honour'. He was very well known in sporting circles, had won the Grand National in 1863 and 1864, and had bred what Sir W. B. Thomas called, 'that famous hound, the Coventry Rambler, probably one of the greatest foxhounds that ever went out hunting.'

When they reached Tranby Croft that evening, Lycett Green, Stanley Wilson, Lord Somerset and Captain Arthur Somerset went to Lord Coventry's dressing-room – Lieutenant Berkeley Levett had refused to go with them. In front of these witnesses, Lycett Green told him that Gordon-Cumming had been cheating. Lord Coventry was the senior Courtier present. Instead of taking the obvious course of going to the master of the house, Mr Arthur Wilson, who was entitled to be informed, and pointing out to him that unless his family immediately withdrew their accusations the consequences would be very serious indeed, and particularly for the Prince, he, like all the rest of them who had been consulted, was not prepared to take the responsibility of doing anything about it. True he was Master of the Royal Buckhounds, but he had never played baccarat before, and he was slightly deaf. He said the matter was so serious and as difficult that he would like to consult Lieutenant-General Owen, 'Ducky', Williams because he was friendly with both Gordon-Cumming and the Prince – and was another 'thorough going man of the world', a familiar and popular figure at race meetings and in yachting circles.

Lord Coventry fetched the general from his room, and Lycett Green repeated his accusation to him, adding that five witnesses were prepared to swear they had witnessed the cheating. The effect on the general was extraordinary: he was 'shocked and overwhelmed with a sense of calamity', as he explained later, and at once said that the Prince must be informed.

That was his immediate reaction, disregarding all other considerations. It did not occur to him to resent this civilian stranger's accusation against the honour of a brother officer who had been his close friend for many years, or even to see that he had a fair chance to defend himself. He didn't even enquire into the matter further. He obviously didn't think at all, he only saw that the Prince, who had a horror of scandals, was about to be involved in one unless someone did something about it quickly. He was well aware how vulnerable the Prince's position was, having been his equerry when the Aylesford scandal nearly broke, and Lord Randolph Churchill had threatened to publish his intimate but harmless letters to Lady Aylesford, the general's sister.

They all knew that there would be a public outcry now if it were noised abroad that the Prince had presided at a baccarat table and consorted with gamblers and swindlers :

'Wrap it up how we may,' Captain Somerset said, 'the whole difficulty is that the Prince of Wales took part in the play.'

If Gordon-Cumming disputed the charge, if he resented it so that there was a row between him and the Wilsons, there would be no way to prevent the scandal coming out. The only possible course, they decided, was to make him admit that he was guilty and let him creep out into the night, and upon that condition get the Wilsons to agree to maintain silence about the whole affair.

Lord Coventry agreed that they should go to the Prince; Captain Somerset disagreed, thinking they could settle the matter among themselves. Lycett Green, whose belligerency had been growing in proportion to the number of people he involved, said he refused to keep silent about it, and he would denounce Gordon-Cumming at the Doncaster Races in the morning unless he were made to sign a document admitting his guilt, a document that would be a protection to his accusers if at any future time he should proceed against them for slander. 'I will not be a party,' he said, 'to letting Gordon-Cumming prey on society in future' – words not appropriate for an accusation of cheating against a man who had been playing with unblemished reputation for more than twenty years, so he must have had something else in mind, probably his notorious seductions of young women.

What was to be done? It was obvious that this emotional young man, if he were not stopped, would spread the story further – he had already told so many people. As the price of his silence General Williams proposed, and Lycett Green agreed, that Gordon-Cumming should be made to sign a document undertaking never to play cards again.

'The Prince must be told,' the general insisted, 'because it was principally his money that was unfairly won.' Captain Somerset objected that in view of the importance of the whole thing this was immaterial. The general then said, 'If we don't get in first and tell His Royal Highness, Gordon-Cumming will!' This impressed Captain Somerset as a valid reason and he gave way – it would have been difficult to make Gordon-Cumming admit he was guilty if he had got to the Prince first and managed to persuade him that he was innocent.

So General Williams and Lord Coventry went to the Prince. They made a grave mistake by doing so without first carrying out a simple investigation of the charges, for it would have revealed that so far from there being five witnesses to an act of cheating, as they had been led to believe, these witnesses did not agree about what they thought they had seen, though all had been intently watching.

They now made an even graver mistake. Although they had heard only Lycett Green, who had the tacit support of Stanley Wilson whom they had not questioned separately, and although they had not heard Gordon-Cumming's version of the story or even told him of the accusation made against him, they took it upon themselves to inform the Prince that 'the evidence they had heard was absolutely conclusive and they did not believe Sir William Gordon-Cumming had a leg to stand on.'

At that time even Lycett Green had detailed to them no specific action of his that could be called cheating, three of his witnesses they had not even seen, and yet they persuaded the Prince that Gordon-Cumming was guilty, that the evidence – which they had not heard – was conclusive. They had lost their heads and were falling over themselves to serve the Prince, but by behaving in this way they did him a great disservice.

The Prince, if he had not been persuaded at the outset of Gordon-Cumming's guilt, if he had known of the confusion in the evidence, might have demanded an immediate apology from the Wilsons for treating his friend and their guest in this way. It would have been better for all of them. As it was he accepted what his advisers told him and agreed that a document signed by Gordon-Cumming undertaking never to play cards again, and signed by all who were in the know, undertaking to observe silence, would be a possible way out of the difficulty. Meantime, as Gordon-Cumming still knew nothing at all about it, he suggested that they should inform him.

Lord Coventry and General Williams therefore went to look for Gordon-Cumming and found him in the smoking-room. Lord Coventry said, 'Something very disagreeable has happened. Some of the people staying here object to the way you play baccarat,' and he went on to explain that Lycett Green and four others were accusing him of cheating, and that the Prince had been informed.

Gordon-Cumming appeared to be as astounded as everyone else had been on hearing this accusation. He peremptorily and indignantly denied the charge, saying that it was a foul and abominable falsehood, and that it was impossible for him to lie down under it.

'You are my two old friends,' he said. 'I wish to place the matter entirely in your hands. I will do whatever you think best. Who is it that accuses me?'

They told him Lycett Green, Stanley Wilson, Berkeley Levett, Ethel Lycett Green and Mrs Wilson.

'Surely' he said, 'as men of experience you are not going to believe the statements of these boys against me?'

They replied that denial was utterly useless in the face of the overwhelming evidence of so many totally unprejudiced people. He then asked them to arrange for him to see the Prince. At that moment, dinner was announced.

They all went in to dinner as usual. Gordon-Cumming's face was like a mask. He spoke to Captain Somerset, who turned away from him. Apart from that, nothing appeared on the surface to show that anything was wrong. There was rigid code of behaviour observed by the Marlborough House Set: appearances must always be kept up, and nothing discreditable must be mentioned in front of servants.

After dinner the guests, including Gordon-Cumming, signed the visitor's book in the hall, and he took an autograph book belonging to another Wilson daughter, too young to be allowed to appear, to the Prince and got him to sign it for her. Then there was conversation and music until about eleven o'clock – but no baccarat. Instead the Prince went into a small drawing-room and received Gordon-Cumming's accusers together with Lord Coventry, General Owen Williams and the two Somersets. Lycett Green repeated his accusation.

The Prince turned to Berkeley Levett and said, 'I believe, Mr Levett, you saw it too?'

Levett replied that he was in the same regiment and that he wished to be left out of the affair. The Prince, understanding his embarrassment, did not insist. He addressed a few formal questions to the rest of the company, dismissed them, and sent for Gordon-Cumming.

He was received in the presence of Lord Coventry and General Owen Williams. He said, 'I have asked for an interview with your Royal Highness, as I have heard that certain people in the house have brought a foul and abominable charge against me of having cheated at cards. I utterly and emphatically deny that I have done anything of the kind.' He appealed to his years of honourable service, hoped the Prince would not believe his detractors, appealed to all who knew him. . . .

'What can you do?' the Prince said. 'What can you do against so many? It is very shocking, but there is only your word against theirs.'

Gordon-Cumming replied that he intended to confront his accusers at the races in the morning and grossly insult them.

From this course, that would have immediately precipitated the scandal, the Prince dissuaded him: 'What good would that do? There are five of them . . .'

It was obvious to Gordon-Cumming that he could not justify himself in this way without involving the Prince. He came out with another suggestion :

'I wish to submit my case to my commanding officer or to the Commander-in-Chief.'

General Williams at once intervened, for this would delay the signing of the document that Lycett Green was demanding. He said with some irritation.

'You are at perfect liberty to apply to the Duke of Cambridge if you wish, but I assure you he will not be as lenient to you as Lord Coventry and myself.'

'Then what am I to do sir ?' Gordon-Cumming asked. 'Something must be done. Your Royal Highness will see what a terrible thing this is for a man like myself who has attempted to lead, for twenty-five years, the life of an officer and a gentleman.'

The general suggested he should leave them while they discussed the matter. When he had gone they drew up the document for him to sign.

Half an hour later they sent for him again : the Prince was no longer in the room. Lord Coventry told him that after consultations they had decided that the only way to avoid a scandal was for him to sign a document they had prepared.

He read it, and protested, 'Why, it would be taken as an admission of my guilt !' They admitted that it would, 'And you still wish me to sign ?'

They pressed upon him the absolute necessity that he should do so because it was the only way a horrible scandal could be avoided. 'Unless you sign, your accusers will publish the story to-morrow morning on Doncaster racecourse.

'But what do they say I did ?'

They couldn't tell him, because Lycett Green had not told them of any specific action to which he took exception. Consequently there was nothing he could explain, nothing he could dispute, nothing he could deny except the general accusation of cheating, and this he continued to do most strenuously and emphatically.

'You are my friends,' he said. 'What do you advise me to do ?'

'If I were in your place,' General Owen Williams assured him, 'I should sign this document,' and they both insisted that he would have no chance at all against five witnesses who were agreed upon the facts, and that the evidence was so overwhelming that it couldn't be opposed.

'Would it be any satisfaction,' he asked, 'to two honourable gentlemen like yourselves that I should sign ?'

Again they insisted that there was no alternative.

The Wilsons' ultimatum, of course, was directed also against the Prince, Lord Coventry and General Williams himself, all of whom had an interest in the scandal not being noised abroad – and Gordon-Cumming could get them all out of trouble, they thought, by merely signing the document. No wonder they exercised extreme pressure! Apart altogether from the question of the Prince being involved if the scandal came out, he had a very strong motive to submit to the ultimatum that his friends were pressing upon him : he knew that if the accusation were made public in the morning, his denial would never catch up with it : innocent or guilty he would be ruined, the smear would remain and he would never be rid of it, but if everyone kept silent . . . It was a tempting thought. And so at last, protesting all the time that he was absolutely innocent – he signed. Immediately doubts assailed him. 'If this is for the purpose of keeping it a secret,' he commented, 'it will defeat its own ends : it is very well known that I play cards a good deal, and my refusing to do so will excite comment. It even debars me from playing 6d and 1/- rubbers of whist in the barracks.'

'I'm afraid it does,' said General Williams.

He then asked who had originated the idea that he should sign that document; they told him it was Lycett Green who needed it as protection in case he should one day proceed against him for slander, and it was the price of his silence.

'You must leave Tranby Croft very early in the morning,' the general added, picking up the document.

'But that too will excite comment !' he protested.

'Then you'll have to think of a suitable excuse.' They both shook hands with him, and left.

As soon as the Prince received the document he summoned everyone concerned, including their host, Mr Arthur Wilson : he read it aloud, signed it, and requested all present to sign it too, promising secrecy. 'But I must tell you, gentlemen,' he added, 'that Sir William Gordon-Cumming strongly denies the charge.'

'Oh, does he, sir ?' Lycett Green retorted, 'Then have him here and I'll tell him to his face that he's a cheat and a liar !' He was pacified when it was pointed out to him again that by signing the paper he had practically admitted his guilt.

'This will be no secret, sir,' Captain Somerset commented.

The Prince seemed surprised : 'Not when gentlemen have given their word not to divulge it ?'

'It's impossible, sir. Nothing in the world known to ten people was ever kept secret.'

This is the document that was signed :

In consideration of the promise made by the gentlemen whose names are subscribed to preserve silence with reference to an accusation which has been made in regard to my conduct at baccarat on the nights of Monday and Tuesday the 8th and 9th September 1890 at Tranby Croft, I will on my part solemnly undertake never to play cards again as long as I live.

(Signed) W. Gordon-Cumming.

Albert Edward P.
Coventry.
Owen Williams.
Arthur Wilson.
A. C. E. Somerset.
Edward Somerset.
E. Lycett Green.
A. Stanley Wilson.
Berkeley Levett.
R. D. Sassoon.

Early next morning Gordon-Cumming went alone on foot to the station and returned to London. He left a letter for Mrs Wilson saying that he had an important engagement in London which required his attendance, and he regretted he was compelled to leave so early that he was unable to wish her goodbye.

He also left a slightly incoherent letter for General Owen Williams :

Tranby Croft, September 10th.

Dear Owen, – I hope you'll take an opportunity of telling the Prince of Wales how entirely I was guided in my action yesterday by his advice, and yours and Coventry's. While utterly and entirely denying the truth of the allegations brought against me, I so thoroughly see now for my own sake as well as that of others it is essential to avoid an open row and the scandal arising therefrom. It is difficult for anyone, however innocent one may know himself to be, and however unstained his character may be, to come well out of an accusation brought by numbers against me alone, and I shrink therefore from doing as perhaps I ought and covet a full and thorough investigation. What a cruel blow it is to me to know that any men, even if almost strangers to me, should tell me that I have deliberately cheated them at cards, or to feel that you, like His Royal Highness, Coventry and you, against whom never a word has been said, should have been called on to advise me on such a charge and possibly believing yourselves, from the fact of my signing that paper, I am in any way unfit to associate with you and men like you. Of course my word is passed as regards cards, but it was quite unnecessary. I should never under any circumstances have touched them again. As regards the money I won this week, I feel it impossible to take it. I believe it was mostly won from the Prince. Sassoon need know nothing as to whether I received it or not and as HRH will doubtless insist on paying it, it should hitherto be disposed of in any way he may think fit, to a hospital or other charity. I intend to fulfil my engagements in Scotland and elsewhere as if this had not occurred though with a sore heart. This I owe to myself. Again thanking you and Coventry,

> I am
> Yours sincerely,
> (Signed) W. Gordon-Cumming.

CHAPTER THREE

An Appeal to the Royal Courts of Justice

Only three days had passed since Gordon-Cumming had left his house in Harriet Street, Lowndes Square, honoured and respected by the highest in the land, admired for his courage and his military record in two campaigns, intimate friend of the Prince of Wales; and now he had saved himself from immediate ruin only by the ignominious compromise urged upon him by his closest friends. When he wrote the letter which he had left at Tranby Croft to be shown to the Prince he still believed that the men to whom he had appealed for advice were trying sincerely to help him to the best of their ability; he had no idea they had already hopelessly compromised him in the eyes of the Prince by their assertion that he was guilty.

The reply to his letter came by return: it destroyed whatever hopes he might still have entertained that his friends would believe his pro-testations of innocence. Evidently Lord Coventry and General Owen Williams, having impulsively assumed and proclaimed that Gordon-Cumming was guilty, had to go on assuming it. This was the letter the general wrote just before leaving Tranby Croft:

> Tranby Croft, Hull. September 11th, 1890.
> Dear Cumming, – I have shown the letter I received from you this morn-ing to the Prince of Wales and Lord Coventry.
> (Signed) Owen Williams.

The rest of the letter was signed by the Prince of Wales and Lord Coventry as well as by General Owen Williams:

> We have no desire to be unnecessarily hard upon you, but you must clearly understand that in the face of the overwhelming evidence against you, it is useless to attempt to deny the accusations. So long as you comply with the conditions you have signed, silence will be strictly maintained so far as we are concerned. In this we have dealt with you as old friends, and in your interest, but we must plainly tell you that we consider we acted as leniently as we possibly could under the painful circumstances of the case. As a matter of course you will receive a cheque from Mr Sassoon for the money owing to you with which procedure we all agree,

and it will now rest with you to dispose of it as you may think fit.
          (Signed) Albert Edward. Coventry. Owen Williams.[1]

Greatly discouraged by this letter, Gordon-Cumming wrote a short note
to the general in reply :

> 2, Harriet Street, Lowdnes Square,
>   Friday September 12th, 1890.
> Dear Owen, – Your letter received today. I had hoped that you at all
> events would have seen your way to giving me the benefit of any doubt
> in the matter, but it seems this is not to be. The secret is in the hands of
> too many people to remain one long, and (I) have little before me to make
> life worth living. I suppose in the meantime I must try to live as of old.
>   Yours all the same, W. Gordon-Cumming.[2]

Then he made a last appeal to the Prince :

> Sept. 12th, Harriet Street, Lowndes Square, S.W.
> Sir, – The receipt of General Williams' letters destroys every lingering
> hope I had that there was yet a few among those cognisant of what
> happened at Tranby recently who believe notwithstanding the positive
> manner in which certain men asserted my guilt that I was innocent of
> what was imputed to me on that occasion. I shall not trouble Your Royal
> Highness with a repetition of my remarks in my letter to General Owen
> Williams and known to you, but (what) I do wish to point out to you in
> particular is this : the secret is already in the minds of far too many, I
> fear, to remain one long, but the main thing that would serve to drive me
> either to death or worse would be the knowledge that your Royal Highness
> is now in any way altered (in) your manner or love to me when we meet,
> as meet we must, if I am to continue to live as I have hitherto lived in
> the world. It is useless my repeating my promise made. That alone, by
> preventing my continuing even to play moderate whist with my brother
> officers I have up to now played, will be the subject of much comment,
> but what I again wish to point out is, the only hope I have of remaining
> in the eyes of the rest of the world an untarnished English gentleman,
> is that the said world should not be aware of any alteration in the anxious
> and friendly manner with which you have so long honoured me, and the
> forfeiture of your esteem is, sir, believe me, the cruellest blow of all. I
> must apologise for writing to your Royal Highness at all, and you must
> be well aware that I write in no way wishing to dictate to you, but I can-
> not help making this final appeal to show how utterly it remains in your
> power to utterly damn, morally and physically, one who has ever been
> a loyal and devoted subject to your Royal Highness. I do not write with
> any hope of receiving an answer to this letter, and ever only remain, sir,
> your obedient servant, – W. Gordon-Cumming.[3]

As he had expected, he did not receive an answer to this letter, but General Williams wrote advising him to cancel his proposed visit to the Earl of Mar, suggesting it would be embarrassing if he were to meet the Prince there. He replied thanking him for his very great kindness in giving him this advice, which he had taken.

In winter he usually went big game hunting in Africa or India, but now he was unwilling to leave England, not knowing what might come out during his absence. As if he felt the need to present a brave front to society, he went the usual round of the country house parties where baccarat was regularly played : on one occasion, at the Arthur Sassoons' house near Brighton, where Captain Somerset was also a guest, his refusal to play aroused the suspicion of his hostess as he had always been the first to suggest a game.[1]

Whenever he met General Owen Williams they greeted each other as if nothing had happened. Once, in the crowded hall of the Marlborough Club, he met Lord Coventry who shook hands with him and passed on. He entertained at his Scottish estate, Altyre, and he was frequently seen in the company of a young American woman, Florence Garner, to whom he became engaged.

Then the inevitable happened. He received an anonymous letter, dated 27th December, from 4 rue de la Concorde, Paris which was the address of a club he belonged to. It read :

> On commence à parler beacoup ici de ce que c'est passé à Newmarket cette été de votre triste aventure. Si vous venez à Paris ou à Monte Carlo soyez très reservé et *ne touchez pas une carte*. On a trop causer en Angleterre.

The only signature was '*Quelqu'un qui vous plaint*' – someone who pities you. It might be translated : 'They are beginning to talk much here of what passed at Newmarket this summer and of your sad adventure. If you come to Paris or Monte Carlo be very reserved and *do not touch a card*. They have talked too much in England.'

He had no idea who had written the letter. He sent it at once to General Owen Williams, asking him to let the Prince of Wales know about it. The general returned it with a long rambling comment – that he was absolutely at a loss to understand it, and did he know why it had been written, and had he the slightest suspicion of who the author was, and that '*on a trop causer en Angleterre*' was not true, and that the reference to Newmarket showed that the writer had the vaguest idea of any rumour and it was very indefinite, but it was beyond his comprehension that any rumour should have been heard, however vague, and that he was confident the incident had not been mentioned by any of those present at the time and he promised to let Gordon-Cumming know if he heard even a whisper of it. The general was obviously determined to close his eyes to the obvious implications of the letter – that the affair was being talked about in Paris and therefore would soon be known in England.

And indeed it was. A fortnight later he was writing again to the general reporting that a lady had informed him the affair was being talked of in London : in this letter he again questioned the general's wisdom in having persuaded him to sign the document which had turned out to be quite useless as the promise of secrecy had not been kept, and he warned the general that he would 'fix on' anyone who repeated the slander.

The general was still unwilling to face the truth : he replied asking Gordon-Cumming to find out from the lady exactly what she had heard and from whom, so that he could endeavour with Gordon-Cumming to stop the rumour which must necessarily be very vague. He assured him there could be no doubt that there was an absolute necessity for him to sign the document as otherwise there would have been no loophole for the avoidance of a horrible scandal, and that his solitary assertion, being vitally interested, would have been of no avail against the assertions of his accusers, and therefore he had no chance of fighting. 'Now, on the contrary,' he concluded, 'as an accusation is made, you can, of course, fight, but I would strongly advise this as a last resort in as much as the less notoriety about the affair the better.'

Gordon-Cumming now telegraphed the Prince, asking for an interview, and he also wrote to him as follows :

Sir, – I have telegraphed today to your Royal Highness to ask if you would grant me an interview on Monday. I am most unwilling again to address you on the subject of the affair at Doncaster, but information I have recently received to the effect that the whole story is the subject of comment in the Turf Club and elsewhere leaves me no alternative but to do so. It is clear, as I feared all the time, that the promise of secrecy made has been broken by those concerned. I have the honour to be your obedient servant, W. Gordon-Cumming.[5]

The Prince acknowledged the telegram, but declined to see him.

The long period of suspense was over, the period of hoping against hope, though he never believed it, that nobody would talk and that the affair would gradually be forgotten. Until that moment he could not have fought back without involving the Prince : now nothing could save him from being involved.

Having decided to fight, Gordon-Cumming wasted no more time. The first thing he did was to release Florence Garner from her promise to marry him. Then he went to his solicitors, Messrs Wontner & Sons, and consulted them about what steps to take to clear his name. Next he went to Lord Coventry and asked him what exactly he was supposed to have done. Even now Lord Coventry didn't know, but he did recall that his accusers were Lycett Green and Stanley Wilson, he wasn't sure who else.

No doubt Messrs Wontner's had pointed out that it was important for them to have details of what he was accused, for, in reality, the charge of cheating was the charge of committing a criminal offence. St John Wontner had been concerned in the High Court proceedings six years earlier which had found the playing of baccarat in public to be illegal. Wontner was one of the leading solicitors specialising in criminal work in London and ultimately was appointed solicitor to the Metropolitan Police. Therefore Gordon-Cumming next tried Berkeley Levett, thinking also that he might be persuaded to act as an intermediary between himself and the Wilsons. He sent his servant with a note for him to the Bachelors' Club, asking him to call.

Berkeley Levett came round to Harriet Street that same afternoon. Gordon-Cumming led him into his sitting-room, and said, 'I suppose you know what I want to see you about? The story is all over the town.' This is how Levett describes what followed :

> I concluded what he meant. He said, 'What do you propose to do?' I said, 'What is there to do?' He said, 'Could you not say you were mistaken? I do not ask you to withdraw, but could you not say you were mistaken?' I said I would say I was mistaken for his sake and the regiment, but I knew there was one man who would not.
>
> He then said, 'Surely you cannot believe this of me?' I said, 'I must believe my own eyes.' He said, 'What do you think you saw?' I said, 'I saw you adding counters.'
>
> He then asked me to go and see Mrs Wilson, to see what could be done. I said I would, and that I would telegraph to Stanley Wilson in Yorkshire. That is all that took place.

To bring this rather prosaic description to life, we have to recall that the scene was taking place between an extremely embarrassed young man and a senior officer who was his friend and who was grasping at a last chance, short of an appeal to a jury, to save his honour. Gordon-Cumming's version was that Levett didn't say he had seen him adding counters, but only 'I thought I saw something . . .' This is how

he described the scene – and the discrepancies between his account and
Levett's are notable :

> When Mr Levett entered the room I said to him, 'You are aware that the
> whole of this story is all over the town?'
> He said that he was, and expressed his extreme regret, and said that
> Mrs Wilson was in a great way about it. I made some remark that that was
> all very well now, but that their statements had brought me into this
> tremendous trouble, and that if they still adhered to the statements they
> had made, it would go hard with me, as there were five accusers to one.
> Then I said to him, 'You must have been mistaken in thinking you saw
> anything of the kind. For Heaven's sake, what did you see?' He said, 'I
> thought I saw something.' I said, 'What?' and he shuffled and said, 'I
> don't quite know.'
> I then said, 'Now look here, you are a friend and brother officer of mine.
> Will you go to Mrs Wilson and tell her that you have seen me, and see if
> anything can be done in the matter?' because I had hoped at this time
> that my accusers would have made a formal retraction of the accusation
> they had brought against me.

Gordon-Cumming says he added, 'Did you not think when you heard
that I was to be watched on the Tuesday night – did you not think of
doing something friendly in the matter?'

Levett couldn't answer. It must have been apparent to him that he
had missed the one crucial moment when he could, and should, have intervened effectively, instead of playing that stupid scene with Stanley
Wilson, rolling on the bed, and telling each other how sensational it all
was: no doubt the good fare at Tranby Croft, and the relaxed
atmosphere of the convivial evening, had had something to do with it.

Gordon-Cumming had already written to Lord Coventry referring
to the story that was going around to his detriment, and mentioning
particularly that people were saying he had confessed his guilt by signing
the paper which, as Lord Coventry very well knew, was absolutely
untrue as he had persistently denied the charge, that he still did and
would continue to do so. As secrecy had not been maintained, he was
about to do what he should have done at the beginning – put the affair
in the hands of the regiment. He was informing Lord Coventry because
it was on his advice that he had signed the paper that had only served
to put him in a worse position than before.

Now he wrote to him again, marking his letter private, and sharply
reproaching him for his bad advice in the past. It seemed to gall him
that Lord Coventry was again going to be asked for his advice at this
critical stage in his affairs. Then he sent a note to Berkeley Levett,

begging him to do all he could for him, and went to see his commanding officer, Colonel Stracey. To him he related everything that had happened from the beginning.

Colonel Stracey, who had heard nothing of it, said he should have reported the matter to him as soon as it happend. As he had not done so, he must leave the regiment at once. 'How could I have told you?' he objected. 'The case was referred to the Prince of Wales, and everyone was sworn to secrecy.' He stressed the fact that from the very first moment he had consistently and indignantly repelled the accusation, but that in a moment of weakness, pressed by the Prince of Wales, Lord Coventry and General Williams, he had signed a promise never to play cards again, being anxious, almost at any cost, to avoid a scandal which, however it went, must damage someone. He now found that the secret had not been kept and that the story was being talked about. He had consequently instructed his solicitors to commence an action against all who had been his accusers, and he now placed his commission in Stracey's hands pending the result of that action.

On the morning of 26th January he called on General Owen Williams who had been away. The general said he had come up to town expressly to consult Lord Coventry, as the story had come out very suddenly, and to go with him to see the Prince. Therefore he could say nothing at present, but he requested him to call again at five o'clock that afternoon.

When he got home he found a note from Berkeley Levett saying that nothing could be done. His young friend had gone straight to Mrs Wilson, who was in London, on the Sunday night, told her of his meeting with Gordon-Cumming and had a long talk with her : she remained firmly of the opinion that if any of them went back on their words they would be lost. Nevertheless, he had telegraphed Stanley Wilson : he came to town on Monday and saw him at St James's Palace where he was on guard duty. The result of their conversation was that he too found it impossible to contemplate going back on what they had said.

Gordon-Cumming answered the note as follows :

Dear Mr Levett, – As you say nothing can be done, I suppose I must carry it to the bitter end in a Court of Law. I am quite certain you had nothing to do with it, and I am quite certain you had no animus against me.

At five o'clock he was at General Williams's house in Hill Street as arranged. He found the general and Lord Coventry there waiting for him. Again he asked their advice about what he ought to do : they said that now the affair had become public they had no advice to give him. He asked if any record had been kept of the events at Tranby Croft. Lord Coventry said the general had written an acount, or *précis*, at the time or shortly afterwards. He pulled a paper out of his pocket and read it aloud. It began with a list of the guests at Tranby Croft, and then :

On the evenings of the 8th and 9th September, the party played at baccarat. After returning from the races on the 10th inst., Mr Lycett Green (having previously taken counsel with his father on the matter) made a statement to Lord Coventry to the effect that his brother-in-law, Mr Wilson, had told him on the evening of the 8th that Sir William Gordon-Cumming systematically placed a larger stake on the table after the card had been declared in his favour, than he had originally laid down, and when the cards were against him he frequently withdrew a portion of his stake, by these means defrauding the bank. This conduct had also been noticed by Mrs Arthur Wilson – who informed her husband of what she had seen – Mrs Lycett Green and Mr Levett having also been acquainted with the facts. It was agreed that they should all carefully watch the play on the following night, when Sir William Gordon-Cumming was again observed most distinctly to repeat the same practices. Lord Coventry, on hearing this, consulted General Owen Williams as to what steps should be taken in the matter. Mr Lycett Green repeated this statement to both of them, in the presence of Lord Edward Somerset, Captain Arthur Somerset, and Mr Wilson, and added that those who had watched were quite prepared to swear to the accuracy of the report. The matter having thus been placed more or less in the hands of Lord Coventry and General Owen Williams, they decided that it was imperative upon them to inform the Prince of Wales immediately of what had occurred, and after mature deliberation they agreed to suggest to His Royal Highness that, for the sake of all concerned, and for society at large, it was most desirable that the circumstances should not be allowed to transpire outside the immediate circle of those already acquainted with the facts, but, as a condition of silence, Sir William Gordon-Cumming must be made to sign an undertaking never again to play cards for the rest of his life. His Royal Highness, having been placed in possession of all the details of the case, and this suggestion being made to him, agreed that such a solution was possible. Lord Coventry and General Williams then went to Sir William Gordon-Cumming and informed him that he was accused of cheating at baccarat. This charge he denied emphatically, and begged to be allowed to see the Prince of Wales, who consented to see him, provided Lord Coventry and General Owen Williams were present. The interview took place. Sir William again denied the truth of the accusation, but was told it was utterly useless to attempt a denial in the face of the distinct evidence of so many totally unprejudiced persons, whose interest it was that no scandal should have happened in the house. The Prince of Wales afterwards saw Mr Lycett Green, Mr A. Wilson, Mr Levett, Mr J. Wilson, Lord Edward Somerset, Captain Arthur Somerset, and Mr Sassoon, all of whom were acquainted with the circumstances of the case, and listened to their verification of the account which had already been given him.

It was pointed out to these gentlemen that an *exposé* would mean a horrible public scandal, and as it was most expedient that this should, if possible, be avoided, they were asked whether they would be willing to keep silence with regard to what had taken place on condition that Sir William Gordon-Cumming signed an undertaking never again to play cards for the rest of his life. To this they all agreed, and declared that they would do their utmost to prevent the matter from transpiring. Lord Coventry and General Williams then saw Sir William Gordon-Cumming, and explained that the only possible condition on which silence could be maintained would be that he should sign the undertaking before mentioned. At the same time they clearly pointed out that his signature to this would be a distinct admission of his guilt. Quite understanding, he signed the document, which was afterwards signed by the gentlemen who were cognisant of the facts, and then given to the safe keeping of His Royal Highness the Prince of Wales. Sir William Gordon-Cumming left Tranby Croft early the following morning.

These circumstances were not known to Lady Coventry, Lady Brougham, Mrs Owen Williams, Miss Naylor, Lord Craven, Count Henry Lutzow, nor Mr Christopher Sykes, all of whom were staying in the house at the time.

The above is an accurate statement of all the facts of the case.

Whatever might be thought of this 'accurate account' and the amusing way it dignified the general's panic and Lord Coventry's befuddlement as 'mature consideration', it was certainly an accurate account of what they had told the Prince, and upon which the Prince had formed the conviction that the accused was guilty.

Gordon-Cumming listened to it all attentively, and took the strongest exception to the sentence which said they had pointed out to him that signing the document would be a distinct admission of his guilt : he said that on the contrary it was he who pointed out to them it might be taken, or that some people might take it as an admission of his guilt whereas he had admitted nothing of the kind and consistently maintained his innocence. The whole *précis* was a revelation to him of what had been going on behind his back : he learned for the first time that before telling him anything about the accusations his 'friends' had assumed that he was guilty and, on their own confession, had gone to the Prince and got his approval for the document he was to be made to sign : it was only too clear now that the sole purpose of their pretended friendship had been to persuade him to sign this document to satisfy a comparative stranger who was threatening to cause a scandal that would involve the Prince if his demands were not immediately acceded to.

He went home in a fury, and wrote a near-despairing letter to General Owen Williams reproaching him for his bad advice in persuading him to sign the document: informing him also, what Lord Coventry knew already, that he had placed the whole matter in the hands of his commanding officer, Colonel Stracey.

Next morning, 27th January, as nothing more could be expected from his friends, he went to Messrs Wontner's in St Paul's Chambers, and instructed them to demand a retraction of their derogatory statements, and an apology for making them, from Lycett Green, Stanley Wilson, Berkeley Levett, Mrs Arthur Wilson and Mrs Lycett Green, or an action for slander would be commenced.

As the *précis* that had been read to him would necessarily be an important document in the case, he wrote and asked for a copy. Lord Coventry replied:

Carlton Club, 4th February, 1891. – Dear Sir William, – I found your letter on returning from hunting last night. I will communicate your request to General Williams, and I feel there will be no objection to supplying you with a memorandum. – Yours, Coventry.[6]

Meanwhile the general, who had at once destroyed Gordon-Cumming's letter, so little to his credit, wrote one in return that was probably the most sincere and human he had yet written to him:

Temple House, Great Marlow, Bucks. Wednesday, January 29th. My Dear Bill, – There is nothing left but to place yourself, as you have done, unreservedly in Stracey's hands, and now all must depend, as you say, on the attitude of those who made the accusation to Coventry. You are quite at liberty to tell Stracey that you signed the document under extreme pressure and the promise of secrecy, but that you never acknowledged for a moment either to Coventry or myself the truth of the accusation against you. You signed on the strongest advice on the part of Lord Coventry and myself who were deputed to present you with the ultimatum, and who were absolutely certain that unless you did so the accusations would immediately be made public. Therefore your signature was the only possible hope of the avoidance of a horrible scandal with which we believed you would have no hope of contending with the possibility of success. The statement of the case drawn up at the time mentions the fact that Coventry and I clearly explained to you that your signature was tantamount to an admission of guilt, but while acknowledging this you signed as the only way out of the impasse but in no way made any acknowledgement that you were guilty, but on the contrary strongly asseverated your innocence. – Yours ever, Owen Williams.[7]

It so happened that on the following day, having received this letter, he met Berkeley Levett in Piccadilly : he still couldn't quite shut off all hope that his young friend would do something for him. 'I have your letter,' he began, 'saying that nothing can be done . . .'

'And I have received a nice communication from your solicitor this morning,' Levett countered.

'Yes, I know,' he said, 'but that needn't go on. What are you going to do with it ?'

The answer, of course, was, 'I've sent it to Lord Coventry.'

'Why are you all so dreadfully *acharné* against me?' Gordon-Cumming asked.

'No, not *acharné* . . .' he answered, and that was all they found to say to each other.

Colonel Stracey, in the exceptional circumstances of the Prince being involved, consulted his brother officers about what ought to be done.[8] Opinion was sharply divided. It was hotly debated whether Gordon-Cumming should be thrown out of the regiment at once or be allowed to attempt to justify himself.[9] The Prince's younger brother, the Duke of Connaught, who was Colonel-in-Chief of the regiment, insisted that Gordon-Cumming must be crushed : Stracey opposed him on the grounds that they hadn't yet heard the whole story and that he ought to be given a chance, whereupon the Duke expressed his strong disapproval, went off to Portsmouth where he was stationed, and refused to come back to discuss the affair with the Prince who urgently requested him to do so.[10]

Stracey went to the Adjutant-General of the Forces, General Sir Redvers Buller, and requested permission for Gordon-Cumming to retire at once on half-pay. Buller listened to all the details and he too was perplexed about what to do, but at last, for two reasons, first because it was Gordon-Cumming himself who, though tardily, had first reported the matter to the military authorities, and secondly because the Prince, knowing all the circumstances, had sanctioned his remaining in the regiment, he granted Stracey's request : in this exceptional case, Gordon-Cumming was to be allowed to retire on half-pay upon the understanding that if he did not succeed in his action the terms of his retirement would have to be reviewed. He wrote to Mr Stanhope, Secretary for War, and informed him of this decision.[11]

Colonel Stracey sent for Gordon-Cumming, told him what had been agreed, and added that for him to have signed the promise never to play cards again was unpardonable : 'Because you signed that document,' he said, 'you will never put on a sword again in the regiment. If you bring a successful action you will be allowed to retire : if you fail, you will be dismissed the service.'[12]

Mrs Wilson and Ethel were very friendly with Gordon-Cumming's sister, Lady Middleton, who also lived in Yorkshire. It seems that Mrs Wilson tried to get her to use her influence with her brother to dissuade him from resorting to law, for on 7th February Lady Middleton wrote from her home at Birdsall, Yorks :

Dear Mrs Wilson, – I have word from my brother in answer to my letter deprecating law. I fear I must try personal influence, but he says, 'mind you, my conduct is in no way a menace to them. The worst is I feel they are acting perfectly conscientiously in the matter and they believe they did see me resort to foul play. There can be no side wind. I never saw young Wilson before, L.G. only about twice, and Mrs A. W. and her daughter have always been more than friendly.' I think he must be wild at so-called old friends so readily believing him guilty. My Lord and I find it impossible to do so, though equally difficult to distrust you, of course. It is a wild mystery, many such, as I have said before, have condemned innocent men, but Oh Mrs Wilson, if I had thought your son or husband was doing such a thing I would have warned him privately, for your sake. I go up to London tomorrow with my Lord to help and comfort. – Yours, E. M. Middleton.

I do not know where we shall be, but will let you know, if you wish.[13]

CHAPTER FOUR

Behind the Scenes

The Wilsons, when they saw they would have to face an action for slander, consulted the solicitor in whom the Prince had the greatest confidence – Mr George Lewis. He occupied twenty-two rooms at Ely Place, Holborn, a very old part of London where the watchman still cried the hours of the night and the premises were locked and barred at nine o'clock every evening. It was said that half of the aristocracy were conducting their affairs and solving their problems according to his directions, and with his help escaping from embarrassing human and financial problems : through his own private eye detective agency, more efficient than Scotland Yard, he knew more about other people's business, both in the world of society and in the underworld, than any man living : he was supposed to be the original of Dickens's Mr Jaggers, the all-powerful lawyer in *Great Expectations*.

In court he looked like a Hebrew Voltaire, his expressionless face masking his quick intelligence : he was a brilliant advocate and a relentless cross-examiner. In his small private office he was like a father-confessor. 'If people come to me in trouble,' he said, 'they don't leave without feeling comforted and helped.'[1] His business was to save society from the consequences of its sins. Once he had accepted you as a client he furthered your interests with ruthless efficiency – he believed it was his duty to do so.

He seldom made a note, relying on a prodigious memory, and he had long ago given up keeping a diary, though all lawyers were supposed to keep one, because he saw that it would be the repository of too many embarrassing secrets.

'Let me tell you,' he said in an interview, 'that no novel was ever written, no play ever produced, that has or could contain such incidents and situations as at the present moment are securely locked up in the archives of my memory and which no man will ever discover.' His clients' papers were kept in a gas-lighted strong-room in the care of an elderly and trusted janitor : the files and deed-boxes were marked only by ciphers, the names on them being all turned to the wall.[2]

It was natural for any of the Marlborough House Set to go to George

Lewis for advice : the Prince had already consulted him about the Baccarat Scandal, Berkeley Levett had been sent to him by Lord Coventry. The Wilsons therefore also went to the small inner sanctum at Ely Place and told their story. 'This great man,' Lady Brooke wrote, 'smoothed down anything approaching a scandal touching Royalty or the aristocracy.'³

Mr Lewis was particularly expert at settling disputes out of court, and scandalous affairs without a scandal, but this one had gone too far before he was called in : he decided that in order to clear the names of all his clients there was nothing left to do but fight the case. He answered Messrs Wontner's letter for each of the defendants in identical terms. The one he wrote for Berkeley Levett was that Messrs Lewis and Lewis were instructed to say that there was no single statement that Mr Levett had made with respect to Sir William Gordon-Cumming that he was not prepared to substantiate in a Court of Law or elsewhere. Under these circumstances he was prepared to meet Sir William Gordon-Cumming before any tribunal, but the responsibility of such an enquiry would rest upon Sir William Gordon-Cumming.

When any citizen makes a complaint that he has been slandered he is entitled to know what it is substantially that is alleged against him, so Mr Lewis's first problem was to prepare the Wilsons to answer 'interrogatories' that would be sent by Messrs Wontner's and to get them to agree upon what it was exactly that they had seen, for each claimed to have seen something different, and their stories didn't agree. To preserve the effect of a fivefold accusation, he wrote out a general accusation, giving no details, which each of them signed as a personal statement : 'I saw the plaintiff cheat at baccarat by placing a larger stake on the table after the cards had been declared in his favour than he had originally laid down.' Since this was a charge of the criminal conduct of cheating the law in 1891 laid upon those alleging this the burden of proving it beyond reasonable doubt. The fact that it was a civil case did not diminish this burden of proof.

He then proceeded to interview the other players who had taken part in the game of baccarat at Tranby Croft : none of them would say that he had seen, or that he had suspected, any cheating. The nearest approach to it was a statement by Captain Arthur Somerset who said, 'I can only remember once I noticed Gordon-Cumming pushing his chips about with a pencil but I thought it was merely nervous excitement on his part, and no supposition of foul play occurred to me.' Mr Lewis couldn't use this information. It would have been of more use to the opposing counsel as suggesting what the Wilsons, Mrs Wilson in particular, had really seen and mistaken for cheating.

As counsel for the Defence, Lewis briefed Sir Charles Russell, one of the most outstanding personalities at the Bar and a close friend : he had been Mr Gladstone's Attorney-General. Lewis had the very highest opinion of his abilities : 'He has no equal as a cross-examiner,' he said. 'He has no equal as an advocate; there never was a greater man at the English Bar.'[4]

The brief had to be a very detailed document, not only putting counsel in possession of every scrap of information he might require, but suggesting what points might usefully be made to strengthen the case he would have to present in court, and giving him a line of action which could, however, be modified during the hearing of the case if events should take an unexpected turn. The line Mr Lewis took was to assume Gordon-Cumming was guilty and that his cheating was a wicked abuse of the Wilsons' hospitality.[5]

When he sat down to write it, he started with several very great advantages – he knew from the letter received by Mrs Wilson from Lady Middleton what line Gordon-Cumming and his counsel would be forced to take in court – that the Wilsons were people of integrity honestly mistaken. He indicated this for the benefit of his counsel, and also drew attention to one of Gordon-Cumming's phrases in his letter quoted by Lady Middleton, that his conduct was in 'no way a menace to the Wilsons'.

'Why,' commented Lewis, 'should it have occurred to him that his conduct in bringing this action should be looked upon as a menace unless he actually felt that it was, and that in truth he wished to frighten these young people and by intimidation to get some sort of a retraction, however slight ?'

Another solid advantage was that the two courtiers, Lord Coventry and General Williams, who were as determined accusers of Gordon-Cumming as the Wilsons were, could pose as having acted as his old friends in his best interests, so they had to be justified and supported although they were not his clients : but he warned counsel to be on his guard, 'one may think they made up their minds too quickly . . .'

With regard to the Prince of Wales, Mr Lewis instructed, '. . . we are desirous that the Prince of Wales's name should not be introduced unduly into the case, and Mr and Mrs Wilson would be glad to avoid alluding to HRH's name except it be imperatively necessary. Probably on the part of the plaintiff there will be no such feeling, but Mr and Mrs Wilson regret extremely that during HRH's visit such an occurrence should have taken place in their house, and that HRH's name should be dragged through this trial which they feel certain must be some annoyance to HRH. 'We are aware,' Mr. Lewis continued, 'that it is impossible to avoid reference to HRH because some of the defendants admit they uttered the slander before him, but so far as it is possible to avoid dragging the Prince of Wales's name into the controversy we, on the part of the defendants, are most anxious to do so.'

He next turned to General Owen Williams's letter of 28th February to Gordon-Cumming in which he had said, 'You are quite at liberty to tell Stracey that you signed the document under extreme pressure and the promise of secrecy, but you never acknowledged for a moment either to Coventry or myself the truth of the accusation against you. You signed on the strongest advice on the part of Lord Coventry and myself who were deputed to present you with the ultimatum . . . your signature the only hope of avoiding a horrible scandal etc . . .' 'Nobody could doubt,' Mr Lewis commented in his brief, 'that it was an indiscreet letter. No one can doubt that it is a letter to be regretted . . .'

He sent for General Owen Williams. After half an hour with the astute Mr Lewis, the general professed himself ready 'to swear in the witness-box again and again' according to the brief, 'that no pressure was put upon Gordon-Cumming by the Prince, by Lord Coventry or by himself, and that the words 'horrible scandal' had no reference, direct or indirect, to the fact that the Prince of Wales was one of the party, that he believed, and still believes, Gordon-Cumming was guilty of cheating and consequently could not have meant by his language to exculpate him though he might have wished to give him some little help with the military authorities.'[6]

Mr Lewis went on to indicate to counsel that in the witness-box Gordon-Cumming 'cannot hesitate to answer that he believed General O. Williams to be a man of profound honour, integrity and truthfulness,' and therefore his counsel will not be able to contend that his explanation is not true. He added that the Prince had authorised him to state that he put no pressure on Gordon-Cumming either.

He then wrote a description of the house party at Tranby Croft for counsel's benefit, detailed the various acts of cheating the defendants had seen, and continued :

Many observations have been made with reference to the course that was adopted. It was suggested that the proper course would have been to have ordered Sir William Gordon-Cumming out of the house and to have informed the military authorities with a view to an enquiry being held into his conduct, but it must not be forgotten that General

Owen Williams and Lord Coventry were not called to judge of the conduct of W. G. Cumming in their own house – they were the guests of Mr and Mrs Arthur Wilson and they were called upon to judge what course should be adopted towards another guest who had been guilty of such conduct in the house of their hostess. If it had occurred in their own house they might have warned Sir W. G. Cumming out at once: they had no such power in the house of Mr and Mrs Wilson and therefore it may naturally have occurred to them as one course to avoid the scandal of such a thing having taken place in their hosts' house, and to see, if silence were kept, that every possible care was taken of those into whose houses Sir W. G. Cumming might go by drawing his sting and preventing him ever playing cards and cheating at other houses.

And again they had to consider what should be done with their friend. There may be people who would say he ought to have been dealt with in the harshest and most severe manner, turned out of the army etc., but that course of conduct might have been pursued by people who were strangers to Sir W. G. Cumming. You cannot in a moment turn out of your heart the feelings that you may entertain for an old and valued friend, and it would occur to any kind-hearted person to see whether there was not some middle course short of absolute destruction to him, and it is quite intelligible that they should seek the middle course which they ultimately adopted.

He quoted the relevant correspondance, and concluded:

. . . we need hardly say how painful it is to Mrs Wilson and the other members of her family to be drawn into a controversy such as this. They have not sought the enquiry, nor have they done anything to produce it. They are not the accusers. The plaintiff must take the entire and sole responsibility of having dragged them into Court and compelled them to come forward to establish his guilt. For the defendants are determined, now that the plaintiff has dared to suggest that their statements made on the 8th and 9th September are not true, to contest this case to the very last and not to allow the plaintiff's conduct to escape the fullest enquiry. The following evidence will be adduced on the part of the defendants . . .

and he detailed what each was prepared to say in the witness-box.

Besides methodically preparing the case, Mr Lewis had to face the problem that if it were heard in a Civil Court the Prince would be brought in as a witness: he was most unwilling to appear because it would inevitably provoke a hostile reaction from the press and from the country. The two most obvious courses were firstly to persuade the Wilsons to withdraw, secondly to persuade the military authorities to reverse their decision and hold an immediate enquiry: if they pronounced Gordon-Cumming guilty there would be little point in having a civil trial. He therefore sent General Owen Williams and Lord Coventry to General Buller to protest against him being allowed to leave the army by retiring upon half-pay without any imputation on his character.

The London Correspondent of the *Manchester Courier* wrote that he was in a position to state

> that the Prince of Wales is profoundly annoyed at being concerned in the transaction, but it is quite incorrect to assert that Mrs Wilson and her daughter 'let the cat out of the bag'. A lady of the Marlborough House set was told the story, and forthwith related it to her bosom friend, who happens to be a bitter enemy of Sir William Gordon-Cumming. Consequently before forty-eight hours were over, all London knew the secret. Sir William, it seems, is determined, notwithstanding that much influence has been brought to bear upon him to desist, to carry the affair to the law courts, and this will lead to revelations concerning the fearful amount of private gambling now going on in England, which will startle the public.

This was typical of many similar articles. It was natural it would be thought that Mrs Wilson and Ethel had betrayed the secret as they were the only two concerned who had not been asked to sign anything. If Gordon-Cumming had not lost his head he would surely have insisted that they should be included also in the pledge of secrecy. The 'lady of the Marlborough House set' was, of course, Lady Brooke, and this carried with it the implication that the Prince had violated the pledge by telling her. In a letter to *The Times* on 9th February 1911 Lady Brooke wrote,' The subsequent funeral [following her stepfather's death in Scotland] and deep mourning prevented me for a long time joining any social gatherings so that I was among the last to hear of what, at that time, set Society agog.' The 'bosom friend' may or may not have been Louisa, Duchess of Manchester – (she was not yet 'an honest woman'): there were many others whom Gordon-Cumming had offered and who would have been only too glad to get their own back.

The London Correspondent of the *Yorkshire Post* wrote:

> There were strong rumours at the clubs yesterday of a development of the gaming scandal which will have the effect of quashing the legal proceed-

ings which Sir W. Gordon-Cumming has instituted. I am not in a position to indicate precisely the nature of the occurrence to which the rumour refers, but I may say that the story in circulation obtains wide credence in quarters where the whole facts of the affair are known.

Meanwhile the Queen had asked to be informed what steps had been taken, adding, 'The Prince thinks the scandal about Sir William Gordon-Cumming ought to be taken up by the miiltary authorities.'[7]

Buller accordingly wrote to her secretary, Sir Henry Ponsonby, and reported :

Lord Coventry and General Owen Williams came to me and protested against him being allowed to retire upon half-pay as if nothing had happened when he was a convicted cheat. I said that I absolutely declined to take action against him upon street rumours. If Lord Coventry or General Williams would give me a charge against Sir William Gordon-Cumming in writing or definitely rehearse before his face or to his colonel, I would take action, but until I had evidence to go on I would not interfere. Lord Coventry and General Williams at this time refused to appear against Sir William or to tell me who would.[8]

Two days later, Buller received a letter from them : although it was signed by them and addressed from the Carlton Club, it was actually a statement prepared by Mr Lewis formally acquainting the military authorities with the charges.

The effect was immediate : Gordon-Cumming was informed that his retirement on half-pay would not for the present be acted upon, that he was suspended from all duty, and that a military enquiry had been ordered to enquire into the charges against him. He replied on 9th February to the General Commanding the Home District :

I have the honour to acknowledge receipt of copies of (1) Of charges brought against me by Lord Coventry and General Owen Williams. (2) Of a letter from the Adjutant-General relative to my application to go on half-pay, and in which he says it is necessary that I should clear my character from imputations contained in the charge. I have the honour to inform you that I have taken the necessary step to appeal to the highest tribunal by desiring my solicitors, Messrs Wontner to issue writs for slander against the persons who have brought the accusations against me, and have urged them to endeavour to fix as early a date as possible for a hearing of the case. I have taken the liberty of asking Messrs Wontners to advise you themselves of the action I have thus taken. – Yours obediently, William Gordon-Cumming.[9]

On the same date, Messrs Wontner's wrote confirming that action had been taken which must lead 'to a full enquiry in the clear atmosphere of the High Court of Justice.'

. . . no step, we submit, of more absolute submission of his honour of
character could have been adopted by him. He denies most positively
that he willingly made an admission of guilt, but while placing himself
in the hands of those believed to be his true friends and in whose judgement he thought he would be safe, he declared from the instant of the
accusation made against him its absolute untruth and prepared to take
steps to force an enquiry. That this is so will be shown from a letter or
letters of General Owen Williams, and it will be ultimately shown that
he only yielded what now is shown to be his better judgement to the strong
pressure of those whom he could not resist. When, however, he found that
this foul accusation had been made public property, he left himself in the
hands of his regiment, placing his application to retire on half-pay with
his commanding officer, he instructed us to take the speediest and most
effectual steps to bring about a thorough and exhaustive enquiry into
the truth of the allegations against him, and made openly at the time but
behind his back and which, we submit, he was induced not to resent,
improperly, by those who acted as his friends and counsellors on the
occasion, and who now for reasons that the future will reveal, turn themselves into his accusers. We submit that in view of the coming enquiry
in a Court of Law, any military enquiry should be suspended. – We have
the honour to be, sir, Your obedient servants, Wontner & Sons.[10]

Buller reported to Ponsonby that he had received Messrs Wontner's
letter and had consulted the Lord Advocate-General about it, who said
it would be in his opinion unfair to allow a military enquiry while the
civil action was pending; and so he had ordered that no military enquiry
was to be held at present. Lord Coventry and General Williams escaped
from the ignominy, which they had brought upon themselves, of
appearing at a military enquiry to accuse an old friend of acts of cheating of which they knew nothing except what they had heard from
others. It would have been more natural if they had come forward as
his defenders, particularly as they had both taken part in the games of
baccarat in question and found nothing wrong with his play.

Buller continued his report to Ponsonby:

I have reason privately to believe that although Lord Coventry and
General Williams state that Sir W. G. Cumming practically admitted his
guilt when signing the paper, yet he now states he can produce letters from
one or both of them admitting that he was throughout insistent on a
stout denial of the truth of the accusations. This is between you and me
but it throws a sidelight on the question, so I thought I might mention it.

He added a private note:

To turn to quite another subject, I hear that the Prince of Wales is condemning my action in the Sir William Gordon-Cumming case in loud and unmeasured terms. You may have heard nothing about it, which I hope is the case, for it is not a satisfactory subject, but in case you have I might say that one story is often only good until another is told, and that I am satisfied that I have done my duty with discretion. . . .

Ponsonby scribbled in the margin of this note that he had heard nothing and probably should hear nothing – but in the following week the Prince wrote to him that he considered Buller's conduct 'throughout this unfortunate and deplorable business has been to say the least of it most extraordinary. If he had acted promptly and decisively at the beginning and told Stracey to act so all this public scandal and especially in the press would have been avoided and no question of a civil action would have even been thought of.'[11]

His personal secretary, Sir Francis Knollys, also wrote saying :

Buller, after calling up the witnesses decided to stifle all military enquiry, and leave the matter to be settled by civil law. . . . The civil action cannot come on before November, George Lewis tells me, and in the meanwhile this scandal is to be kept hanging over everyone's head and at the end of nine or ten months the whole affair is to be raked up again because Buller chooses to throw his mantle over Cumming; refusing to have any sort of enquiry or court martial leaves the matter to be settled by a civil court. According to the line of conduct he has adopted, every officer, NCO or private against whom a disgraceful charge is brought can evade it for months by merely getting hold of a solicitor and bringing a civil action against his accusers.[12]

Mr Lewis put forward a proposal through the *Pall Mall Gazette* that a tribunal, perhaps of three colonels, should be set up to take the sworn evidence and decide the case in a judicial manner, so that Gordon-Cumming might have the means 'of bringing his accusers immediately to book and establishing his innocence without the law's long delays.' This scheme also came to nothing.[13]

He indicated in his brief what points counsel should make in court with regard to these transactions – that it was impossible that Gordon-Cumming could have had a more favourable tribunal before whom to appear than one composed of his brother officers, but he seems to have shrunk from it; and, of course, the fact that two of his closest friends, and the Prince, believed him to be guilty would build up a strong presumption that he was so.

The next plan was to get the trial prejudged by an enquiry to be carried out by the Guards Club. We learn from Knollys, 'the Guards Club are going to take the matter up and there is to be a special meeting on Friday next to consider the situation. It will be proposed at the meeting to nominate a committee of ex-Guardsmen, but members of the club, to enquire into the case and to report to the club thereon. This may possibly do some good.'[14]

But at the special meeting a motion to empower the committee to conduct its own enquiry was defeated, and a motion to suspend judgement was carried by 79 to 49. The Prince was extremely angry. He wrote to Ponsonby:

> The decision of the Guards Club is a terrible blow to the Scots Guards; and I feel most deeply for the officers who have the honour of their regiment so much at heart. Should Cumming, by any legal quibble, win his action, I think nearly every officer would leave the Regiment.[15]

Sir Francis Knollys explained:

> The great object is to put an end to the action, and to prevent the Prince of Wales being called into the witness-box; and the best way to have achieved that end would have been for the Guards Club to have turned him out, (Sir William), and the Marlborough and Turf could have followed suit. There would then, in all probability, have been an end of the whole affair, and people in that case could have talked about the case being pre-judged as much as they liked.

He added a postscript:

> I am sure you will understand that if possible the Prince *must* not go into the witness-box in a case of this sort.[16]

Ponsonby had a rather painful interview with the Prince who was indignant because Colonel Stracey had abstained from voting, and also because his brother, the Duke of Connaught, had refused to intervene. When asked about this, the Duke explained to Ponsonby:

> No one feels stronger *against* Sir G. Cumming than I do, but as colonel of the regiment I have felt all along that I must be perfectly fair and impartial and that it would be placing the Prince in a very unfortunate situation were I to put undue pressure on the regiment with the object of crushing G. Cumming. Being the Prince's brother it was more than ever incumbent on me not to allow myself to be used in a manner that might cause the world to think that Cumming was to be sacrificed to save annoyance to the Prince. I told Colonel Stracey what I thought he *ought* to do, and when he did *not* do this I expressed my disapproval of his action most strongly.[17]

The Queen agreed with the Duke. She had hard words to say about the Prince encouraging gambling, so hard that he refused to visit her except on the understanding that gambling would not be mentioned. Lord Rowton, acting as mediator, wrote to Ponsonby that the Prince was much pained and much grieved by the Queen's sentiments, and very sorry on that account, but that he was sensitive and hard words would do harm. He should ask the Queen to be gentle, especially as he was in a position to assure Her Majesty practically that baccarat was a thing of the past. He should prevent angry words between Queen and Prince. It would only lead to another scandal and perhaps frustrate the desired end.[18]

Ponsonby's own opinion was that the decision of the Guards Club was lucky because, had they ejected Gordon-Cumming, everyone would have said it was because of pressure from Marlborough House.[19]

And indeed, the Prince's friends had now got him into a most unenviable position. First Lord Coventry and General Owen Williams by assuring him at the very beginning of the affair that Gordon-Cumming was guilty and the evidence against him conclusive : he was certainly entitled to believe that these two trusted advisers had investigated the charges and knew what they were talking about, whereas they had done nothing of the kind. Thus the Prince had felt all along that he was the injured party because, through no fault of his own, he found himself involved in a scandal, and also because it was chiefly his money that Gordon-Cumming was supposed to have unfairly won.

Then other friends, particularly Sir Francis Knollys, had easily fanned his indignation and led him to make the various attempts to prevent the accused obtaining a hearing in the Civil Court where he himself would have to appear as a witness. Everything that had been done, supposedly in his interest, had made the situation worse. Articles appeared in the national and international press hostile to the defendants and critical of the Prince. The *New York Times,* which had always been favourable to him since his visit to the United States, described the scandal as vulgar and disreputable, and deplored his manoeuvres to get the trial prejudged, prophesying that there would be political repercussions.[20]

For the attitude of the press, Mr Lewis blamed Gordon-Cumming, claiming that he had tried to prejudice public opinion by means of false and misleading statements to the newspapers, and he suggested in his brief that counsel might desire to cross-examine him with regard to these matters.[21] The first newspaper to take it up was the *Hawk,* followed, more explicitly, by the *World, Truth,* the *Star, Land & Water,* and others. Mr Lewis himself wrote an article and had it published in the *Pall Mall Gazette,* 'to state on the very highest authority the exact truth on certain aspects of the case.' In this he defended the Prince and put the case sympathetically for the Wilsons.[22]

On 4th February, Queen Victoria wrote from Windsor to her eldest daughter, the Princess Royal, widowed Empress Frederick of Germany :

> I have to thank you for two dear letters of the 22nd. I must at once correct an error which you seem to have made in thinking Bertie wishes to shield this horrid Mr Cumming. On the contrary he is most anxious that he should be punished. The incredible and shameful thing is that others dragged him into it and urged him to sign this paper which of course he never should have done. He is in a dreadful state about it for he has been dreadfully attacked about it.[23]

She was referring not to Gordon-Cumming signing the paper but to the Prince also signing it, and being unnecessarily involved. She wrote again on 18th February :

> I have asked Sir Henry to write to you about this dreadful 'card' scandal, so that you may understand it. It is a sad thing Bertie is dragged into it, but people think good will come out of it and that it will be a shock to society and gambling, lies etc.[24]

Captain Somerset, who hadn't seen the Prince since Tranby Croft, met him coming out of the Marlborough Club and was shocked to see that all one side of his beard had gone grey – it was the first sign of age that he had shown.

Any hope which might have been entertained that the Wilsons would agree to settle the affair by withdrawing their accusations were dashed by the appearance in several newspapers of a Press Association release headed, 'The Baccarat Scandal' announcing that '. . . acting in consonance with the opinion of the Royal Personage who has been mentioned in connection with the matter, it is stated in well-informed circles that there will be no cross-examination and no attempt to prove the allegations; that an apology will be tendered, etc. . . .' This was printed in the *Daily News* and the *Echo.*[25]

Messrs Lewis & Lewis at once denied that there was any truth in the statement, and began an action against both these papers. They both printed retractions, but the *Echo* at the same time repeated the original paragraph with a scathing attack in a leading article : it had been impracticable to delete them, the proprietor explained, because of the way the type had been set up :

The Baccarat Scandal is to be hushed up. . . . It is, no doubt, a very comfortable arrangement for all parties immediately concerned, especially for the exalted personage who condescended to act as banker at the Tranby Croft gambling table, but it is certainly discreditable . . . too likely to create a widespread impression that the facts are uglier, perhaps, than they really are. . . . But the nation has a right to expect that a prince who pitches the key-note to society should recollect that his evil example is tenfold more mischievous than that of the common run of men . . . the spectacle of a prince presiding at a gambling table is far more demoralising than the circulars of betting touts. . . .

The sense of justice is shocked when a couple of street urchins are sent to prison for playing pitch-and-toss whose offence in its essence is no wise distinguishable from that of peers and princes. . . .

At the very end there was a note in small print, 'Since the above was written, we have been informed that the statement on which the article is based is without foundation. The case will, it is now asserted, be defended to the last.' The origin of this announcement issued by the Press Association was never revealed : the fact that Mr Arthur Wilson was appointed High Sheriff of Yorkshire at this time seemed to confirm that some negotiations had been going on, and that a journalist had reported them prematurely. It all helped to build up public interest in the affair.

Both sides now did their utmost to have the case heard as soon as possible, Gordon-Cumming to clear his name, his opponents because they assumed, quite wrongly, that he would put off for as long as possible the inevitable day upon which he would be judged guilty before the nation of being a cheat and a swindler.

As counsel for Gordon-Cumming, Messrs Wontner & Sons first approached Charles Gill, who had been making a name for himself in the criminal courts; and then, as his senior, Sir Edward Clarke. After long and anxious consultations they decided that Gordon-Cumming was telling the truth, and that he was innocent. They accepted the brief.

Sir Edward was at the opposite pole from the Prince of Wales in his birth, upbringing and education. His father was a silversmith with a small shop, in King William Street in the City of London, above which the family lived. Edward as a lad had served in the shop and at night slept behind the counter. His parents sent him to school and took an interest in his education, but when by his industry he had secured for himself a small job in the India Office and then threw it up to study for the Bar, they bitterly opposed him. By winning scholarships and working as a law reporter for the *Morning Herald* and as a parliamentary reporter for *The Examiner* to augment his income, he completed his studies and in 1864 was called to the Bar. In 1866 he married, also against the wishes of his parents : it turned out very happily and he had several children.

In 1868 he had his first important brief as a junior counsel. From that day his earnings steadily increased and in a comparatively short time he had reached the head of his profession. It was said that Charles Dickens was the first to recognise his unusual talent when he heard him speaking at a public meeting in the provinces.

His appearance was not impressive. This is how he described himself :

He was below middle height, and of sturdy figure. His strong features gave the face a stern and almost harsh expression, and the brown eyes, which might have softened it, were half closed under heavy brows. In his youth and early manhood, he was not a favourite with men or with women; his painful earnestness gave him an unattractive severity of appearance and manner; but in later life prosperity mellowed him, and the saving grace of humour displayed itself in some of his later speeches.[26]

He enjoyed the confidence both of the profession and of members of the public : no member of the Bar stood higher in the general estimation; his integrity and his fairness to client and to opponent alike had never been questioned. In 1886 he was appointed Solicitor-General in the Salisbury Government : the existing rules allowed him to continue his career at the Bar at the same time, so, in spite of his high office, he was able to accept the brief to defend Gordon-Cumming.

His opponent, Sir Charles Russell, was a more flamboyant character and had much more in common in his tastes and pursuits with the Prince of Wales and his set : he was a member of the exclusive Jockey Club, owned the racehorse *Miss Shylock* – a winner at Lewes that year – and was something of an expert on form. He always travelled with a pack of cards and would play at anything with anybody. He was five years older than Sir Edward Clarke, was born in Northern Ireland of Catholic parents, and called to the English Bar in 1859. His appearance was striking. This is a description of him by his sister-in-law, Lady Gilbert :

My first recollection of Charles Russell is seeing him walk into the drawing-room of our house in Belfast, and he comes before me still as I saw him then. His figure was tall, square-shouldered, and splendidly set up, the head noble and striking, crowned with a curly crop of crisp chestnut hair. The brow and eyes were his great distinction, the whole face square and powerful, the nose well chiselled, the mouth rather large and full of strength. The dominating brow was pale as ivory, and the penetrating grey eyes were alive with transparent light and sweetness. Although it was a grave serious face, the frequent and singularly charming smile was all the more fascinating when it appeared.[27]

His first successes were on the Northern Circuit, then Mr Lewis gave him his first chance to distinguish himself in London and thereafter briefed him in many of his most famous cases. Other barristers may have been better authorities on points of law but none could express them with more telling effect. A classic example of his shrewd and powerful cross-examination was his exposure of Pigott, the forger, which cleared the great Irish leader Parnell from an accusation that would have ruined his career – it was an exposure made possible by Lewis's brilliant detective work. They were a formidable team. With exuberant energy Russell extorted verdicts from the juries: he had an actor's talent for focussing all attention on himself, making them forget what had been said on the other side. Whenever he appeared in Court it was Russell, not the judge, who was the centre of attention: 'It was a pity,' a colleague remarked, 'that he was not more tolerant of the judges.'

He had more than a touch of Irish blarney, an Irish brogue which he valued highly, and depths of Celtic emotion to draw upon when required. On one occasion he was proving so convincingly that his client, an alcoholic, was practically an abstainer, that a junior counsel on the other side burst out laughing: 'Young man,' he said, 'if you do that again I'll have you taken out,' and he went on, unruffled, to win his case.[28]

Of English juries he had but a poor opinion. 'An Irish jury enjoys the trial,' he said. 'They can follow every turn of the game. They understand the points of skill; the play between an Irish witness and an Irish Counsel is good fun, and they like the fun, and they don't mind the loss of time. With an English jury it is different. They are busy men and they want to get away quickly. The great thing in dealing with an English jury is not to lose time. Mere *finesse* they don't appreciate; go straight at the witness and at the point; throw your cards on the table.'[29]

He always gave the impression of being completely sure of himself and of the rightness of his case – but he did admit that Sir Edward Clarke, who had got the better of him several times, was 'a clever little attorney.' One of these cases was the trial of Adelaide Bartlett in a poisoning charge when she was acquited of murder by the skilful advocacy of Clarke. Sir James Pagett, the distinguished Surgeon commented, 'in the interests of science will she tell us how she did it.'

An announcement that the case would be heard by Lord Coleridge, the Lord Chief Justice of England, added to Clarke's anxieties because, while admitting his pre-eminence as a jurist, he distrusted him as a man. His opinion was based upon the methods Coleridge had used while he was a practising attorney. This is what he wrote about him :

> John Duke Coleridge . . . was tall and graceful, moving always with a certain slow dignity. His face was of classic outline, and the clear complexion and the soft blue eyes gave it something of feminine beauty. A drawing of this face with its benign and almost holy expression would have served as a likeness of the 'Seraphic Doctor', and it was not strange that the Western circuit should have called Coleridge 'good John'. . . . But seen from the back he made a very different impression. He had a curiously long and shiny neck and I never walked behind him without thinking of the angel who brought down on the species which he for the moment employed as his disguise the decree that on their bellies should they go henceforth, and wondering why an exception should have been made in this case. And indeed Coleridge was more subtle than any counsel at the Bar. His cross-examination was always painstaking and ingenious, and the more closely the witness was entangled in the net the more suave and gentle was the manner of the cross-examiner. But the main characteristic of the process was its studious unfairness. Coleridge was in the habit of repeating a witness's answer or quoting it in a subsequent question. And somehow the phrase as repeated or quoted was not exactly the same as the witness had first used. The change was very slight, not sufficient to provoke comment. The witness, led quietly along from one admission to another, did not realise until the operation was over how completely he had given his case away.[30]

During April the Lord Chief Justice's Court was converted into a new courtroom with raised bench, witness-box, and chairs instead of the usual seats. On 13th May it was announced that the case would be heard on 1st June. Readers of *The Times* were warned that spectators would be admitted only by ticket, that a number of visitors would be accommodated on the bench, that thirty seats had been reserved for the press, and that the remaining places would go to members of the bar, witnesses and special guests.

A short time before the case came on, Clarke received a visit from Mr George Lewis who brought him a message from Marlborough House to the effect that it would be unpleasant for the Prince if it were known that he travelled about with his own baccarat counters : would Clarke be content if copies were produced for the trial of the same size and colour but without the gilt feathers on the back. Clarke went to Marlborough House, compared the originals with the copies, and said for the purpose of his opening speech he would be quite willing to use the plain counters, but he would make no promise of concealment.

CHAPTER FIVE

Standing Room only

On 1st June 1891 the *Manchester Guardian* announced :

> The hearing of Sir William Gordon-Cumming's action for libel against
> Mr Wilson and others will begin today in the Lord Chief Justice's Court.
> Everything is being done to make the affair a success. Special rows of seats
> for 'distinguished visitors' have been provided; the Prince of Wales will
> be present; and sensational disclosures are confidently expected by society.

For months past the authorities had been besieged by applications for
places as if they were the managers of a theatre where there was to be
an important première. It was the Prince, of course, who was the attraction. Long ago Barnum had told him, 'It is you, sir, who will be the
greatest show on earth,' (and not Barnum's widely advertised circus.)

We know a great deal about what happened during the hearing of
the case because of the large number of very observant journalists who
were present. To begin with the *Pall Mall Gazette* :

> Before the iron gates in the Strand were open, people had begun to
> assemble in the courts, and at half past nine a cluster of fashionably
> attired people gathered round the doors at the Lord Chief Justice's
> Court, in which the *cause célèbre* was to be heard. Admission to the court
> was by ticket only, and the stalwart janitors at the doors refused all
> applications from men and beseechings from women who came unpro-
> vided with the open sesame of the Lord Chief Justice with a stern relent-
> less negative.
>
> The cause was not timed to open before eleven o'clock, but nearly
> every inch of available public room was taken half an hour before that
> time. . . . Upon the long bench close upon a score of chairs were arranged,
> a seat on the left of the judicial chair being reserved for the Prince of
> Wales. The court presented an appearance which, save for the dignity of
> its fittings and its rows of learned looking law books might almost have
> been taken for a theatre at a fashionable matinée. . . . Round about the
> doors were a flock of the junior Bar for whom there seemed to be no hope
> of entrance until a fortuitous circumstance gained it for them. It so hap-
> pened that on this particular day not a single special juror who had been
> summoned had failed to respond to the call of duty. The twelve necessary

for the course of the action were soon in the box to 'well and truly try the issue joined,' and all the others remained in the court fearful and yet hopeful as to their chance of being allowed to stop there. They were not left long in doubt. . . . The Associate issued the cruel edict, 'All jurors in waiting go to Court number three. Follow the officer please. . . .'

A rush of barristers not employed elsewhere, journalists, and artists from the illustrated journals, took their seats as they vacated them. Ushers and doorkeepers were kept busy conducting society women in brilliant summer costumes and gentlemen in frock-coats to the reserved seats until the whole of the space on the floor and in the galleries was filled. The first to take his seat on the bench was Mr Lawson of the *Telegraph*, and he was soon surrounded by a bevy of smart ladies.

A bright fine sun streamed through the skylight upon a gallery filled with ladies in the gayest of summer dresses and dainty bonnets, all looking as exactly interested as though they were going to witness a wedding instead of a trial. Many of them had provided themselves with opera glasses, others carried lorgnettes : they amused themselves by spying out the counsel as they arrived.

What was it like to be present on this particular day? The Special Representative of the *Pall Mall Gazette* answers, 'We here inside, the favoured few . . . who have won paradise in the shape of an *entrée* to the Lord Chief Justice's Court, we are very hot and very crowded and we feel more like *sardines à l'huile* than anything else . . .'

A more learned confrère reminds us that this is indeed an historic occasion : except for the brief incident of the Mordaunt Case, in which the Prince had voluntarily entered the witness-box to clear himself from blame, no heir to the throne had appeared in court since Prince Henry, later the public idol and victor of Agincourt, was committed for contempt of court by Judge Gascoigne in the year 1411. On that occasion, according to Shakespeare, his father, King Henry IV, exclaimed,

> Happy am I that have a man so bold,
> That dares do justice on my proper son;
> And not less happy, having such a son,
> That would deliver up his greatness so
> Into the hands of justice.

The *Star*, that advertised itself as 'The evening paper with the largest circulation,' informs us :

It was ten minutes to eleven when Mrs Arthur Wilson, dressed in black with hat to match and wearing a blue fox boa, took her seat in front of Sir Charles Russell. By then the jury were sworn in and Lady Coleridge arrived carrying her useful fan with which she, on the occasion of another big trial, tapped her slumbering husband while he drowsed through a weary address to the jury.

Then, just when the public had finished admiring the peach-like complexion, the ivory teeth and the smart attire of the Chief's young wife, all lorgnettes and opera glasses were levelled dead on the chair on the left of the judge's seat, for the Prince of Wales wearing a black frock-coat and a big smile had located himself there with Sir Francis Knollys behind him.

The *sardine à l'huile* confided to his notebook, 'We are witnessing the great society drama unfold, we are gazing on the countenance of our Prince and we are (presumably) happy.' He tells us that Gordon-Cumming, who had come in early, was sitting beside his solicitor, Mr St John Wontner, 'his firm, set, handsome features steadily composed to the deadly issue . . . his complexion tanned by travel and adventure to a deep permanent red; the row of defendants, much more nervous and much less distinguished than the man they accuse, but with a certain clearness and decision of type not uninteresting in its way.'

They sat very quietly together, silent and not looking about them. Before their eyes was a large escutcheon with the words inscribed round it, *Honi soit qui mal y pense* – 'Shame be to him who thinks evil,' but undeterred by the writing on the wall, they prepared to implement their accusations. Mr George Lewis, who had escorted them in, was beside them. Captain Somerset was on the other side of them – seeing little prospect of gaining admission, he had aranged for Mr Lewis to subpoena him as a witness so that he would be provided with a seat.

In front of the group of fashionable ladies on the bench, 'close to the footlights,' as Sir Edward Clarke described it, one of the judge's daughters-in-law, Mrs Gilbert Coleridge, sat with a sketch-book on her knee busily at work sketching the chief actors in the drama, occasionally gazing intently through her opera glasses at one of her subjects and then bending over her work again.

At 11.05 the usher called for silence. All stood, including the Prince, while the judge entered through the door at the back of the court : Lord John Duke Coleridge, Lord Chief Justice of England. He and the Prince bowed low to each other : he was tall and gracious with a fine scholar's face and a classic profile : he moved with slow dignity : he was the very model of a Lord Chief Justice.

Lord Coleridge was seventy. He had held his high office for eleven years and he was tired of his profession. He no longer desired to be a judge. He wanted to pass his declining years in his beautiful garden at Ottery St Mary in Devon, 'But,' he had confided to a friend, 'my wife is bright and young, so fitted to adorn the society in which she moves, that to take her from it . . . for my own delight would be a very selfish thing to do.' She sat smiling beside him now in her smart costume and wearing a little hat with towering plumes.

Lady Coleridge, indeed, divided the honours of the Court with her husband. She looked as charming as ever, she nodded and smiled all round, the Court and galleries all sparkled with her friends, and as the case was opened she borrowed the pencils and paper of the Lord Chief Justice at her elbow with delightful audacity. (*Pall Mall Gazette*)

There was first a routine matter to be disposed of : Sir Charles Russell got up and asked that a certain action might stand out of the paper till the present momentous trial had been concluded. Permission being granted, everyone settled down to enjoy the greatest society scandal of recent times.

For a moment while the jury stood up to be sworn, all eyes turned to them. A sensible, commonplace, but not particularly bright looking dozen were these good men and true, with an unfair proportion, perhaps, of broken noses, but with sound untarnished reputations. (*Pall Mall Gazette*)

Lord Coleridge looked round him with a benign, almost a religious expression, waiting for silence. The well-known beauty, Margot Tennant (who later married Mr Asquith who was the second silk for the defendants. He became Prime Minister in 1908) inadvertently let fall her small lace handkerchief : it fluttered down from the gallery onto the heads of the people below. He began in a voice of musical sweetness, addressing the Counsel for the plaintiff :

COLERIDGE : Sir Edward Clarke, His Royal Highness, the Prince of Wales is in attendance, and I am sure you will agree with me that it is not desirable that he should be kept waiting longer than is necessary. Perhaps you may be able to indicate how long His Royal Highness will be required to remain ?

Clarke replied that he could not say then with absolute certainty whether His Royal Highness would be called as a witness for the plaintiff, but they should certainly desire to consult the convenience of His Royal Highness. This reply provoked Coleridge to remark, 'His Royal Highness attends not as a spectator, but on the summons of the parties.'

Mr Charles Gill then defined the issues to be tried by opening the case to the jury on the written pleadings : he was very much younger than his senior, and half a head taller.

When he had finished, Sir Edward Clarke rose to make his opening speech : he was listened to with concentrated attention. His task had been made the more difficult because Mr Lewis had managed to avoid stating what the precise charges against Gordon-Cumming would be. Messrs Wontner's had applied to the courts to make him divulge this information, but the decision had gone against them : they had appealed, and again lost, so Clarke had to make his opening speech in defence of his client without knowing what his opponents would say against him. He began quietly and cautiously, feeling his way :

> May it please your lordship, gentlemen of the jury – you heard from the statement of the pleadings which has just been made by my learned friend, Mr Gill, who with me has the honour and responsibility of appearing for Sir William Gordon-Cumming in this matter, what is the question for you to decide. It is a simple question, aye or no, did Sir William Gordon-Cumming cheat at cards?

He showed at once that he was leaving the way open for the defendants to withdraw their accusation, and that he was trying to make it easy for them to do so :

> In opening this case to you I shall as far as possible avoid any comment upon the conduct of these persons who have been concerned in the matter and through whom this accusation has arisen; and if it be necessary to make comments, they must be made by me at a later stage of the case. In opening this case to you I desire to put, as simply as I possibly can, and without attempting to distribute blame amongst any of those who are mentioned, the circumstances out of which this accusation arose.

He described Sir William's military record, his devotion to duty, his long-standing friendship with the Prince, his ample means,

> He now finds himself in court here to face an accusation that he,

after a life hitherto so spent in the enjoyment of privileges and advantages such as I have pointed to, suddenly descended to cheat at cards, to attempt to rob one or two of his oldest friends. Now, gentlemen, it is a grave accusation, and one that wants to be seriously considered.

He then pictured the scene at Tranby Croft, and explained how baccarat is played, commenting, 'It seems to me to be about the most unintelligent mode of losing your own money, or getting somebody else's, I ever heard of.' (A ripple of laughter ran round the court, Lord Coleridge smiled rather grimly and there was a faint flicker of amusement on the Prince's face.) He said that some of the players were old hands and some complete novices, and he gave details of the system upon which Gordon-Cumming was playing. As early as Monday evening, 8th September, the Wilsons had been in communication with each other about their accusation that Gordon-Cumming had cheated, but 'not a syllable had been said about it; no sign had been given in their behaviour to Sir William Gordon-Cumming that there was any sort of suspicion of this kind in their minds; and on the evening of Wednesday the 10th, when he was going to dress for dinner, Sir William Gordon-Cumming was astounded by receiving a visit from Lord Coventry who told him that people who were in the house were making statements with regard to his cheating at cards, and that it was a very serious matter . . . He peremptorily and absolutely denied the charge.'

Lord Coventry and General Owen Williams naturally thought, when circumstances of this kind occurred, that there should be left on record a full and complete account of the whole matter, giving, as they said, an accurate account of all the circumstances. They signed that document, and handed it to the custody of His Royal Highness, the Prince of Wales, in order that it might be kept with the undertaking which I now have in my hand. Sir Francis Knollys was good enough just now to hand it to Mr Lewis.

He was about to read the document when Russell commented that it would not be evidence against the defendants who were no parties to it, 'but,' he continued, 'as I gather my learned friend intends to call those who did prepare it, namely General Owen Williams and Lord Coventry, I have no objection, on that understanding, to its being read.'

As counsel may examine, but not cross-examine, witnesses they call, this would have prevented Clarke from cross-examining the two courtiers: he therefore replied that he intended to call only General Williams, 'as I must leave somebody whom I shall have the opportunity of cross-examining.' He explained that he was not saying that certain statements in the document must be taken as absolutely conclusive evidence against the defendants,

> but it is, as you will readily see at once, gentlemen, of cardinal importance in this case; for when two persons, who because of their experience and position in society were considered to be persons who safely might be consulted with regard to a case of this kind, deliberately set down a full statement of the transaction as they knew it, it is most important for the jury, who have to judge what did take place, to see what their account was.

He proceeded to read the document, known as the *précis*, that had been read to Gordon-Cumming at the general's house in Hill Street, disillusioning him about the quality of the two courtiers' friendship for him, and throwing him into a state bordering on despair. This time he listened without displaying any emotion.

> The Prince sat firmly in the red morocco chair assigned to him on Lord Coleridge's left, his arms folded, his face impassive save for an occasional and very faint smile. (*The Daily Chronicle*)

When he had finished reading, Clarke laid the document down, and commented:

> The last sentence, that it is an accurate statement of all the facts of the case, can hardly perhaps be accepted now, because it is only right I should tell you at once that the defendants in their answers to the interrogatories have denied the agreement to watch Sir William Gordon-Cumming, which is specifically stated in the memorandum to have been made; and it is certainly the fact, and I shall prove it by General Owen Williams, when in the box, that with regard to the suggestion that signing this document was a confession of guilt, that that suggestion was made by Sir William Gordon-Cumming, who objected at first because, he said, it would be a confession of guilt; and then they said it might be so, but there was no other mode of escaping a horrible public scandal.
>
> Gentlemen, I said I would make no comment on the behaviour of persons who were concerned in this case, but ... how these gentlemen can have imagined that this arrangement would prevent the matter

being mentioned, I cannot conceive. This is signed by gentlemen only; but there were ladies cognisant of the matter, and it would be difficult for them to keep the secret. Some of the men who knew the secret were married, and it would be impossible for them to keep it. . . . the one mistake that Sir William Gordon-Cumming made in this case, which he most deeply regrets . . . was that he took the advice of those men whom he thought his friends, and consented to make, what was not so great a sacrifice perhaps, a sacrifice of playing cards in the future, in the hope that he might avoid that scandal which they seemed so to dread, a scandal which he supposed, and as was represented to him, might be of most unhappy consequences to society at large. But, gentlemen while he signed that, as I told you, he from beginning to end asserted his innocence of the charge; and I dare say it will occur to you if Sir William Gordon-Cumming had been thinking more of himself, and less of those who honoured him with friendship; if he had been the common cheat – which he must have been if, in these circumstances and in that company, he had tried to get money from his friends by dishonest means – he never would have signed a document like that. He, if a guilty man, would have been prepared to meet the accusation whenever it came and face it out to the end; and the fact that Sir William Gordon-Cumming signed that, regrettable as it is from the inferences which have already been drawn from the fact since it has been published, is, I submit to you, no sort of evidence that he admitted himself, or knew himself, to be guilty of this offence. But the importance of this document is to my mind very much greater than this. Did His Royal Highness the Prince of Wales, and General Owen Williams and Lord Coventry, believe when that document was signed, that Sir William Gordon-Cumming had cheated at cards at Tranby Croft? It is a question of vital interest . . . or did they think, as they say, that the only way of avoiding a great public and social scandal was to get him to sign this, and in consideration of a promise of not playing cards in the future on the one side, to get a promise of secrecy on the other?

He reminded the jury that His Royal Highness was a field-marshal in the army and familiar with the rule that when an officer's conduct is impugned it is his duty to report the imputation made upon him to his commanding officer and demand that there would be an investigation at once : it was impossible, he said, for His Royal Highness and General Owen Williams not to do this if they believed him guilty. And Lord Coventry was bound by regulations and rules of honour as strict as those which affect the army: if he had believed Gordon-Cumming guilty he would have had no right to let him remain a member of the clubs, the Carlton, the Turf and the Marlborough, to which he himself also belonged.

It is impossible to conceive that these three gentlemen, His Royal Highness, General Owen Williams and Lord Coventry, at the time that document was signed, believed that Sir William Gordon-Cumming was guilty. If they did not believe him to be guilty, why did they allow him to sign it? Because, I fear, there was pressing on their minds, and urged by them in the strongest terms – terms almost of menace against Sir William Gordon-Cumming – the belief that the mere mention of the fact that at the Wilsons, at Tranby Croft, the Prince had been banker at a baccarat table would be of itself such a social scandal that any arrangement was necessary in order to prevent its coming out. There is nothing in the whole course of this case which carries any imputation upon the Prince of Wales, or those who were at Tranby Croft with him at the time; but that is the meaning, and the only meaning, of their forcing Sir William Gordon-Cumming to sign this document; and the very fact that they did so is the completest proof that they themselves did not then believe he had been guilty of the offence.

He then made an important point – that according to the record, Mr Lycett Green's original accusation was that Gordon-Cumming had not only added to his stake after he had won, but that he had also withdrawn part of his stake when the cards went against him, an accusation more difficult to meet and answer: the defendants had now withdrawn it, so the accusation upon which Lord Coventry and General Owen Williams had formed their opinion, and which had frightened them into making Gordon-Cumming sign the undertaking, no longer existed.

He explained again the system upon which Gordon-Cumming had been working, the *coup de trois*, which, he said, might easily have been mistaken by inexperienced players for cheating, whereas it was in fact an ordinary procedure of the game. He pointed out that the stakes were constantly under the observation of the croupier and the banker, who had to estimate how much was on the table before deciding upon his own play, but no experienced person had seen any irregularity. He concluded:

I am here to defend that soldier's honour. I am here to defend it by his evidence, and by such careful examination of the circumstances which are alleged against him as I hope and believe will satisfy you that the accusation was one not founded upon fact; honestly made, perhaps, but if so an honest mistake – that it is an accusation which, when it is brought here and examined before you, cannot stand and cannot be upheld against Sir William Gordon-Cuming. The issues are heavy ones for him. If the accusation be upheld against him, if you find it to be proved, there ends in this court that career of honour and of public service which his thousand friends hoped would be continued for many splendid years to come. He must go away, degraded from the profession to which he belongs, exiled from the friendship and companionship of those he has known as friends, and in another land, and perhaps under another name, seek some career which may dim, but cannot efface, the memory of these transactions.

I do not ask you on his behalf for sympathy, or even pity. If he is guilty of this offence he deserves no sympathy; if he is innocent, the sympathy will come to console him for the agonies of the time that has gone by before he was able to meet this accusation in court. I do not ask for pity. Pity, indeed, if he were guilty of this, all of us would feel for the man who, after such a career, passed into darkness, and of whose past life his friends would never speak, of whom they would think only with a sigh. But that pity would follow, not prevent, the punishment.

I hope for a very different result than that. From the moment when he knew that this charge was being talked about from lip to lip, he claimed to be tried before the best and highest tribunal that this country can give; no bastard imitation tribunal of justice where laymen pretend to be judges, with assessors sitting to decide upon a question of this sort, but before the Great Justiciar of England, the man who inherits and sustains the proudest traditions of the English Bench, and before that special jury which, after all, is the best tribunal for the ascertainment and judgement of facts that anyone has ever been able to invent.

Gentlemen, the issue is in your hands. You will not be moved from your duty of impartial judgement by appeals on one side or the other; but I do trust that Sir William Gordon-Cumming may go away from this Court, when your verdict is given, back to the life of honour and repute that he has led hitherto among his fellows, that he may still wear in your service, and in his country's service, a sword that has never been stained but with the blood of his country's foes, and that he, as he risked his life for you and yours in the times gone by may, in his hour of peril here, find protection in your instincts of justice.

When he sat down there was what the *Pall Mall Gazette* called, 'a great stir in the Court' and an obvious sensation, 'but no demonstration calling for any reproof.'

Gordon-Cumming now entered the witness-box, a tall soldierly figure. His grey eyes scanned the Court, recognising a friend here and there. He leaned against the front rail of the box, resting his arm upon it, and as he did so he appeared to turn his back on the Prince of Wales. There was a mutter of protest from the crowd.

The examination-in-chief began – a series of questions put to him by his Counsel with the object of giving him an opportunity to put his case in his own words. He said, answering the opening questions, that he was the fourth baronet in line, forty-two years of age, with a seat in Scotland and a residence in London, and that he had been in the army twenty-three years. He described his service in the Zulu War and in the Egyptian campaigns, serving with the Guards Camel Corps in the Gordon Relief Expedition. He had been honoured with the acquaintance of His Royal Highness the Prince of Wales for the last twenty years and for the last ten years with his friendship.

All this had been mentioned in Clarke's speech, but the jury, in arriving at their verdict, were supposed to consider only the evidence they had heard from the lips of the plaintiff and the defendants. Therefore Clarke took him through the principal events of his stay at Tranby Croft. First he was asked to define the nature of his acquaintance with the Wilson family – he had been to entertainments at their house in London, he had been once before to Tranby Croft, in 1885, before Ethel was married, and he had seen her and Mr Lycett Green at York after their marriage.

Then he described the game of baccarat on the first evening, where everyone was sitting, and that His Royal Highness took the bank.

And on this occasion, did you play your 'system'? – Most of the evening, I did.

Just tell me what you usually did in regard to that, what you did on this occasion, the system of staking. Suppose now that a coup is coming off? – When I stake a £5 counter and win, that would represent £10, and I should then add a third counter in front of me, which would represent a second coup of £15.

If you stake £5 and win, a £5 counter would be coming to you from the bank, and you would add another £5 counter, making three £5 counters, or £15, making that your stake for the second coup? – Yes.

If you won that, would you go on to the next coup in the same way? – I really cannot say. I had no system about that.

At all events starting with £5, winning, and adding another £5 counter to it upon the second coup, you would win £15, and that would represent a win of £20 upon the two coups? – Exactly.

COLERIDGE : If he stakes and wins he gets £30.

CLARKE : Of the stakes, £10 is his own money. Of the first £10, £5 is his own.

RUSSELL : He gets £5 on the first coup and £15 on the second.

CLARKE : He wins £20, because of the £15 which is staked the second time, £10 comes out of his own pocket.

COLERIDGE : I see.

The examination continued :

Did you go on that way occasionally during that evening? – Yes.

You kept your tableaux until the end of the evening, and then destroyed them? – Yes.

Without going into detail, may I ask you this; is it important that a banker should know how much there is on one side of the table as compared with how much there is on the other? – Yes; it is advisable he should know.

And when there is a much larger sum on one side of the table than on the other, does the banker sometimes call attention to it, and ask if anyone will put on a higher stake so as to equalise the two tableaux? – Yes.

Do you remember if that happened on both the evenings in question? – It certainly happened on both.

Did His Royal Highness call attention to the inequality of the stake? – Either His Royal Highness or General Owen Williams, one or the other.

What did you do on either of these occasions? Did you stake? – Yes, on both nights.

What did you say? – When either General Owen Wiliams or the Prince of Wales called attention to the stake, I said : 'I will go £25 on the other tableau,' meaning the opposite tableau to which I was sitting.

In that case you would not put down a stake at all? – No.

You would be heard to say that, and that tableau would be considered to be increased by your £25? – Yes.

Did you win £25 more than once? – Once on the first night two or three times the second.

Clarke then went on to the second night's play. Gordon-Cumming again described where everyone was sitting, and said that he helped Lady Coventry with her cards.

On that second evening, did you notice anything about Mr Arthur Stanley Wilson's luck? – I recollect his winning five coups running, but I certainly said nothing.

That was at the time he was handling the cards on behalf of that tableau? – Yes.

Did you make an observation to him upon it? – Yes; I said novices always had luck at cards.

And you had your stakes on all five coups? – Yes.

Clarke then took him through the events of the two days in question, so that he could say that no one had made any comment on his play on either evening and that he had heard nothing at all about it until Lord Coventry and General Owen Williams had come to him on the evening of 9th Septemeber and given him the astounding information that there were objections to the way he had played baccarat : he had emphatically and indignantly denied the suggestion that he had cheated, and told them it was 'a foul and abominable falsehood.'

Then came his description of his interview with the Prince of Wales to whom he had expressed his intention of grossly insulting his accusers – a course from which the Prince had dissuaded him. He described how he had come to sign the undertaking never to play again, under the threat that there would be a terrible scandal if he did not, and that the accusation would be spread all over the racecourse next morning. When he asked who had originated the proposal that he should be made to sign the undertaking, General Owen Williams told him that it was Mr Lycett Green.

How did Sir William back up his counsel's eloquence? With great coolness and steadiness. His nervousness seemed to quit him as he entered the box. His hands left his moustache, and settled quietly on each other; he leaned firmly on the rail; his voice was dry, almost hard; his grey eyes did not flinch. Sir Edward made him repeat verbatim the conversation with the Prince, a striking phrase in which was his declaration that for twenty-five years he had tried to lead the life befitting an officer and a gentleman. (*Daily Chronicle*)

The final questions were :

Did you cheat at baccarat that night? – I did not.
Is there any truth whatever in the accusation against you? – There is none whatsoever, of any sort or kind.

The Court then adjourned. Lord Coleridge and the Prince with Sir Francis Knollys retired through the door at the back of the courtroom to the judge's private rooms for lunch. Lady Coleridge followed with her friends to another room where refreshment had been provided for them.

*

After the recess, Gordon-Cumming again entered the witness-box.

There were ladies everywhere – on the Bench, where they were shepherded by Lady Coleridge and her sister – in the public gallery and in the judge's gallery where Mr Stephen Coleridge had them under his care. They used their lorgnettes on Sir William, they laughed at small jokes, they swept out with motley skirts at lunch, and swept in very late, disturbing Sir Charles Russell's cross-examination, to his great discomposure. The Chief Justice himself, with his grave scholar's face and dignified manner, had to share attention with his wife, sitting close on his right hand, and smilingly alert for all comers. (*Daily Chronicle*)

Russell began by establishing, strictly in accordance with his brief, that Gordon-Cumming believed Lord Coventry and General Owen Williams to be men of the highest integrity – this was to add weight to their testimony that would come later, that they believed him to be guilty.

After lunch Sir Charles Russell stood up, snuff-box in hand, his face grave, one would have said with a touch of commiseration on it. The Cross-examination opened, as is usual with the great counsel, very quietly, but it developed rapidly into a quick and stern encounter of wits, in which the lawyer did not always come off best. (*Daily Chronicle*)

Am I right in the suggestion that you have been on very intimate terms with General Owen Williams for a period of twenty years? – Certainly.

I think you have travelled with him in Africa and India? – I have.

You have frequently stayed as an intimate visitor at his house? – Very frequently.

You have sailed with him in his yacht frequently? – I have.

And have always regarded him as a fast and true friend of yours? – I have.

And have always regarded him as a man of the highest honour? – I have.

And still so regard him? – I do.

You have not been so intimate with Lord Coventry? – No, I have not, I must have known him fully ten years.

And you also regard him as a man of honour? – Certainly.

Russell had to establish next, with the help of the letter Mrs Wilson had received from Lady Middleton, that Gordon-Cumming regarded the Wilsons also as people of integrity.

You have told us that you have been a visitor on several occasions at Mrs Wilson's house at Tranby Croft? – On one occasion only, previous to last year.

On two occasions altogether? – Yes.

And have dined at her house in town? – I have lunched there. I cannot recollect dining there. I have been to her house and met her about town.

Her daughter, Mrs Lycett Green, you have also met? – Yes.

Her son, Mr Arthur Wilson, I think you have not met before this visit? – No.

Mr Lycett Green you did know, but not very much? – No; not very much. They live near York. I was at their house on one occasion.

And you played baccarat that night? – Yes; we played baccarat that night.

It was a family dinner party? – No; very few were there.

You were on your way to Scotland, and you proposed to dine with them whilst waiting for the night mail? – Yes.

There were only three of you at the table? – Three or four.

It was a bit obscure why Gordon-Cumming should have dined with people he hardly knew, but the reason was that Ethel too was very friendly with his sister, Lady Middleton.

The remaining defendant, Mr Berkeley Levett, is a subaltern of your regiment? – He is.

Did you, or have you, Sir William, any reason to suggest that any one of these defendants entertained towards you unfriendly feelings? – None whatsoever.

Or had any cause of quarrel at any time with you? – Never.

You have said, have you not, that the worst of it is you felt they were perfectly conscientious in the matter, and they believed they did see you resorting to foul play? – I did believe so. Pardon me, are you reading any letter of mine? Is that what you wish to imply?

I don't wish to put it in that way, for reasons the Solicitor-General knows . . .

CLARKE : Certainly.

(Russell thereupon admitted he was reading the letter.)

Does it not express your feeling? – Certainly.

It is a letter to a person you don't wish to trouble to come here to-day, and I will read it again : 'The worst is I feel they are acting perfectly conscientiously in the matter, and they believe they did see me resort to foul play.' About this game of baccarat, you have played it a good deal, I have gathered from what you have said? – Yes.

The counters on this occasion ranged from 5s. to £10? – I think there were counters ranging a great deal higher but they were not employed.

The counters that were employed ranged from 5s. to £10? – Yes.

All friends in a friendly party in a country house? – Yes.

You would call it a very innocent game of baccarat? – Yes, I should call it a very quiet game of baccarat.

No discredit to anybody to be connected with such a game? – None whatsoever.

Or to be one of a party playing in such a game? – No.

Or to be known to play such a game? – Certainly not, in my estimation.

You would not therefore call the fact of its being known that General Williams or the Prince of Wales was playing at such a game – you would not call the mere knowledge of that fact a horrible scandal? – No.

And no scandal at all? – No.

These were deceptively simple questions. Through them, Russell had succeeded in getting an admission from Gordon-Cumming that he thought no scandal attached to the Prince of Wales for playing baccarat –

important because, at a superficial level, it seemed to invalidate his motive for signing the document never to play again – the motive that there would be a terrible scandal if he refused to sign and the Prince would be involved, the truth of which events had fully demonstrated. Gordon-Cumming, however, had expressly stated that, 'in his estimation', no scandal attached to the Prince.

Russell now came to the main purpose of his cross-examination – to bring up the accusations against the plaintiff time after time from different angles, in different words, to try to find some weak point in his defence, some inconsistency, some partial admission. The questions were difficult to answer because his accuser was instancing particular coups, and he had no reason to remember these more than all the others.

Mr George Lewis brought Russell a miniature table made of mahogany and placed it on the desk in front of him : it had slots round it and tickets with names on them.

CLARKE : I should point out that this is not a reproduction but a diagram.
RUSSELL : It is not intended to be a model.

He continued the cross-examination :

As we have correctly heard from my learned friend, the game is decided by the possession of the eight or nine, or by the highest card approaching the eight or nine? – Precisely.

The eight or nine are called 'naturals'? – Yes, if they are dealt in the first two cards.
COLERIDGE : If you have two cards, supposing you get a four and a six as the result of them?
RUSSELL : My lord, that would be a very bad hand. In that case you would ask for another card in the hope of getting nine.
COLERIDGE : It resembles *vingt-et-un*.
RUSSELL : I am told it is very much the same. (He continued the cross-examination.)

Then we had another interval of baccarat in which the possible forms of cheating – or the dishonest increase of a stake after a successful coup seemed probable, or had been declared – were exhaustively put forward. Suddenly the counsel's voice was raised to a strong resonant note, and the questions became terribly pointed. Did not Sir William stake £5 at the first coup on the evening of the eighth, the opening night? He did not recollect? Did he not receive £15? Sir William's answer was firm and comprehensive. If he staked £5 he won £5, if £15 he won £15, and from that position he could not be moved.

Then as to the position of the hands. They were folded the one over the other in the attitude in which Sir William disposed them in the witness-box, and under them were his counters, the stakes being some inches further on to the centre of the table. Did he not slip two additional counters from his pile to the stakes after a successful coup? Various ways were suggested – that he had a broad carpenter's pencil under which they were slipped – that the means used were the sheet of paper on which he recorded the tableaux. Sir Charles paused between the inquiries, and leant back eyeing his witness steadily. But Sir William stood to his guns. (*Daily Chronicle*)

There were again a number of questions concerning where the various people were sitting on the second night. Then Russell handed a photograph up to Gordon-Cumming at the same time explaining to Lord Coleridge, 'It is a photograph, my lord, of the table and the room, but it appears that the chalk line on the table was erased.' He continued :

Would that give a reasonable idea of the table on the second occasion? – I think the chalk line was nearer the edge of the table, otherwise I think it is correct.

There was a clearly marked chalk line there? – I think there was. (After a pause) I remember there was a chalk line on the second night.

Do you recollect on the second night that Lady Coventry was exceptionally lucky? – No, I cannot say I remember whether she was or not.

Did you advise her as to whether she should or should not take cards? – Yes, several times.

Do you recollect one occasion when in her original two cards she had a hand in which she had either six or seven? – I cannot recollect any particular occasion at all.

I put it to you because it was after this coup that the incident you mentioned took place, and the banker called attention to the stakes. Did you advise Lady Coventry not to take a card, and did you increase your stake after you saw her cards by adding to the £5 one £10 counter over the line? – No, I did not.

I put it to you, was it not on that occasion that the observation was made about the manner of staking? – I cannot recollect when the observation was made about people putting down their stakes.

I put it to you whether you were not paid £5, and you said, 'Owen there is £15 more to come here'? (Gordon-Cumming noticed he had slipped in the word 'more' and corrected him,) – No; my observation was, 'Owen, there is £15 to come here,' because I had not been paid at all.

What was your stake? – To the best of my recollection it was £15 that I had put down.

The counters are of different colours according to their nominal value? – Yes.

Did you, after this incident, with your pencil, push an additional stake across the line? – An additional stake after the cards had been dealt?

Yes? – No.

He was then asked whether he had noticed Mr Lycett Green leaving the table, sending a note and coming back again – which he had not.

Now, I do not know that I need go into the matter in greater detail. I cannot fix this with reference to the note being brought in because you say you have no recollection of it. I put it to you whether, later in the evening, you did not increase your stake on several occasions after the cards were dealt? – No; on no occasion.

Sometimes after a card was favourable, and sometimes after the banker declared what his point was? – Never; not on any single occasion.

You mentioned, as accounting for the position of your hands over your counters, that it was with the view of keeping them from falling off the table. Is it not the fact that you kept a considerable quantity of counters in your pocket? – Yes. Not a considerable quantity, but a certain amount.

Was there any considerable winner but you? – I cannot say, but I should suppose not.

Two hundred and twenty-five pounds, I think you said? – Yes.

Russell now tried to demonstrate that his behaviour after he was accused was proof that he was guilty. He began by reading passages from General Williams's *précis*, describing how he and Lord Coventry had told him of the charges against him :

That is the substance of the interview. Did you ever learn what was the charge against you further than that conversation? – No. Further than that I never knew the charge against me, except that they had seen me cheating.

Did you ever ask? – I did not, except on the occasion of the interview, when they said they didn't know.

What were you told? – I was told that five persons made the charge. I asked who they were – not then, but after the interview with the Prince of Wales and General Owen Williams. I was told there and then.

Why did you not tell us that before? – Because I was not asked.

Do you now say that at your interview with Lord Coventry and General Williams you did not learn who your accusers were? – I cannot say whether I did or not.

If you had asked who your accusers were in so serious a matter, surely you would have remembered what the answer was? – I cannot recollect.

Did you ask to be confronted with them?

This was actually a very tricky question, and Gordon-Cumming fell for it. It would never have occurred to him to 'ask to be confronted with' his accusers. His intention was to seek them out himself and grossly insult them, as he told the Prince, who, however, dissuaded him from this course. We know also that General Williams exerted himself to persuade him not to have a show-down with his accusers, or else why should he have written just before leaving Tranby Croft, 'I so thoroughly see now for my own sake as well as that of others it is essential to avoid an open row and the scandal arising therefrom.'? But he was taken off his guard by Russell's question, and he answered quite simply that he had not asked to be confronted with them.

Russell, having scored a point that seemed to put Gordon-Cumming in a bad light, kept on hammering at it.

Sir William Gordon-Cumming, as a lieutenant-Colonel and a man of the world, in a matter of this kind did you need any suggestion as to what you ought to do? – I had lost my head, Sir Charles, on that occasion. If I had not lost my head I would not have signed that document.

I am not coming to the document yet. I am at an earlier stage. You were told that five persons had charged you with cheating at cards. You did not ask what those particular acts of cheating were? – I cannot recollect whether I asked or not. I learned the names at the second interview.

But here is a most serious charge. Surely your first question would be, 'Who are my accusers?' would it not – I think I was told who they were, but I was told a subsequent investigation would take place.

Were you not told at the later interview that Mr Lycett Green objected to signing the paper, and wished to have it out and be confronted with you?

This again was a tricky question. The truth seems to be that Lycett Green had first insisted that the document be signed or he would immediately spread the scandal. Only after Gordon-Cumming had signed it he demurred and wondered if it might after all not be sufficient protection for him; and the only time he could be said to have asked to be confronted with Gordon-Cumming was when they were already adding their signatures and he was perfectly certain the courtiers wouldn't allow it because all their work would have been undone.

Were you not told that? – No.
Did you ask to be confronted with Mr Lycett Green? – No.
You knew that your own brother officer was one of the accusers? – Yes.
Did you ask to be confronted with him? – I asked to be confronted with nobody.
You knew that Mrs Wilson your hostess, was one of your accusers? – Yes.
Did you ask to be confronted with her? – I asked to be confronted with nobody.
Why not? – I cannot tell. It was an act of folly on my part, but I did not do so.

He might have answered that he had declared his intention to confront his accusers on the first public occasion and grossly insult them, but that the Prince and General Williams had dissuaded him. Rather than drag the Prince into the argument, he let it pass.

Sir William Gordon-Cumming, I want to know this. Do you pledge your oath that at the later interview with General Williams and Lord Coventry, you did not hear that Mr Lycett Green wished to be confronted with you, and wished to have it out face to face? – I have no recollection of it.
Is that all you have to say? – I have no recollection . . . (after a pause) But I may go further, Sir Charles, and say emphatically that no such suggestion was made.
Now, I want to ask you whether you were not told who your accusers were at the first interview? – I cannot recollect.

COLERIDGE : I think the information may have been volunteered to me, but I have no recollection whether I asked or not.

Russell continued his cross-examination :

Now, as to the challenge of Mr Lycett Green to confront you – let me see if I appreciate what you say. You say that you do not recollect that you were told that, at the interview with Lord Coventry and General Williams? – No.

This was ridiculous really, and probably only Russell with his overpowering personality and enormous self-assurance could have put it over. Gordon-Cumming received no such challenge. Obviously if Lycett Green had been so minded he could have gone directly to him and had it out with him : he had preferred to involve all these people instead.

Suddenly the cross-examination shifted to the charge and the signature of the incriminating paper, and again there was a pitiless hail of interrogatories, such as these : Did you ever ask what the charge was? Did you ask who your accusers were? Did you ask to be confronted with them? And finally, How did you, an innocent man, come to sign such a document? Most of these questions were steadily answered, though Sir William's recollections were vague, but at the last the witness rather lost his habitual phlegm. In a rapid eager monotone, he declared that a pistol had been put at his head, that he had lost his head, that he had done under impulse what he had ever since regretted. (*Daily Chronicle*)

Russell continued :

I understand your point to be that, because you were not advised to seek an encounter with your accusers, you did not think it right to seek it? – When a man is in the position I was, Sir Charles Russell, he is not responsible for his actions. I had a most horrible charge made against me, and I virtually lost my head on that occasion.

You were cool enough to ask to see the Prince of Wales? – Certainly; it was my first thought.

And he agreed to see you in the presence of Lord Coventry and General Williams? – I think so.

But you think you lost your head? – I consider I did.

Did you, with this accusation hanging over you, ask the Prince to write his name in the year book of one of the young ladies of the house? – I did, immediately before dinner.

You don't seem to have lost your head very much? – Pardon me, there is no losing one's head in a simple thing like that.

Russell then passed to an aspect of the case that was a source of embarrassment both to the Prince and General Williams. As officers of the army – the Prince was a field marshal – they should have reported the accusation without delay to Gordon-Cumming's commanding officer, Colonel Stracey. Not only had they failed to do this : they had rejected Gordon-Cumming's proposal that it should be done. It was a serious breach of the military regulations. Clarke had made the point that they must have believed him to be innocent : it would have been inexcusable to have allowed him to remain a member of his regiment and of his clubs had they believed him guilty.

Do you recollect also whether at the interview with the Prince you said anything about referring the matter to your commanding officer, the Duke of Cambridge? (He was in fact the Commander-in-Chief.) – I have no recollection of using the Duke of Cambridge's name.

Do you recollect General Owen Williams saying to you in reply, Certainly, by all means, if you think right? – No.

And did General Williams, an old friend of twenty years standing, add, 'But I am afraid he will not be so lenient to you as we are'? Did he say that? – I have no recollection of his saying anything of the kind.

But in this matter of social life or death, surely you can recollect whether it was said? – I cannot recollect it.

Again Gordon-Cumming may have been trying to shield the Prince, or perhaps he was growing tired. The next few questions were about his meeting Mrs Wilson on the stairs, and his leaving Tranby Croft early on the morning of the 10th.

Now, I put one question which I ask you anxiously to consider. Do you suggest, as has been suggested by learned counsel today, that Lord Coventry and General Owen Williams advised you to sign that paper, and asked you to leave the house, believing you to be an innocent man? Did they so believe you? (There should have been an objection here, because a witness cannot be asked what somebody else believes. He answered quite correctly,) – I am totally unable to say.

And as you stand there now, are you unable to say? – I am perfectly unable to say. I have had no conversation with either of them since, except on one occasion, and they never expressed any opinion as to my innocence or guilt.

So that you are quite unable to say whether in advising you they were advising you as an old friend whom they believed to be innocent? – I had a communication from them, the gist of which was, to the best of my recollection, that there was no possibilty of believing other than my guilt from the fact of there being five to one against me. I received that letter two days after leaving Tranby Croft.

Then the suggestion made on your behalf that these gentlemen could not possibly believe you guilty was not yours? – I do not understand.

CLARKE : I am responsible for making that statement in opening the case.

Russell then went through the events of the evening from the time he was first accused, leading up to his interview with the Prince of Wales and to his signing of the undertaking :

He was perfectly cool and collected throughout the tedious ordeal, and at no time allowed himself to be confused. When Sir Charles Russell rose to cross-examine there was a trace of nervousness, but he frankly replied to the interrogatories and admitted that on the fatal evening when he had been charged with cheating he had done many foolish things, chief among them being the signing of a paper practically admitting his guilt, but he declared that lying under such a foul charge no man could be expected to be responsible for his actions. (*Daily Express*)

Sir William Gordon-Cumming, why did you, as an innocent man sign that paper? – Because it was put to me by those two friends of mine, on whom I placed implicit reliance, that I had no chance of clearing myself; that, however often I reiterated my innocence, I had no chance of proving it against five witnesses. I was told that a horrible scandal would follow, in which my name, my regiment, and everything would suffer unless I signed that paper.

You were told that the scandal would be all over the place? – Yes.

The horrible scandal would be that you, an officer of the Guards, had been accused by five witnesses of cheating at cards? – Probably the word scandal was used by General Williams – a scandal to which the name of the Prince of Wales and of other persons would be attached.

How? – It would not be desirable that the name of the Prince of Wales should be associated with a game of baccarat with an officer who had been accused of cheating by his hosts or by the people of the house in which the Prince of Wales was staying.

I think you told me that it was an innocent game? – It was a scandal for a man in my position.

And to avoid that scandal you signed that paper? – Yes, to avoid the scandal I signed the paper, and I have never ceased to regret that I did so.

Now I ask you again, do you not know that, rightly or wrongly, these friends of yours were advising you as they thought best in your interests as a guilty man? – I was not aware on what grounds they gave their advice.

Do you think they were honestly advising you? – I think that nothing could have been worse than that advice they gave me, and nothing could have been more unwise than my following it.

I was not asking whether the advice was good or bad. Did you not know – did you not believe that it was the advice of men who were advising you in your interest, and in the belief that you were guilty? – No; I do not think they believed it at the time.

You did within twenty-four hours? – That is a different thing. I had signed the paper in twenty-four hours.

Were you not warned by General Williams that you were not to meet the Prince of Wales? – No. I was by letter, not warned, but requested.

You made reference to a letter from General Owen Williams? – Yes.

Within twenty-four hours of the accusation? – Yes.

Have you that letter? – No. I think I destroyed it directly I received it.

Why? Have you destroyed all the letters you received at the time? – Most of them.

On what principle did you destroy some and keep others? – On no principle.

Would you be able to recognise a copy of the letter which you destroyed? (A copy was handed up to him).

CLARKE : This document has never been disclosed before, and I do not know whose custody it came from.

RUSSELL : Its authorship is apparent on the face of it. May we take it that that was the letter you received, Sir William Gordon-Cumming? I think this is the gist of the letter I received.

CLARKE : The witness says that that is the gist of the letter he received. In the absence of any information as to where the copy comes from, I object.

COLERIDGE : In his evidence the witness says he destroyed the letter, and he says now that this is the gist of it.

CLARKE : In the case of the letter of Sir William Gordon-Cumming which it is proposed to read there can, of course, be no objection, nor will there be if Sir Charles Russell will say who produces this letter.
COLERIDGE : (brushing aside the objection) It may have been picked up in the street.

The objection no doubt arose because, when General Owen Williams was called upon by Messrs Wontner to supply copies of the relevant documents, he ignored the request and allowed his correspondence to be used only by Messrs Lewis & Lewis. This unethical behaviour Clarke found particularly distasteful. The cross-examination continued :

Before I read this letter, am I right in saying that you signed the promise on the advice of Lord Coventry and General Williams, and on their advice alone ? – Yes.

Nobody else advised you ? – No.

You do not suggest that the Prince of Wales did ? – I did not see the Prince of Wales after the one interview.

I now read two letters . . . The first from you to General Williams :- 'Thursday, Sept. 11th – Dear Owen – I hope you will take an opportunity of telling the Prince of Wales how entirely I was guided in my action yesterday by his advice and yours and Coventry's . . .' Why did you speak of the advice of His Royal Highness – Because I believed that the document was submitted to the Prince of Wales before being sent to me.

[Russell continued to read the letter.] 'While utterly and entirely denying the truth of the allegations brought against me, I thoroughly see how, for my own sake as well as for that of others, it is essential to avoid an open row and the scandal arising therefrom. It is difficult for anyone, however innocent he may know himself to be, to come well out of an accusation brought by numbers against one alone etc.*

You wrote that letter, just read, and left it to be given to General Owen Williams on the morning of your departure ? – I did.

He then read the answer, signed by the Prince, General Owen Williams and Lord Coventry, and dated 11th September, saying they had dealt with him as old friends and in his interest, but they considered they had acted quite as leniently as they possibly could under the painful circum-

---

*The complete letter is on pages 37-8. Russell misread the date : it was actually 10th September. Slight differences in the text of the letter are obviously due either to mis-reading or to mis-transcription.

stances of the case – mentioning also that he would receive a cheque for his winnings.

Have you disposed of it ? – The money is in my possession.

As a fact, the cheque has been paid into the bank ? – But the money is in my possession.

RUSSELL then turned to Lord Coleridge and said, 'Perhaps it would be a convenient point here to adjourn ?

COLERIDGE : Have you any further questions to put to the witness?
RUSSELL : I have indeed.
COLERIDGE : Then we will adjourn.

That evening Sir Francis Knollys wrote to Sir Henry Ponsonby,

I was all day in Court with the Prince, and so far the case has, I think, gone dead against Cumming. He was under cross-examination by Russell for a couple of hours and when the Court adjourned Russell said he had not nearly done with him. He, Russell, conducted the cross-examination very ably and cleverly. I thought Cumming would have been able to take up a much stronger position than turned out to be the case. It will last for another couple of days, and the Prince will be in the witness-box tomorrow. But as he is called by the Solicitor-General they won't be able to cross-examine him, or, I hope, ask him disagreeable questions.

CHAPTER SIX

The Prince in the Witness-Box

On the following day, 2nd June, when the hearing of the case was resumed, the courtroom was again crowded. Long before the great clock in the Strand had struck the appointed hour of eleven, every available seat had been taken, and the perspiring janitors could scarcely force their way through the crowd of barristers in the corridors whose privilege it was to be present at important trials but who were refused admittance.

The most intense interest continues to follow the baccarat trial. Nothing else is talked about at the clubs and little else is read but the hourly bulletins of the evidence. The expectation of the Prince's appearance in the witness-box served to fill the court the moment it was thrown open and not a seat or an inch of standing room was afterwards to be obtained. (*Daily Express*)

The *Globe* tells us that because it was a dull day the ladies wore more sombre costumes. Many had provided themselves with luncheon packets and flasks which were quickly hidden away under the seats.

The sitting opened with a curious little incident. The Prince of Wales, instead of coming in with the Lord Chief Justice, entered before him by himself, and the stir his appearance made caused those in front to rise. The greater part of the Court rose as well, under the impression that the judge had come in, and then abruptly sat down again with a laugh when it was found that the Majesty of the Crown and not the Majesty of the Law was in question. The Court knows but one king – the presiding judge. (*Daily Chronicle*)

Then there was a pause. The Special Representative of the *Pall Mall Gazette* had a theory that women, however many people are looking at them, have a thousand pretty little expedients for carrying off the situation, whereas a man, even the most accomplished of men, can only unbutton and button his gloves and his coat and preen himself like a great fowl. To test his theory, he took out his stop-watch and noted that the Prince stroked his beard for exactly seven minutes. 'Nods and smiles of recognition to a friend or two among the galaxy on the stage – bench, I mean – relieved His Royal Highness, and presently Lord Coleridge

95

entered and they exchanged bows and a few smiling remarks. With that His Royal Highness composed himself in the red armchair, and after a glance at the railed box at his elbow in which he would soon have to appear, resigned himself to go through with the day's proceedings.'

The bench presented a striking picture. In the middle, on the dais specially constructed for the occasion, sat the Lord Chief Justice of England, his intellectual face beaming from behind his gold spectacles at the row of eminent counsel before him. The 'Chief', as he is irreverently called by his subordinates, dearly loves to try a *cause célèbre*, and yesterday he was completely in his element. And on his left was the Prince of Wales, looking very anxious and worn, and no wonder. . . . Immediately behind him was his faithful secretary, Sir Francis Knollys who sat calm and motionless the whole day through.

The *Pall Mall Gazette* tells us that Gordon-Cumming 'stepped back into the witness-box, fresh and collected. Nothing but the tint of his gloves was changed from yesterday.'

The cross-examination was again very searching. Sir Charles had dropped to a minor key, but his questions were packed with vital matter. There was first a letter of Sir William's, dated three days after the scandal, in which the writer, addressing General Williams as 'Dear Owen,' hoped that he might have given him the 'benefit of any doubt in the matter.' 'Then,' asked Sir Charles, 'did you doubt that the Prince, the General, and Lord Coventry believed you guilty?' 'No,' said Sir William, with his steady look into the counsel's eyes, 'I did not then doubt.' 'Or that these men had acted in your interests,' pressed Sir Charles. 'And in their own,' put in the witness calmly, with just a touch of acidity in his tone. 'How in their interest?' caught up the counsel. 'Well, they did not wish to be associated with a scandal.' 'But how was an innocent game of baccarat scandalous?' And so the keen fencing went on to the point where the counsel presses home Sir William's admission that he knew his friends believed him guilty. (*Daily Chronicle*)

Now, at all events, we have got to a time when, if you had ever thought it, you could no longer entertain the respect of those men whose friendship you had enjoyed. You had reached that point? – I beg your pardon.

When you received these letters you had reached the point of knowing that you no longer retained the respect, as an honourable man, of these men whose friendship and esteem you valued? – If I had been guilty of the offence, yes.

But you believed that they thought you guilty? – I had no reason to doubt it.

Of course you knew – although it was, perhaps, a comparatively unimportant matter, that you were regarded by these five persons as having been guilty of dishonourable conduct? – Apparently, as they accused me of being so.

Why did you not, even then, take steps to assert your innocence and to vindicate yourself by bringing yourself face to face with your accusers? – Because I considered that, having taken that very fatal and foolish step of signing the document, it would be impossible to succeed, as many people would think me guilty whether I was or not.

Sir William Gordon-Cumming made an admirable witness. If he had deliberately rehearsed for the part, he could not have done better. Leaning easily on the rail, his grey-gloved left hand resting easily on the bare right, perfectly dressed, his tones equable, firm, neither over-hurried nor over-deliberate, cool, but not too cool, Sir William faced the fire of the most deadly cross-examiner in England much as he would have faced his foe on the battle-field. It was a sight to see the man look thus, and act thus, knowing as one did that this supreme test had come at the end of nine months of agonising suspense, and that its issue was social life or death. Once, and only once – when he came to speak of the signing of the document which he admitted amounted to a confession – did his steady composure give way, and his measured speech change to a rapid flow of broken words, appealing, almost pitiful, in their tone. (*Illustrated London News*)

Then what has altered the position of things from the 13th September, except the fact that somehow or other this very melancholy story has become public property? – After signing the paper and committing the act of gross folly, as I characterised it yesterday, and after a reflection of twenty-four hours, I saw the mistake I had made. But on the assurance by letter from General Williams that by no possibility could it come out except to the persons immediately concerned, I lived for some time in a fool's paradise, hoping and believing that that would be the case.

Then, although in the eyes of these once valued and esteemed friends, you were a dishonoured man, you were content to remain so if secrecy were continued? – It does not follow that because these five believed me guilty that I was guilty. I knew perfectly well I was not.

Pray attend to my question? – I have answered your question.

I assure you you have not, Sir William Gordon-Cumming. Although you knew – rightly or wrongly – that in the eyes of these gentlemen, whose respect and esteem you valued, you were a dishonoured man, you were content to remain so? – I was not content to remain so.

Attend! Attend! You were content to remain so, so long as secrecy continued? – I had no alternative.

Then I ask you again the question to which I have not yet got an answer. What has since taken place which has altered the position as it was when these letters arrived in September, except the fact that this story has become public property? – The mere fact of its becoming public property was quite sufficient for me.

Was that the only reason? – Are you asking me my reasons for taking these proceedings?

I am asking the question which I have put to you. I will repeat it now for the third or fourth time, and hope you will kindly attend. You have told me that when you received these letters in September you then became aware of the fact that you were regarded, rightly or wrongly, by these esteemed friends as a dishonoured man, and you have said in effect that you were content not to take proceedings provided secrecy was continued . . .

CLARKE : Those were not the words of the witness.

RUSSELL : In effect.

CLARKE : When my learned friend says 'in effect', I know what he means.

The cross-examination continued.

My question is, what is the altered condition of things except the breach of the secrecy and the story becoming public property? – The thing had become such public property that I thought the matter would at once be taken up by my clubs, by my regiment, and by my friends.

That is your answer, and that is the answer I expected you to have given long ago.

Sir Charles had what he wanted. There was that kind of low sigh and unsettling of people in seats which marks a point in a law court. (*Pall Mall Gazette*)

Now and then in this correspondence with 'O.W.' there cropped up a phrase favourable to Sir William, such as an admission that he had all along denied the charge, and that he had signed the document under great pressure. The most painful passage was a reference to an interview at barracks with Mr Levett, the young subaltern in the Guards, who was one of Sir William's accusers. Witness's and counsel's version of this strange talk varied amazingly. According to Sir Charles, Sir William used such

1. GEN. O. WILLIAMS.	11. ARTHUR WILSON.
2. LORD COVENTRY.	12. CHRISTOPHER SYKES.
3. LYCETT GREEN.	13. COUNT LUDSKEW.
4. BERKELEY LEVETT.	14. MISS NAYLOR.
5. MRS LYCETT GREEN.	15. MRS. GEN. O. WILLIAMS.
6. LORD A. SOMERSET.	16. MRS. A. WILSON.
7. REUBEN SASSOON.	17. LIEUT. COL. SIR C. GORDON CUMMING
8. LORD E. SOMERSET.	18. H.R.H.
9. STANLEY WILSON.	19. COUNTESS COVENTRY.
10. TYRWHITT WILSON (EQUERRY)	20. LADY BROUGHAM.

The Tranby Croft house party. The key has been wrongly dated September 11th. Alternatively, was there a cover-up? Sir William Gordon-Cumming had departed on foot alone for Hessle Station, early on the morning of September 11th. He certainly was not a guest of honour requiring to be seated between the Prince of Wales and the hostess, Mrs Wilson. Furthermore, a close examination of his positioning suggests a contrivance reflecting the circumstances of the previous night.

The drawing room, scene of the first night's play. For this photograph a different tablecloth has been used. While baccarat was being played the uneven tables were covered by a tapestry cloth of variegated colours.

The table in the billiard room used on the second night. When this photograph was taken the original chalk line had been erased. A new line was drawn which should have been nearer the edge of the table.

(Right) Sir William Gordon-
Cumming

(Below) Sir George Lewis in 1893

The Prince of Wales leading in his Epsom Derby winner, Persimmon, after the race in 1896. The horse won the St. Leger in the following September, at Doncaster. It was for this race that the house party was held at Tranby Croft, near to Doncaster, in 1890.

phrases as, 'For God's sake, try and see what you can do,' and 'I know that I am asking you to do a fearful thing.' According to the witness he said nothing of the kind. According to Sir Charles, Mr Levett's reply to the overtures was that for Sir Williams's sake and that of the regiment he would gladly do something, but that he could not disbelieve his own eyesight. According to Sir William, Mr Levett had hesitated when pressed to state what he saw at the baccarat table, and finally admitted that he did not quite know. 'Was not the door locked?' asked Sir Charles, adding another touch of melodrama to this strange story, and again there came back the steady 'No.' Sir Charles leaned back, and took a long breath – 'You swear to that, Sir William?' and not for the first or the second time there was no flinching in the reply. (*Daily Chronicle*)

One of Russell's hardest tasks was to explain away General Owen Williams's letter to Gordon-Cumming admitting that he had been coerced 'by extreme pressure' into signing the undertaking never to play cards again, and under threat of immediate exposure by those whose 'ultimatum' he and Lord Coventry had brought to him. It was for the defendants' case, as Mr George Lewis had said, 'a letter to be regretted.'

Russell, following his brief, took the line that it had been written in response to one of Gordon-Cumming's appealing for help (which could not, however, be produced) because he was sorry for him and wanted to help him with the military authorities. Russell could safely do this because it was fairly certain that neither the jury nor the public knew that, so far from wishing to help him with the authorities, they had demanded an enquiry and volunteered to come forward as his accusers. Perhaps Gordon-Cumming still hoped to be friends with them again when he had won his case, but the most probable explanation was again that he was anxious not to involve the Prince, who had advocated the military enquiry.

What Sir Charles wanted to get at was clear to everybody, to the man in the witness-box equally with the rest of us. The touch of the old forensic hand appeared in the success with which he got him to say what he wanted in spite of himself. The object was simply that Sir William should confess that he sat quietly under what he admitted to be tantamount to a *peccavi* as long as he thought it would not get about, and that it was the fact that it did get about with all that this implied, and no loftier motives whatever, which led to Sir William taking these proceedings. . . .

There were curious glimpses into the social torture chamber during these passages : now it was some letter of Sir William to a friend which was sad reading, then it was an anonymous correspondent, a warning line from Paris or Monte Carlo signed 'someone who pities you,' warning him that rumour was busy in his old haunts. . . . Sir Charles suggested that Sir William himself had said and written despairing things, 'It's all out, it's all up with me. There is nothing before me but to cut my throat. Life will not be worth living now.' But some of these, amid something of a sensation, Sir William flatly denied. (*Pall Mall Gazette*)

I may ask you in reference to this matter whether you did not correspond not only with General Williams, but also received two letters from Lord Coventry? – Yes.

And you have given Lord Coventry a subpoena *duces* to produce them? – I believe that is so.

I merely put that to you for the reason that one of them is marked 'Private'? – I do not think there is anything in them that I should object to being read.

Russell read the first letter, which was that of 25th January, advising Lord Coventry that because the story was now in everybody's mouth, and being told unfavourably for him, he had no choice but to see Colonel Stracey about it. Russell then turned to the second one:

The next letter is marked, '6.45. Private. Carlton Club . . .
COLERIDGE : As the letter is marked private . . .
RUSSELL : We have taken the best advice, and I have begun by asking the gentleman if he had any objection.
COLERIDGE : What could a gentleman say?
RUSSELL : We have had the advantage of consulting a legal colleague who is not now in the case and of considering among ourselves. If your lordship will read the letter . . .
CLARKE : I do not think my learned friend is aware that I have not known the contents of these letters.
RUSSELL : I am not bound to show them.
COLERIDGE : I do not say there are no cases in which a private letter may not be read. The writer himself may destroy the privilege. I do not say there are no such cases, and it is for the learned counsel to determine. I only ask you, have you decided? And only ask whether to read a letter marked private is *prima facie* not desirable?
RUSSELL : We have decided. I should like to take the suggestion your lordship has made. We think that the particular letter does come within the description of your lordship: it is not connected with anything else but this case, and it is addressed to Lord Coventry, whose conduct, although no unworthy motives are alleged, is impugned.
COLERIDGE : I have said all I can say.
RUSSELL : My lord, I very anxiously did consider the matter and I

was not content with the opinion of my colleagues on the matter. I went outside that advice and asked advice elsewhere, with the result ... I ought to tell your lordship, Lord Coventry felt the same difficulty, and it was for that reason I sought advice, and it was for that reason also that I prefaced the question to Sir William Gordon-Cumming whether he desired the letter not to be read.

COLERIDGE : That is outside the question. A gentleman cannot say that he objects to anything being read, especially when his honour is concerned.

RUSSELL : I am put into a position of some difficulty, I confess.

COLERIDGE : I am only anxious that a Court of Law should be conducted on principles of fairness and honour.

RUSSELL : I have suggested, by the tenor of my cross-examination, that this gentleman was content to remain without taking any proceedings so long as he thought secrecy might be maintained.

CLARKE : I think this crowns the impropriety of the course which has been taken in this matter. My learned friend has chosen to put a question as to a letter which is marked 'private'. I should have thought that the unbroken traditions and the rules of conduct of a case in the profession would have been that, before any such letter was referred to at all, private communication would have been made to me, as counsel on the other side, with regard to its contents.

COLERIDGE : I do not say anything about that. Sometimes cases may arise in which the word 'private' must be treated with utter scorn. For instance, a letter may be marked 'private' for the very purpose of annoyance, and the word private in that case does not deserve to be respected. I have not read this letter; I am not in the least degree acquainted with its contents; but I wish to say now that I am very anxious to do anything so long as confidences between gentlemen shall not be broken.

ASQUITH : May I say a word on this point ?

CLARKE : It is not a question for argument.

ASQUITH : The only observation I was wishing to make is that my learned friend, Sir Charles Russell, and all our colleagues have fully considered this point, and if we had not come to the conclusion that this letter falls within the category of letters referred to by your lordship – wherein, by the mere marking of the word private at the top, privilege could not have been effectively claimed – we should not have dreamed of introducing it in cross-examination.

COLERIDGE : I have called attention to the point for counsel to consider.

RUSSELL : We bow to the suggestion your lordship makes.

COLERIDGE : If the plantiff wishes, he is entitled to have the letter read.

GORDON-CUMMING : I really forget at the moment the contents of that letter.

RUSSELL : Will you give me that letter, Lord Coventry, please?

CLARKE : Wait a moment please!

Sir Charles thought there was a gleam of hope in the Lord Chief Justice's words, and again Lord Coventry had to bring out the letter. The usher was taking it to the witness, when Sir Edward Clarke interposed, and seizing the letter declared that if it was now to be put to the witness it was a scandalous proceeding. (*Exeter Evening Post*)

RUSSELL : I was going to say, will you read that letter and then see whether he wishes it to be read.

CLARKE : I say it is the most unfair course I ever remember to have seen pursued.

RUSSELL : Do I understand your lordship to say if Sir William Gordon-Cumming desires it to be read, it can be produced?

COLERIDGE : There are many cases in which a man has written privately, and under such circumstances ought not to be deprived of the right of not having the letter read. I am sorry I interfered. All I did was to ensure that the learned counsel should consider the point before anything was done.

Sir Charles apologised, and spent the next few minutes in pouring abuse on the devoted head of Mr George Lewis and his satellites on the solicitors' bench. One particular expression was so hearty that it floated up to the bench, and the ladies smiled behind their fans. The Prince of Wales smoothed his beard, and Lord Coleridge busied himself about the drawer of his desk. (*Exeter Evening Post*)

The public watched this display for some minutes fascinated, and then Clarke rose and said,

CLARKE : I understand my learned friends have considered the point, and they do not press it.

That was the conclusion of the cross-examination, and although it had ended in this unseemly way it was a brilliant performance. Gordon-Cumming, however, had not wavered in his defence. The public, from being inclined to be antagonistic at the beginning, were now decidedly in his favour. On the other hand, Russell by his line of attack had been able to stress some thirty or forty times in his majestic style, for the benefit of the jury, the presumed dishonourable behaviour of Gordon-Cumming and, almost as many times, the integrity, or the respectability, or the leniency, of General Owen Williams and Lord Coventry.

> It was the sword against the pen. The lawyer armed with the weapon of attack, the soldier warding off the thrusts as best he could and occasionally making a hit, to the great delight of the junior barristers present who always like to see one of their leaders smartly answered by a witness. (*Pall Mall Gazette*)

Clarke now had an opportunity to re-examine his client to allow him to comment on one or two matters that had arisen. He dealt first with Gordon-Cumming's small act of kindness that had been used by Russell to prove that he had not lost his head :

> You were cross-examined yesterday, Sir William, as to whether on the evening of the 10th September, after dinner, there was a conversation at Tranby Croft, and whether you asked His Royal Highness to put his name in Miss Wilson's birthday book ? – Yes.
> There was a Miss Wilson who had not come out, and she wished to have His Royal Highness's name in her birthday book, and you asked him to give it ? – I did.
> And were you that evening in conversation with the other people in the house in the usual way ? – Quite in the usual way.

He was asked about the length of the interviews at Tranby Croft with General Williams and Lord Coventry, and with the Prince of Wales, and whether at any of these interviews any detailed statement had been made to him as to the allegations. To which he replied that no detailed statement had been given to him, and that he had not been aware that General Owen Williams had written a *précis* of what had occurred, until it was read to him much later – on the 26th January. His comment on the *précis* was that the accusations had not been defined to him as clearly as General Williams stated, and that he had taken great exception to the passage in it saying that signing the undertaking would be a distinct admission of his guilt. Clarke commented that General Williams in his letters had continued to address Gordon-Cumming as 'Dear Bill' or 'My Dear Bill'. His final question was,

A number of letters of yours have been produced written to General Williams, and some to Lord Coventry. Have you, through your solicitors, applied to these gentlemen for copies of the letters written to you, and have you failed to obtain them? – I believe that is the case.

The *Pall Mall Gazette* Special Representative continued, (he seems to have missed Clarke's re-examination of Gordon-Cumming, his attention having been diverted to another part of the courtroom,)

The plaintiff's cross-examination lasted without interruption till one o'clock, save for the timely entrance of Lord Coleridge's ancient clerk bearing a tumbler of ice whence, from time to time, the learned judge carefully extracted a piece, conveyed it to his glass with a skill which evidently won the admiration of the ladies on his right who watched the operation with intense interest, and thought, perhaps, as the heat was intense, how nice it must be to be a judge and drink iced water in the morning with all the world of fashion looking on. But all eyes were soon diverted from the ice to the witness-box. Precisely at one o'clock the Solicitor-General called his second witness, the Prince of Wales.

The *Globe* says that the interest thus awakened was evidenced by a subdued noise caused by a general endeavour to get an advantageous position.

The heir apparent rose at once from his chair and, declining the offer of Lord Coleridge who politely whispered to him to remain seated, he stepped into the witness-box and took the oath like the humblest of his future subjects . . . This sign of deference to the law must have gladdened the heart of many an honest radical as the Prince kissed the testament . . . and stood up in the box and gave his evidence like any other man. The Solicitor-General was courteous in the extreme . . . (*Pall Mall Gazette*)

Your Royal Highness has known Sir William Gordon-Cumming for twenty years? – I have.
    Am I right in saying for the last ten years at least, he has enjoyed Your Royal Highness's favour? – Certainly.
    He has been a guest at your house? – On several occasions.
    And did that friendship – intimacy – continue unimpaired and undisturbed up to the 9th or 10th September of last year? – It did.

The Prince stood with one hand easily resting on the rail, his head a little down, his attitude free and not undignified. His voice was a little hoarse and rough, and somehow had a queer unfamiliar note in it; but the replies were given with great readiness, and even rapidly. (*Daily Chronicle*.)

On the second evening, sir, General Owen Williams, I believe, acted as croupier? – Yes.

Is it a fact, sir, at the end of the second evening's play, Sir William Gordon-Cumming showed you his tableau, and a remark passed as to his winnings? – I think so.

And at the time that that tableau was shown and the remark made, I take it that nothing had occurred to give you the smallest suspicion as to his play? – Nothing whatever.

It was not, I believe sir, until the evening of the 10th that any communication was made to you in regard to the alleged bad play? – No.

May I ask by whom the communication was first made to your Royal Highness? – By the Earl of Coventry.

And before dinner on the evening of the 10th, your Royal Highness had heard no statement from anyone except the Earl of Coventry? – From nobody.

May I ask if your Royal Highness remembers whether the statement made to you by Lord Coventry purported to be the statement of an individual, and, if so, whether that individual was named? – Of individuals.

Of whose? – Of three gentlemen and two ladies.

Then, in the first instance, it purported to be a statement to which all five of them could speak? – Exactly.

I believe your Royal Highness did not see any of the five persons mentioned until after Sir William Gordon-Cumming had had the honour of an interview? – I did not.

At that interview Sir William Gordon-Cumming emphatically denied the charge? – He did.

It was thus clear that the Prince had judged Gordon-Cumming to be guilty, and agreed to the undertaking never to play again being submitted to him for his signature, entirely on the advice of Lord Coventry and General Owen Williams, without himself hearing any evidence, or seeing any of the accusers until later. The rest of the questions were about the *précis* which, he said, agreed with his recollection of what had been stated to him.

Sir Charles took the Prince out of Sir Edward's hands with some airiness. 'You' took the place for the most part of 'Your Royal Highness' and 'Sir' which had interlarded the Solicitor-General's questions. But Sir Charles was tender with his witness. Only once did His Royal Highness betray any impatience. It was when Sir Charles was questioning him about a conversation with Mrs Wilson after and about the critical incident at Tranby Croft, did she say this? Did she say that? Said the Prince shortly, 'She said very little.' With that, the subject dropped. (*Pall Mall Budget*)

Now, had you, sir, seen those three gentlemen, and heard the statement with reference to these ladies, before you were called upon to express any opinion as to the signing of the memorandum? – Yes. (This answer contradicted what he had said to Clarke. He quickly corrected it by adding) Previous to the signing of the memorandum, (which was not what Russell had asked him.)

May I ask whether that paper was the suggestion of yourself, or was it a suggestion made by somebody else in which you acquiesced? – I acquiesced. The suggestion was made by Lord Coventry.

I need hardly ask you. You were greatly distressed at the occurrence? – Most certainly. (This reply is described as being 'in a deep throat note.')

Sir Charles evidently wanted the Prince to admit that he had deemed Sir William Gordon-Cumming guilty, but oddly enough he beat about the bush. Had not General Owen Williams asked His Royal Highness if he believed the accusers' story? suggested Sir Charles. 'I never remember his asking any question of the kind,' he said decisively. Yes, His Royal Highness had been much distressed about the matter. Did he recollect Sir William making any reference to the Duke of Cambridge? He was certain he had. Quite certain. Did he desire to act in the circumstances of the case as leniently as he could to Sir William Gordon-Cumming? 'Most certainly,' said the Prince, louder and more emphatically than he had as yet spoken, and for once holding up his head. But he had not met Sir William since? The Prince nodded assent. Had he intimated that he could not meet him again? Everyone strained to hear the almost muttered reply, 'I cannot.' (*Pall Mall Budget*)

He had spoken in such a low voice that one reporter thought he answered, 'It would be more agreeable not,' and the official version says there was no reply. That terminated Russell's cross-examination.

The Prince was stepping out of the box, everybody feeling that, through timidity or prudence, two great English counsel had neglected to obtain some very essential light on the case, when he was briskly summoned back by a small gentleman rising from the back of the jury-box and asking in a sharp clear voice with a cockney accent, 'Excuse me, your Royal Highness, I have a question or two to ask you.' The Prince was happily equal to the occasion. He wheeled round smilingly, and stood to attention. The sharp voice spoke again in dead silence, and, in firm tones, asked the two questions for which everybody was thirsting, but which both Sir Edward and Sir Charles had curiously omitted. (*Daily Chronicle*)

This may have been curious to the public but, in fact, the second question should have been disallowed by the judge because that went to the very question that the jury had to decide on the evidence, but not on an opinion.

THE JURYMAN: Are this jury to understand that you, as banker on these two occasions, saw nothing of the alleged malpractices of the plaintiff?

In a situation like this, the Prince was at his best. He answered the juryman thoughtfully, as if to an equal, without a trace of condescension:

THE PRINCE: No; it is not usual for a banker to see anything in dealing cards, especially when you are playing among friends in their house. You do not for a moment suspect anything of the sort.

THE JURYMAN: What was your Royal Highness's opinion at the time as to the charges made against Sir William Gordon-Cumming?

The Prince 'made a French gesture with his arm and shoulder,' and replied:

They seemed so strongly supported – unanimously so – by those who brought them forward, that I felt no other course was open to me but to believe what I was told.

The little juryman sat down with the same marionette motion with which he had risen, and the Prince bowed, smiled again, and quitted the box, leaving his plucky interrogator the hero of the hour. Everybody laughed, but everyone was pleased. . . . (*Daily Chronicle*)

. . . except possibly Sir Edward Clarke, who didn't like the Prince's suggestion that although he himself had seen nothing wrong, Gordon-Cumming might still have been cheating. He got up and remarked to the Prince's retreating back, 'I take it the answer to the first question is 'No.'

The answer to the second question was curious, because it is open to everyone to disbelieve or to believe an accusation against a friend, even if it seems strongly supported: but the Prince, besides being someone, was the representative of a form of government. Probably, in a matter like this, affecting the future of the institution of monarchy, he did not feel himself free to hold a personal view. In this sense his answer can be understood. He was not a fighter for lost causes : he had to reflect the opinions of the majority.

This is clearly seen in a parallel case. As President of the Father Damien Fund, to discover a cure for leprosy, he immediately dropped the Father Damien part of it when he heard that a discreditable story was in circulation about him. He said, according to Frank Harris, secretary of the fund, 'Such stories are always believed, and I can't afford to be laughed at . . . We may believe what we please, but I have to consider public opinion.'[1]

So the bold juryman who interrogated the Prince of Wales has been identified. He hails from South London and is a member of the Camberwell vestry. Mr Goddard Clarke, for such is the name of the 'good man and true', is a successful man of business who devotes his spare time to parochial work. He is, withal, a sound Liberal. The London Water Supply is a topic on which Mr Clarke is well primed. He is a member of the Society of Arts, the London Chamber of Commerce, a Fellow of the Society of Chemical Industry. Beyond these offices Mr Clarke is Treasurer of the Camberwell District Local University Extension Scheme, and he is a Liveryman of the Cooper's Company, while much time is given by him to religious work. (*Pall Mall Gazette*)

Upon Sir Edward Clarke's application, the Prince was informed that his further attendance would not be required. Then the Court was adjourned. Apparently the Prince did not lunch with Lord Coleridge on that day, for it was reported that he left the building immediately by the Carey Street entrance, and that an enormous crowd of people were loitering about every possible approach to the Law Courts in order to catch a glimpse of him as he made his exit.

The judge and his friends retired to the judge's luncheon room and those left behind commenced to picnic it out in court. It was indeed a veritable picnic, perhaps the first that has ever been held in a law court, but there was no alternative. To leave one's seat and issue forth to the refreshment rooms in search of food would be to lose one's seat for the remainder of the day, for a surging crowd was eager for admittance and ready to fill the places of those who left the court.

The idea suddenly occurred to some inventive barrister to hail one of the obliging officials of the court and bid him bring whiskies and sodas and sandwiches, biscuits, beer, and even stout, from the distant luncheon rooms. To carry out the idea was the work of a few moments. The ushers soon returned, laden with food and drinks, and in a moment the occupants of the back bench were camping out in primitive fashion on desks and forms as if they were on the river at Maidenhead, instead of in the Royal Courts of Justice in London. Long before the Chief returned, all vestiges of it had disappeared. (*Pall Mall Gazette*)

When the case was resumed, Clarke called his last witness, General Owen Williams.

General Owen Williams, who succeeded His Royal Highness, is tall, military, moustached, well-made. He holds himself straighter in the box than any other witnesses have done. But for something a little mincing in his speech, he is in manner and appearance a very proper general, and such he was voted by the spy-glass wielders in the gallery. (*Pall Mall Gazette*)

Clarke began in his usual way, establishing the fact of his long friendship extending over twenty years with Gordon-Cumming who was frequently a guest at his house and a fellow visitor with the Prince of Wales. Then he confirmed that the general had been an ordinary player on the first evening at Tranby Croft, and croupier on the second, which meant that he shared the bank and was therefore interested in its losses or gains. The first time we had heard any suggestion of foul play was when Lord Coventry came into his room at about 7 p.m. on the evening of 10th September.

I ask you a question now to be answered 'Yes' or 'No.' It depends on your answer whether I have to follow it up. Prior to the dinner hour on the evening of the 10th, did you hear any statement as to the alleged facts by anyone other than Mr Lycett Green? – No.

And when Mr Lycett Green made that statement, I understand Lord Coventry and you were both in the room listening to it? – We were.

Did you on that evening, or at a later time, and when, set down in writing that statement? – At a later time I set it down in writing.

And set it down accurately? – As well as I could remember.

The document was handed to him. He identified it as being the account in his own handwriting of what Lycett Green had stated to him.

I believe you and Lord Coventry considered that, in these circumstances, it was your duty to inform His Royal Highness of what took place? – That was so.

But before informing His Royal Highness of the matter, did you agree to make a suggestion to His Royal Highness as to the way it should be dealt with? – No. (This was evidently not true because, when Clarke insisted, he admitted, 'I think it was proposed to make this suggestion . . .')

Did you make that suggestion before you went to see His Royal Highness? – I think I made it to Lord Coventry before the interview with His Royal Highness.

At the time you made that suggestion, had you or had you not seen Sir William Gordon-Cumming? – We had not.

You say 'we'? – Neither of us.

Or heard any statement from anybody except Mr Lycett Green? – No statement whatever except from Mr Lycett Green.

Clarke then took him through his *précis* section by section, noting that His Royal Highness had agreed that Gordon-Cumming should be made to sign an undertaking never to play cards again, and that all should keep silence about it, and that this would be a possible solution. Then Gordon-Cumming had been informed of the accusations and had emphatically denied them. Clarke read from the *précis*.*

'Lord Coventry and General Williams then saw Sir William and explained that the only possible condition on which silence could be maintained was that he should sign the undertaking above referred to.' Had that undertaking been already put into writing by Lord Coventry when it was first mentioned to Sir William Gordon-Cumming? – Oh yes, I believe so.

Now, upon that document being produced to Sir William Gordon-Cumming, did he say anything with regard to its being tantamount to a confession of guilt? – He did.

Did you agree that it would be so considered? – Undoubtedly it would.

Did you tell him that his signature was the only way of avoiding a horrible scandal? – Yes.

That it was the only possible hope of the avoidance of a horrible scandal, and that you and Lord Coventry believed he would have no chance of contending against it with any possibility of success? – That is so.

*Slight textual differences must be due to transcription or mis-reading.

At that time you were under the impression that he would have to meet five witnesses agreed upon the facts? – Yes.

Agreed upon the facts as stated by Mr Lycett Green? – Certainly our impression was that the evidence was so overwhelming that it could not be opposed.

Having gone through the *précis*, which the general admitted he had written while the facts were fresh in his mind, Clarke questioned him about Messrs Wontner's application to him, which he had ignored, for copies of the relevant correspondence:

Is it the fact that Sir William Gordon-Cumming's solicitors asked you to give them copies of letters which you had from Sir William? – Yes.

And you took no notice of this request? – I did not. I had none in my possession.

What about the letters produced to-day? – They were not in my possession.

Certain letters have been produced to-day which were written by Sir William Gordon-Cumming to you, and which I have received no copy. In whose possession were they? – I think in Lord Coventry's.

But you took no notice of the application that was made to you in writing? – No.

Clarke again asked him in whose possession the letters had been. This time he changed his answer and said, 'I cannot say positively, but I imagine they were placed with the other documents which you have just read.' Russell came to his rescue:

RUSSELL: As I understand it, the papers of last September which were immediately connected with the transaction were forwarded to the Prince of Wales, and were produced to me from Sir Francis Knollys.

The general was then cross-examined by Mr Asquith who began by questioning him about the letters:

You received two or three letters from Sir William Gordon-Cumming immediately after the events in September? – I did.

Did you forward these immediately after you received them to the Prince of Wales? – I did.

You have never had them in your possession since? – I have not.

His statement, therefore, to Sir Edward Clarke that he thought the letters were in Lord Coventry's possession was shown to be untrue.

I take it from you that this accusation came upon you as a shock of a very painful kind? – As a terrible shock. (He pronounced it 'slowly and deliberately, ter-ri-ble.')

And there was no predisposition in your mind to believe it? – None whatsoever.

You had seen nothing yourself at the table to excite any suspicion of the play in your mind? – No.

Do you remember on the second night of the play, when you were acting as croupier, the Prince of Wales making any remark to the plaintiff in the course of the play? – Yes.

What was it? – His Royal Highness told him to take his hands off the table or to move his hands further back, because he could not see what the stake was, and it did not look well.

After the historic instance of the last half hour before lunch, the evidence of the plaintiff's third witness, General Owen Williams, fell very flat, and even the lady with the sketchbook showed signs of fatigue, as Mr Asquith slowly and deliberately put the gallant officer through his paces. The Prince had resumed his seat on the bench after lunch, and watched the proceedings with an interested air. . . . (*Pall Mall Gazette*)

I want to take you to the interview in Lord Coventry's room, when you first heard the accusation. Will you tell us again who was present? – Besides Lord Coventry and myself, Mr Lycett Green, Mr. Arthur Wilson Jnr, Lord Edward Somerset and Captain Arthur Somerset.

Were these all that were present? – These were all.

You told us that Mr Lycett Green spoke on that occasion? – He did.

Did he tell you, or profess to tell you, not only what he had seen, but what others had seen? – Undoubtedly.

In their hearing? – In their hearing.

Did they in any way dissent from the account which he gave? – On the contrary.

What do you mean by 'on the contrary'? – They assented to the account.

The pretence here was that several witnesses had assented to Lycett Green's account. Actually, of those present, only one alleged having seen any cheating – Arthur Stanley Wilson.

Now, did Mr Lycett Green tell you of any specific case which he and the others had witnessed, or did he speak merely in general terms? – He did not give any specific action as far as I can remember, but he left no doubt on the minds of Lord Coventry and myself that each and all of the persons he had described as having witnessed cheating had absolutely seen them.

Did Mr Lycett Green, or any of the others, speak of Sir William Gordon-Cumming as having added money to his stake? – Yes, I am sure of that.

No doubt about it? – No doubt about it.

The *précis* has been read, in which mention is made of his having, when cards were against him, withdrawn a portion of the stake. Have you any recollection of any of them saying that? – That was the general idea I had of the information that was given.

But can you absolutely swear that anyone gave that specific information to you? – No.

COLERIDGE : That was the impression made upon your mind? – Yes.

COLERIDGE : Are you sure that what was stated to you was sufficiently clear and definite to make a correct representation of the substance? – Yes.

COLERIDGE : You are absolutely clear as to the fact of the counters being manipulated? – Yes.

COLERIDGE : Both ways? – That is my impression.

Asquith continued the cross-examination :

As to watching, did Mr Lycett Green tell you that he and young Mr Wilson had in fact watched the play on the second night? – That is my impression.

Did Mr Lycett Green tell you that there had been any previous agreement between them to watch? – Mr Lycett Green told me that they had discussed this question.

Who had discussed it? – He and his brother-in-law, Mr Stanley Wilson. He said the others had discussed the matter with him. My impression is that they had agreed to watch. There is no question that they did watch.

He was then asked to say in his own way exactly what happened at the interview with Gordon-Cumming :

We, Lord Coventry and myself, said we had to perform the very difficult duty of informing Sir William Gordon-Cumming of the charge made against him by certain members of the party. Lord Coventry in plain language told Sir William Gordon-Cumming that he had been accused of cheating. He immediately replied indignantly denying the accusation, and demanding, or rather imploring, Lord Coventry and myself to ask His Royal Highness to accord him an interview, which we said we would. I think Lord Coventry told him exactly what the charge was that was brought against him – that of having increased his stake when the cards were in his favour. I think he appealed to us as men of experience to know whether we believed the statement of these boys against himself, who was an old friend of ours.

This was not quite straightforward. Gordon-Cumming did not ask for an interview with the Prince until after they had told him he knew already about the accusations. Bringing the Prince into it was entirely the courtiers' doing.

He was asked whether he had explained to the witnesses, at the interview with the Prince, the suggestion that an undertaking should be signed: he answered that it was in the absence of the Prince, but whether it was before or after their interview with him he couldn't remember.

When you made that suggestion, do you remember that Lycett Green strongly demurred to it? – Yes.

What reason did he give? – Mr Lycett Green said, I think, 'that the matter ought to be settled now because, if it is not, Sir William Gordon-Cumming may, if it is hushed up, at some future time insult me or some member of my family, or bring an action, and we should not have the same advantages that we have at present. Everything is fresh in our memories now, and we can all swear to what has occurred; and I think it would be far better that the matter should be settled at once.' – the idea being that it should be made public.

Did he desire to be confronted with Sir William Gordon-Cumming? – He did.

Did you afterwards tell that to Sir William Gordon-Cumming? – I did.

It is impossible to accept this as a true statement. For the general to have conveyed a challenge for a showdown from Lycett Green to Gordon-Cumming would immediately have caused a row and defeated his main purpose – to prevent the scandal coming out. We know already from

Gordon-Cumming's letter to him just before leaving Tranby Croft that the general had been impressing upon him that it was 'essential to avoid an open row and the scandal arising therefrom.' Perhaps the general misunderstood Asquith's question and thought he was talking about the 'ultimatum' of which he was the bearer to Gordon-Cumming, that the accusations would be published abroad if he refused to sign the undertaking.

> Did you argue with Mr Lycett Green in favour of signing this document? – I asked him to agree to maintain silence with regard to the occurrence if Sir William Gordon-Cumming signed the document which was placed before him. I told Mr Lycett Green that the document would be tantamount to an admission of guilt on the part of Sir William Gordon-Cumming, and that once signed would render him harmless for the future. He was content with the explanation and promised to maintain silence.

He was asked whether, at his interview with the Prince, Gordon-Cumming had made any reference to the Duke of Cambridge and his commanding officer. He replied that there had been a reference, 'and I confess I was a little bit nettled at this remark, inasmuch as I felt we had gone a long way out of our way to deal leniently with him.'

> Do you conceive that in the advice which you gave, and in your whole dealing in this matter, that you were acting in his interests as an old friend? – I do.

Asquith's methods, though less spectacular than Russell's, were not ineffectual. He insisted at some length on the general's friendship for Gordon-Cumming, to imply that such a close friend would never have believed the charges against him unless he had found the evidence overwhelming – ignoring the awkward fact that the general had not taken any evidence: to imply also that the general had been thrown into a state of ter-ri-ble shock not at the prospect of the Prince (and himself) being involved in a scandal, but because his friend had been accused of cheating – a theory hard to swallow; it had to be gradually insinuated, and this took many words and bored the audience who were looking for sensations.

Finally he got round to the crucial letter the general had written, the 'letter to be regretted . . .'

> Can you tell me what were the contents of the letter of the 27th to

which yours was a reply? – I can, if you will let me see my letter of the 28th. (It was handed up to him.) I can now very well remember what was in his letter. He told me that the story was in everybody's mouth, and that there was nothing left for him but to place himself unreservedly in the hands of Colonel Stracey, the commandant of the regiment, and leave the case with him. He asked me to do him the justice that he never acknowledged to Lord Coventry or myself the truth of the accusations that were brought against him. He said that – I forget the exact terms – unless the reports were stopped or contradicted there was nothing left for him but to vanish for ever, or to cut his throat. He reproached both Lord Coventry and myself for having given him bad advice as to signing the document, and in reply I wrote as he requested, saying that he had not in any way acknowledge his guilt, and that he had signed the document under extreme pressure. That is my letter of the 28th January.

He was then briefly re-examined by Sir Edward Clarke . . .

I understand you to say that you told Sir William Gordon-Cumming that the evidence against him was so overwhelming that he could not possibly hope to stand against it? – That was my opinion of it.

At that time had you anything but the statement of Mr Lycett Green and of Mr Wilson, and the tacit acquiescence of Mr Berkeley Levett? – Nothing whatever.

That was the evidence on which you said you believed it? – Yes.

After a few more questions, Sir Edward Clarke turned to Lord Coleridge, and said, 'That, my lord, is the plaintiff's case.' The Court adjourned.

General Williams, whose evidence closed the case for the plaintiff, was subdued, regretful, but firm. His most impressive statement was that he believed Sir William guilty. (*Daily Chronicle*)

CHAPTER SEVEN

The Juvenile Lead

June 3rd 1891. The third day of the trial.

There is no indication of a subsidence of popular interest in the great case. Directly the iron gates in the Strand were thrown open this morning there was a rush of those who had for some half hour or so been besieging them. They hurried up through the great hall and then came to a full stop again outside the doors of the actual court. The regulations were very stringent. No one must be admitted until all the internal arrangements are complete, and so the expectant crowd pressed round the doors, appearing to enjoy with great gusto the pushing to and fro of some, and the jocular remarks of others. Sandwich boxes were again in evidence, and there was every indication of preparations, on the part of the ladies, for a long day. When at length the doors were opened there was the usual rush for seats, and the gallery was speedily filled.

The seats on the Bench were crowded by the same fashionable society ladies who have watched the case right through . . . and their costumes were certainly distinctively bright notes in the dingy Court. By the way, this trial is really regarded by the fair galaxy the Lord Chief Justice has around him, as a sort of social function of no little enjoyment. For each day that the case has been going on, Lady Coleridge has been giving delightful little luncheon parties in the private room of the Master of the Rolls, while Lord Coleridge himself has entertained the Prince of Wales and Sir Francis Knollys to a similar necessary repast in his own room.

Lady Coleridge looked charming in a black Empire costume, with a white rose-pink-spotted vest, and creamy silver gauntlets. (*Echo*)

The *Star* reporter describes the scene for us, (He seems to have picked up some of the jargon of baccarat!)

The tableau on the right of the Lord Chief Dealer Coleridge was as before, a winning one from the very opening of the game, but it was not until a few minutes before the time to begin that general anxiety as to whether the Lady Chief Justice would again be present were dispelled. From the general point of view, now that His Royal Highness has given his evidence, the interest of the case has departed. He was present in Court again, everyone standing up, when a moment or two after the judge the Prince walked in. But where he sits under the lee of the judge's desk, he is

117

hidden from the view of a good half of the Court. And after all, a prince of the blood royal on the other side of an oaken desk is not an exhilarating spectacle. At all events a beautiful woman is a much more pleasing sight, and Lady Coleridge is beautiful. To-day she came in a new costume, the smartest of arrangements in black velvet, open jacket and white satin waistcoat with gold buttons. She is a charming adjunct to the administration of justice. The pleasant way in which she nods around the Court to her friends, the delightful sense of property she has in the whole proceedings, the infinite amusement with which her smiles and dimples seem to show she regards the whole business, and above all the pretty little cheeky absence of awe with which she behaves under the very eyes of the august Lord Chief Justice, all make the Court pleasant . . . The Wilson family are not accustomed to sitting on the hard oak of the solicitors' bench, so they are provided with bags full of wind on which they balance themselves.

　　Mr George Lewis appears to be the Prince's friend in Court, for they came in together. (*Star*)

Lord Coleridge turned to Russell to open the case for the defendants – but he wasn't there. A messenger was hurriedly sent in search of him. Mr Mathews rose and said he would be there in a minute. Soon Russell came into Court, with profuse apologies for the delay, and at once launched into his opening speech for the defendants. He began by totally rejecting Clarke's suggestion that they might wish to admit they had been mistaken in what they saw and in what they said they had seen :

> . . . and although they would have been glad if, in point of truth and honour, they could have taken that course, they have found it impossible to do so; and so, in no spirit of bitterness towards Sir William Gordon-Cumming, they feel bound to come before you to-day and state upon oath that which they, without that solemnity, have previously stated as far back as the month of September in last year.

He recalled that both Sir William and his counsel had stated they believed the defendants were acting perfectly conscientiously in the matter, and that His Royal Highness, Lord Coventry and General Williams, whether their action was mistaken or not, unquestionably acted honestly, and intended to act honestly and leniently towards their friend; and so the matter was narrowed down to the simple question whether the jury could arrive at the conclusion that the defendants were mistaken in what they saw, or in what would say they saw :

> They made their charges – they stood by their charges. It was indicated that they desired to be confronted with Sir William Gordon-Cumming.

Sir William Gordon-Cumming did not desire to be confronted with them because, he says, he was advised not to see them. When the proposition is made to sign the promise of secrecy, the objection to sign that promise comes from one of the defendants, speaking for the rest. It comes from Mr Lycett Green, who says, 'I prefer to have the matter out now. I wish to be confronted with him. While the matter is clear in the recollection of us all let us have it out.' He then goes on to make the suggestion, which shows considerable sense on his part. 'How do we know,' he said, as General Williams told us, 'that he may not, if this thing is hushed up, hereafter say that this accusation is not well-founded, and is not a true accusation, and after the lapse of time turn round upon us and say we have accused him falsely?' It is only when the assurance is given by General Williams, which corresponds with the statement that General Williams made to Sir William Gordon-Cumming, that the signing of the paper in the terms on which the paper was drawn was a virtual admission of his guilt, that Mr Lycett Green agrees with the document and signs it accordingly. The plaintiff accepts the terms – I do not stop to characterise them humiliating and dis-honouring terms – terms by which it is stipulated that, in consideration of these very defendants being silent as to those charges, he, on his part, enters into the degrading and humiliating undertaking that he will never as long as he lives play cards again !

Russell then asked the jury if it was conceivable that an innocent man would under such circumstances bear the odious burden placed-upon him, and said that at no stage in the distressing story had his conduct been that of an innocent and an honourable man.

In a voice hoarse with forensic passion, Sir Charles drew a picture of the conduct of an innocent and a guilty man charged with filching from the pockets of his friends. To the suggestion that there had been solicitude for the Prince's name in connection with the scandal, 'It won't do,' said Sir Charles, pointing at his learned friend on the other side in a way well-known to the Parnell Commissioners. (*Star*)

The great advocate spoke for exactly an hour and three quarters, but his speech can hardly be called one of his best efforts. Beginning in solemn tones, he described the case in which he was engaged as containing some of the most remarkable incidents which he had met with in the whole course of his career at the Bar. Raising his voice and clenching his fist as he spoke of the plaintiff, he flourished as a signal of defiance to the learned counsel opposed to him the variegated bandana which, together with the historic snuffbox, form part of his equipment whenever he goes into action.

Coming then to the events at Tranby Croft, Sir Charles proceeded to instruct the jury in the mysteries of the game of baccarat . . . With the help of two wooden models with which Mr George Lewis supplied him, Sir Charles Russell endeavoured to present to the minds of the jury a picture of what happened on the two nights in question. The first model, marked in white letters 'September 8th' was supposed to represent the table at which the party played that evening, and sundry labels, fastened round the edge, indicated the places occupied by the several players. The second table, round which a line had been drawn with chalk, was similarly provided with the names of those present on the second evening, and excited great interest among the jurors, who were pleased to see something tangible after two days of questions and speeches. Armed with the models, Sir Charles began his lecture upon the game, and before many minutes were over he was talking of 'tableaux' and 'naturals' in a way that was simply astonishing. . . . (*Morning Advertiser*)

He said he did not play baccarat himself but, on the whole, thought it was 'not a bad sort of all-round game,' and then described how Stanley Wilson noticed in front of Gordon-Cumming one counter representing £5 in the first deal in the first coup, and then, after he had won, three counters of £5 each. It was astounding, but it did not enter his mind that it was an act of cheating it would not naturally suggest itself to the mind of anybody, but it startled him, because it struck him as very odd, seeing his neighbour at first with one piece claiming to be paid in respect of three. He had not unnaturally continued to watch closely, and he would tell the jury that he observed in the course of the evening and at intervals, a similar thing repeated. He told Mr Berkeley Levett, who also noticed the same thing :

So next night there were five watchers instead of two. Same result. Again those stealthy fingers were, according to Sir Charles, seen to move forward and drop through an increased stake; once, when the cards were unfavourable, they glided back and slipped three counters onto the reserve pile. It was all dreadfully dramatic, and one did not lose the effect in Sir Charles's skilled handling. (*Daily Chronicle*)

Mr Lycett Green saw acts of cheating, Russell continued, and :

He with difficulty repressed himself. His first impulse was then and there to denounce the cheat. You will recollect in whose presence he was. He left the room after he had seen two distinct acts of this character. His first intention was to write a note to the master of the house, and then, for other reasons, he thought it more prudent to write a note to

Mrs Arthur Wilson informing her of what he had seen, and sends her a note by a servant. He waits outside for some moments in doubt what he ought to do; and, finally, he thinks things might reach a climax, and that he ought to be in the room. He walks back into the room and does not sit down, taking no further part in the play. . . .

Violent tugging of his robe from behind showed Russell he had made a mistake, so he hurriedly added (greatly to Clarke's amusement)

. . . until after a few minutes, and then resumes his seat at the table.

He then described how Lycett Green sought the advice of persons older than himself, his father, Lord Edward Somerset and his cousin, Lord Coventry and General Owen Williams, who decided that the Prince of Wales must be informed :

It has been suggested by my learned friend, and not unnaturally, that Lord Coventry and General Owen Williams seemed very early and speedily to have arrived at a conclusion as to the guilt of Sir William Gordon-Cumming. Perhaps it is not unnatural. It was difficult to believe – you will find it difficult to believe – that these persons, having no ill-feeling to Sir William Gordon-Cumming, and with every motive to prevent a scandal at Tranby Croft, – one of them actuated by a strong motive of comradeship and of service in the same regiment – in making an accusation of a distasteful nature were mistaken. It is not unnatural that they found it impossible to believe that these five persons, all stating that they independently saw acts of cheating, and as to whom no motive of unfriendliness can be suggested – they found it difficult to believe, I say, that all these five persons could be mistaken. But, gentlemen, could any conduct have been pursued more calculated to build up, sustain, and support the statements of these five unprejudiced persons than the conduct of Sir William Gordon-Cumming?

Then the great advocate, with the impression of these facts fresh in his hearers' minds, gathered up their moral and hurled it in sharp ringing sentences, at the plaintiff's head. Here was a man, held to be of honour, accused of the debasing act of filching money from the pockets of his friends. What did he do? He said he was innocent. A guilty man would say that. An innocent man would say that too, but he would say more. He would ask, 'Where are my accusers? What do they say I have done? When and how do they say I did it? Bring them face to face with me. There is a terrible mistake which I can dispel.'

Then, as to the point of the scandal and the hinted desire on Sir William's part to save the Prince from exposure : and again came the courtly note so prominent in this trial. How was the Prince involved in a 'scandal' which simply consisted in playing an innocent game of baccarat and having the misfortune to play with a man who cheated? But if there had been fifty princes (with a slight deprecatory bow to royalty in the red morocco chair) would an innocent man have allowed his honour to be clouded by any such consideration?

As to losing his head, the counsel conjured up the image of the self-possessed, handsome, daintly-gloved and perfectly clothed gentleman whom they had seen in the witness-box. There was no appearance there 'in that cool, clever, intelligent man' of loss of self-possession. (*Daily Chronicle*)

Russell continued :

It did not seem to him to be a matter of grave concern that the Prince, whom he had professed to honour, was erased from the category of his friends; that General Owen Williams, a friend of twenty odd years, and Lord Coventry, a friend of some years, must for the future regard him as a man stained with dishonour. All these things he seems to have been willing to waive so long as the outside world knew nothing of it.

Then came the interval between the scandal and the commencement of the proceedings, and as Sir Charles spoke of it there was scarcely a whisper in Court, 'When did Sir William take proceedings? When, indeed?' There was a pause; and, emphatically striking the pile of legal books before him, Sir Charles replied in thrilling tones, 'Not till he found it was impossible to *slip* out of the army.'

As he proceeded, Sir Charles assumed more of that fierce forensic oratorical manner and keen analytical power for which he is so famed. Here was this man, under an awful stigma, his name had been dragged in the mire of scandal, it was trembling in the social balance; and yet . . . what did he do? He was content to allow himself to be branded as one who had been guilty of cheating, and to remain in the eyes of his friends a dishonoured man; and for what? Simply that the whole matter should be kept secret. (*Echo*)

When he finds he cannot slip out of the army on half-pay without an enquiry, then, and then only, does he resort to this action – an action for damages forsooth, against five people who made the statement last September, and whose statement was tacitly assented to by him, but which he now denies, because no other remedy is open to him. These are the facts of the case as far as it is now my duty to open them. You will hear the evidence which is to be given, and, however painful it may be, it will be your duty, if you believe the evidence to be that of conscientious persons, to give effect to it in your verdict.

There was complete silence as Russell resumed his seat, and Asquith called the first witness for the defence, Arthur Stanley Wilson : he stepped smartly into the witness-box. All attention was focussed upon him – so much had been heard about the alleged cheating, and now, at last, came the turn of the first man who claimed to have actually seen it.

> He was a young-looking dapper boy in irreproachable frock coat and black scarf, with a small, black and lovingly-tended moustache and a very confident manner. . . . (*Daily Chronicle*)

In spite of his sallow complexion, he looked younger than his age, which he gave as twenty-two. He answered Asquith's opening questions with no hesitation or trace of embarrassment – that he was the son of Mr and Mrs Arthur Wilson of Tranby Croft, that he remembered the party there last September, that he had known the plaintiff before because he had stayed at their house, he thought a few years ago. Yes, he knew baccarat, most certainly, having played a good many times before, both at home and in London.

Russell handed him the miniature table marked 8th September and he confirmed that the labels were in their correct places to indicate where the various players were sitting. He explained about the uneven tables, covered with a cloth, how the cards were dealt, how the game was played, what cards you needed in order to win, and how the money was paid. Asquith continued his questions :

You have told us you were sitting next to the plaintiff? – Yes.

Did you observe where the plaintiff placed his stake? – Yes, I did, most certainly. He placed it on the top of a piece of white notepaper which he had in front of him.

Did he do that once, or invariably when you saw him? – I think invariably, but he may have done it once or twice in another way.

But that was his usual practice? – Certainly.

There was no line on the table at that time? – No.

You have told us that the middle table was higher than the side ones were. Where did you and Lieutenant Levett place your stakes? – We both of us placed ours on the higher table.

Before the Prince dealt the cards did you look round the table? – Yes, to see how the people were playing, whether they were playing high or not.

Did you notice what stake the plaintiff had put in front of him? – Yes; when I looked he had one £5 counter on. This was before the deal.

On what was it placed? – On the sheet of notepaper.

What was the colour of the counter? –Red. I looked at the same time all round to see what other stakes were being placed.

He described the first coup, and his surprise at seeing the miracle of the one red counter grow into three on the sheet of white paper. (The Court here grew very still and Sir Edward Clarke took copious notes.) He looked again, and in the folded hands of Sir William saw a red gleam which he took for counters. . . . (*Daily Chronicle*)

Mr Asquith encouraged him, 'Yes, go on?' After a pause, he continued with quiet intensity :

As I looked across at Lord Edward Somerset about to take up his cards, I noticed that Sir William was sitting with his hands in front of him, like this . . . (He held one hand over the other with the thumbs protruding. The people at the back of the Court stood up to see better.) . . . and there was one £5 counter on top of the sheet of notepaper. He was sitting with his hands over the £5 counter in that position, leaning forward. . . .

A juryman who couldn't see properly asked him to turn that way. He did so, repeating the movement of his hands.

. . . then I turned round. Lord Edward Somerset picked up the cards, and he, the plaintiff, leaned over – like this – to see what cards he had got. As I looked at the same time, I saw that he had something red in the palms of his hands, and this I immediately knew could be nothing less than one of the £5 counters. (There was a gasp of excitement from the crowd.) He looked, as I said over Lord Somerset's hand to see what card he had. Lord Edward had a 'natural' – a nine and a court card. Immediately he saw this he opened his hands – like that – and let drop three more £5 counters, and was paid £20 on the coup.

There was an indignant 'Oh !' from his hearers – the young man had the true entertainer's gift for moving his audience while he himself showed no emotion at all : he told his story, as one reporter said, 'With a curious sense of dramatic effect.'

What was the next thing you noticed about his play? – I saw him sitting with his hands in much the same position. I cannot say for certain who was taking up the cards. Whoever it was drew a very bad card, and I fancy we were baccarat, that is, nothing. Immediately he saw this he drew back his hands to his own pile, which was in front of him, to the bottom of the sheet of notepaper, and let fall the counters, I could not see how many, onto his own pile.

COLERIDGE : Before that he had got £5 on? – Yes, he had £5 on. He did not touch that.

Asquith continued :

You were sitting next to Mr Berkeley Levett, and you knew him to be a brother officer of the plaintiff? – Yes.

Did you say anything to Mr Berkeley Levett? – Yes. Directly I saw this I turned round to him and whispered, 'My God, Berkeley, this is too hot!'

Explain what you meant by 'this'? – The withdrawing the hand. The incident which I have just described. Mr Levett said, 'What on earth do you mean?' I said to him, 'This man next to me is cheating.' He said, 'My dear chap, you must be mistaken. You have made some mistake. It is absolutely im-poss-i-ble.' I said to him, 'Well, just look for yourself.' He looked, and a few coups afterwards he turned to me and said, 'It is too hot.'

All this was very dramatic. The witness seemed to enter into the exciting nature of the recital and quite made the ladies hold their breath by the thrilling manner in which he reproduced the startled tones of the scandalised Levett and his own horrified self. There was just that suspicion of a drawl too about his tones which conjured up the gilded young guardsman to the life . . . Then he took his excited audience to the scene in the bedroom. There Levett threw himself on the bed and exclaimed, 'My God! To think of it!' reproducing the heartrending tones of Mr Berkeley Levett when he thought his late captain had cheated. Having brought his evidence up to the point when Mr Levett in despair flung himself dressed upon his bed, the Court adjourned for half an hour much to the satisfaction of all present, owing to the close atmosphere. (*Star*)

All these declarations caused no small sensation in Court, and afforded much ground for speculation during the usual adjournment for luncheon. (*Echo*)

Not a few of the spectators were forced to stand all day long, and some weary barristers at the back were constrained to improvise seats out of a heap of ponderous law books, gathered at random from the shelves of the court. So the rising lawyers of the present sat as it were in judgement upon the great lawyers of the past. (*Morning Advertisier*)

After the lunch interval, Stanley Wilson went back to the witness-box and described how he went to his mother's dressing-room, after leaving Berkeley Levett, and told her he had seen Gordon-Cumming cheating. She begged him to say nothing about it, but he told his brother-in-law, Mr Lycett Green, next morning, mentioning at the same time that a different table would be used for the following night's play that would make cheating impossible.

Asquith then questioned him about the second night's play. Russell passed the second miniature table up to him, and again he was able to indicate where each player had been sitting : the only one he hesitated about was Berkeley Levett. He described the new table as being long, long enough for perhaps twenty people to sit at, but only three feet across, with a chalk line right round it about six inches from the edge.

The play began after dinner with the stakes placed over the white line. By and by, Lady Coventry, who was holding cards, had a seven – a very good card. Sir William, who sat next, looked over her shoulders and advised her not to take a card. Then the watcher declared that he saw Sir William's hands, one above the other, creep up to the white line, as if they were covering something. That was the first stage. The next was that the Prince showed a low card, and cried, 'I'm baccarat' – i.e., nothing. The third was that Sir William flipped up a £10 counter just over the line and behind his red £5 counter. The banker paid, but the £10 was overlooked. Then Sir William : 'I beg your pardon, sir, there's one more tenner you've forgotten.' To which the Prince : 'I wish you would put your counters in a more conspicuous place.' All this story was told with airy self-possession, partly to the jury, partly to the judge. (*Daily Chronicle*)

Asquith continued :

Was anything said by anyone as to confronting Sir William Gordon-Cumming? – Oh yes. My brother-in-law said distinctly that if he did not think himself to be guilty he wished to be confronted with him at once.

I think nothing was said at that time about the undertaking? – No, I don't think there was anything then said about it.

But, later in the evening, was anything mentioned to you about it? – Yes.

By whom? – By Lord Coventry and General Williams.

Was Mr Lycett Green present? – Yes, he was.

Did he concur or object? – No; he objected to the paper altogether. He said he thought that months afterwards it might come up against us; that the plaintiff might bring an action against us, or insult one of us, or words to that effect. I cannot recall the exact words.

What did General Owen Williams say? – General Williams assured him that in signing the paper the plaintiff admitted his guilt.

CLARKE: Do you remember the words used by General Owen Williams? – I cannot remember the precise words now. It is nine months ago.

He treated the Court to a highly dramatic delivery of the talk in which he and others took part, which, if it was a trifle overdone here and there, put plenty of light and shade into his very thrilling story . . . There was only one more incident, the inquiry – which was not put to the Prince of Wales – whether the disclosure had come through him. A brief denial, and the examination came to a close. (*Daily Chronicle*)

The reporters were so affected by his performances that they came out with phrases such as, 'Mr Wilson proved to be the sensation of the day,' and 'Staggering evidence of Mr Wilson,' and '. . . nothing could so arouse and enthral the breathless attention of his hearers!' The general impression was that he was an extremely capable young man, familiar with the game of baccarat, and that he had a clear recollection of everything that went on.

Sir Edward Clarke's cross-examination shed a refreshing light on 'Mr Jack's' early career and accomplishments. The Solicitor-General treated him throughout as a boy – and a rather naughty boy. He had been to Cambridge, but as he had not done much work and had wasted his time, he thought he might as well come away, a conclusion in which Sir Edward discovered his father agreed, 'and took you away,' added the counsel, 'to waste time elsewhere.' Then followed more 'Leaves from a Young Masher's Life.' 'Your occupation?' asked the Solicitor-General. 'I have no occupation,' with a touch of outraged pride; 'only a month at my father's business' – here a touch of modest diffidence, as if the witness were anxious not to make too much of this one black month in a career of white masherdom. (*Daily Chronicle*)

Clarke then questioned him about his previous experience of baccarat: he was extremely vague. Apart from one occasion at Tranby Croft about a year ago when his father had objected to the game, he thought he might have played it at some man's rooms at Cambridge, but he couldn't remember precisely. Asked to mention any one person with whom he would swear he had played baccarat, he could not. After a few more questions he admitted that when he sat down to play at Tranby Croft on 8th September he was a novice – but that he had heard a great deal about it since.

You represent to the jury that you have a clear memory as to the events at Tranby Croft? – Yes.

Mr Lycett Green was your spokesman on that evening? – He was.

You are aware that he did not profess to have seen any false play at all on the evening of the 8th? – No, he did not.

Then he was professing to relate, as to the evening of the 8th, not what he had seen, but what you had seen? – What I had told him. I may have put in a word here or there, but I cannot say.

You would have put in a word if it had been necessary to correct any inaccuracies? – Certainly.

So what he told Lord Coventry on that occasion was the story as you wished it to be believed that night? – Yes.

He agreed that the story had been told three times that night, to Lord Coventry, then to Lord Coventry and General Owen Williams, and again to both of them in the presence of the Prince, and that he had no doubt it was exactly the account that he was then in a position to give. Clarke then read aloud the record that had been made by General Williams, and signed also by Lord Coventry, and affirmed by the Prince of Wales.

Is that a true account of what Mr Lycett Green said in your presence? – It is more or less so. It may not be as to the withdrawing of the stake frequently.

Listen to the paragraph I have read, and answer the question I put. Is the sentence I have read to you an accurate statement of what Mr Lycett Green said in your presence? – I should say, not quite.

Clarke then repeated it sentence by sentence. Stanley Wilson said that the first part, Gordon-Cumming putting on a larger stake after the card had been declared in his favour, was correct. About having used the word, 'systematically', he fancied he had done so but couldn't swear to it, and he didn't think he had said that Gordon-Cumming frequently withdrew his stake. He had only seen him withdraw once.

I take your answer, and we will come back to what you saw. I come to the next paragraph : 'This conduct is described as placing a larger stake after the cards had been declared in his favour, and with frequently withdrawing a portion of the stake when the cards were against him. This conduct had also been noticed by Mrs Arthur Wilson.' Did Mr Lycett Green tell these three gentlemen, at different times, that on the evening of the 8th, Mrs Arthur Wilson had noticed that conduct ? – Yes.

I do not wish to catch you for a moment, and you may not have noticed the exact form of my question. Did Mr Lycett Green tell General Williams, Lord Coventry and His Royal Highness that on the evening of the 8th Mrs Arthur Wilson had noticed that conduct ? – No; I beg your pardon. I thought you said on the evening of the 9th.

By all means put yourself right. I ask now, did Mr Lycett Green in your presence tell these three gentlemen that Sir William's conduct had been noticed on the 8th by Mrs Wilson ? – Certainly not.

And that she had informed her husband of what she had seen ? – Certainly not.

In order to make my meaning perfectly clear I will read the whole passage : 'This conduct had also been noticed by Mrs Arthur Wilson, who informed her husband of what she had seen. Mr and Mrs Lycett Green and Mr Levett having also been made acquainted with the facts, it was agreed that they should all carefully watch the play on the following night.' Is that a correct statement of what occurred ? – No, it is entirely wrong.

No such thing was ever said ? – Certainly not, because the things did not take place at all that were put down.

Clarke completed the reading of General Owen Williams's *précis* : they agree, it is said, to watch carefully the play on the following night, 'when again Sir William was frequently observed most distinctly to repeat the same practice.'

Was anything said by Mr Lycett Green in your hearing to either of these three gentlemen as to withdrawing the stakes the second night ? – No, never.

You said that the *précis* was not shown to you ? – Yes.

You are aware that it was sent to the Prince of Wales and then remitted to Lord Coventry for verification, and that his Royal Highness has himself affirmed it ? – Yes.

Coming to the account which has been given to-day, did you at any time make a memorandum of what you allege took place on these evenings? – No.

You made the observations which struck you at the time. If you had been asked the day after, could you have given a more detailed account? I could have detailed several other acts if I had been asked.

Quite possibly? – I'm certain of it.

You were asked the day following by His Royal Highness? – I may have given more details then.

Will you undertake to say you did? – No; I will not undertake to say I did.

Do you suggest to the jury that any part of such a matter as that could have slipped from your mind? – Certainly. After nine months one is quite liable to forget a few of the facts or forget the details.

Forget the details? – Yes.

He was then questioned about the tables used on the first night: he could not recall whether they were covered by one cloth giving an uneven surface over all of them, or by two separate cloths, or by three, nor could he describe the colour. He couldn't remember how often he had handled the cards himself or how many times they had gone round the table when he saw the alleged cheating; but he identified without hesitation the values of the different counters when Clarke held them up one after the other. He said he didn't use any system, just played as the fancy took him; but he was able to describe the *coup de trois*.

Now, I understand that Sir William Gordon-Cumming had got an ordinary sheet of notepaper on the table, and these counters which he staked, £5 or otherwise, were put on the paper? – Yes; towards the top of the paper.

Towards the end of the paper farthest away from Sir William Gordon-Cumming? – Yes.

That piece of paper was in the clear observation of a good many people? – Certainly.

Including such persons as Lord Edward Somerset? – Yes.

Could Mr Tyrwhitt Wilson see it? – I really do not remember.

Could the Prince see it? – Yes.

Could General Owen Williams see it? – Yes.

Coming to Stanley Wilson's actual accusations of cheating, Clarke asked, referring to an expression he had used in his affidavit,

What is called 'declaring the cards'? – I have never thought about it.

We have heard a great deal of baccarat lately. Will you think of it now, and tell me what is 'declaring the cards'? – I suppose that it is declaring what a particular card is worth.

Of course a player, if he holds a natural, lays down his cards; otherwise the banker declares first? – Yes.

The jury will understand you to say, that in each case the alteration which you allege was made after the banker had declared his point? – Not each time; not the first time.

The first time, the Prince said 'I give cards.' Therefore he could not have a natural. Lord Edward Somerset picked up the cards and looked at them, and then Sir William Gordon-Cumming looked at them . . . – Not the first time. That was the first time I saw him distinctly cheating. I think you will find that by my evidence.

You told us in your evidence that the first thing happened at the very first coup? – I did not say I saw anything. I said what happened.

If you describe what happened, you must have seen it? – I did not say that I saw anything that Sir William Gordon-Cumming did wrong.

You do not suggest that you saw any cheating at the first coup? – Certainly not.

Then I understand that, so far as the first was concerned, you do not represent that you saw him do anything wrong? – Yes.

That being so, I pass from that, and come to the instance in which you say you saw him cheating.

Clarke had him confirm again where each of the players had been sitting, then

You illustrate by putting your hands together the way in which he was holding his hands at the time? – Yes.

Were you leaning over in front of him, or behind him? – We were both leaning over together.

You suggest you saw something red in his hand? – Most certainly I do.

At that time there was a sheet of paper to which you have referred lying upon the table in front of him with a red counter upon it? – It was.

You said Lord Edward Somerset had a natural? – Yes, he had.

You had placed your stake? – Yes, on the higher table beyond Lord Edward Somerset's stake, which was in front of him at the time.

He was only playing in half sovereigns? – Yes. He may have had sovereigns on sometimes.

He put his counters on the table? – Yes, just in front of him.

He did not put them on the sheet of paper? – He may have done that, although I am not quite certain.

Cannot you say? – No. I cannot say for certain.

Did you notice Lord Edward Somerset's first stake in the evening? – Yes.

How much was it? – I think 10/–, but I am not perfectly certain.

Then I understand you to say that on this occasion you saw three more £5 counters on the paper? – Yes, I swear I saw it.

Do you mean to say that, having been upon the table a sheet of white paper with a red counter upon it as Sir William Gordon-Cumming's stake, immediately Lord Edward Somerset had declared a natural you saw four red counters upon it? – There were certainly four red counters upon it. I saw him open his hand, as I have said before, and drop them out.

Put his hands over the paper? – He had kept them there the whole time. I could see the £5 counter underneath. He just lowered his hand, and, opening it, let three more drop out.

And immediately after a natural was declared? – Immediately after he had seen the cards.

Had a natural been declared or not? – I think it was pretty nearly at the same minute, but I could not say for certain. Lord Edward Somerset would put down a natural on the table.

The point is, was the natural declared? You have been asked in this case to give particulars of all that you saw. [He quoted from the affidavit] 'The cheating consisted in the plaintiff increasing his stake after the card was declared in his favour.' Did you use that phrase? – I may have done.

Do you not swear in that affidavit that the cheating consisted in adding to the stake after the card was declared in his favour? Do you mean that it was after Lord Edward Somerset had declared a natural? – He certainly had seen the natural, and I think Lord Edward Somerset had put it down, but I am not quite certain.

I am merely quoting your own sentence? – What I consider is, he had seen the card and he knew it was a natural. It was virtually declared.

Do you know that in every one of the five affidavits this particular phrase has been used, 'after the card was declared in his favour'? – I cannot say.

Do you swear that what was done was done after Lord Edward Somerset had declared a natural? – I cannot swear to that, but I can swear that Sir William saw the card, and if not declared it was virtually declared – it was as good as declared.

COLERIDGE : You maintain your answer is substantially the same – that he had seen the card? – Yes.

COLERIDGE : And that having seen it, he put on more counters? – That is exactly what I mean.

CLARKE : Perhaps, your lordship, it would be convenient here to adjourn. I have much more to ask this witness.

COLERIDGE : You cannot finish to-night?

CLARKE : Oh no, my lord.

COLERIDGE : Very well, we will adjourn.

CHAPTER EIGHT

The Wilsons accuse their Guest

On the fourth day of the trial, proceedings began at ten thirty instead of at eleven : it was generally understood that this was because the Prince of Wales was not expected to attend. Many people arrived late, unaware that the time had been altered. Outside there was mud and rain; but the same crowds were seeking admittance, though the ladies' dresses were less bright. Gordon-Cumming was, as usual, one of the first of the principals to arrive : he sat talking quietly to his solicitor.

> The Wilsons took their seats on their air cushions half an hour earlier to-day, at half past ten, the ordinary hour for the courts to sit. There was a significance in this. It seemed to imply that the suit of Gordon-Cumming against Wilson and others had ceased to be a fashionable function and had become a mere law case.
>
> The Prince did not turn up at the beginning, perhaps he was not coming, but the Lady Chief Justice turned up punctually, looking as charming as ever. It is very interesting to note the Lady Chief Justice's attitude towards the gentleman who presides over the Court. When the Lord Chief Justice came in, the Court most respectfully rose. All the ladies sitting by the side of Lady Coleridge the balcony stalls rose and bowed most deferentially. Lady Coleridge sat quite composed at first. When at last she half rose it was with a roguish little smile to the Chief as though to say, 'though you are My Lord Chief Justice, you are my husband.' (*Star*)

Stanley Wilson again took his stand in the witness-box : he still maintained his confident attitude, but now it seemed to be a strain. An unkind reporter suggested that yesterday was probably the hardest day's work he had done in his life. The renewed cross-examination concerned the accusations of cheating during the second night's play :

> Is your recollection quite definite as to what took place on that evening ? – It is.
>
> How is it that your recollection is quite definite on some matters and not on others ? – It is only natural. I have talked the subject over with my brother-in-law, and I have thought about it very often.

Not being a pleasant subject, you thought of it very often? You have had a great many interviews with your solicitors? – Yes, a great many.

Had you seen Mr George Lewis before you made your affidavit? – Yes.

Who prepared the affidavit? – Mr George Lewis.

At that moment, three minutes after Lord Coleridge, the Prince of Wales entered by the judge's door at the back of the courtroom : the whole Court rose and bowed. He exchanged bows with Lord Coleridge and took his usual place in the red morroco armchair.

Mr Wilson looked a trifle paler than yesterday, but he quickly assumed the *sangfroid* that is such a remarkable characteristic of his demeanor in the box. The Solicitor-General is not so vigorous in his method of cross-examination as Sir Charles Russell, but he displays a remarkable analytical power, which became very marked in his bout with Mr Wilson. Some of the questions brought out interesting particulars – indeed, some the spectators little expected to hear, judging by the slight sensation they created. 'To whom did those counters you played with at Tranby Croft belong?' Mr Wilson hesitated a moment. Then, still with hesitation, 'The Prince of Wales.' There was a whispered consultation between the Solicitor-General and Mr Wontner, Sir W. G. Cumming's solicitor; and the visitors watched intently. What would be the next question? Would Sir Edward ask whether the Prince were in the habit of carrying counters about with him when visiting at country houses? But no. Sir Edward tacked, and turning to another portion of the disagreeable story induced Mr Wilson to say that he would 'stake his life' that he saw the 'foul play'. And yet his mother sat down to play again the second night, and with one whom they had accused of cheating ! (*Echo*)

On the second night did it so happen that all the five persons who knew of the accusation were sitting close together? – Yes, more or less.

What do you mean by that? – Mr Levett was sitting opposite, but whether exactly opposite I could not swear.

You told us yesterday that the table was only three feet wide? – Yes. It was measured a few days ago.

Then Mr Berkeley Levett was sitting immediately opposite to Sir William Gordon-Cumming, and within three feet of him? – Yes, I suppose he was.

Had you mentioned to the rest of the family party the use of the chalk line? – I thought everyone would know.

What did you explain to your mother about the chalk line? – I told my mother that it would be impossible to cheat.

Did you say that to anyone else? – To Mrs Lycett Green.

So this little party sat down with the knowledge or impression that the chalk line was placed on the table to prevent Sir William Gordon-Cumming doing something which he could have done if the chalk line had not been there? – Certainly.

No syllable having been mentioned to Sir William Gordon-Cumming or to his old friends staying in the house? – No, certainly not. What! My word against Sir William's?

Sir Edward said he thought the accusation was founded on his word and on Mr Levett's: Stanley Wilson disagreed. After his interview with Mr Levett he thought it would only be his own word against Sir William's.

How long do you think it was after you sat down at the table before you noticed anything? – I cannot tell. Perhaps twenty minutes or half an hour after I sat down I noticed something.

So far as you knew, you were the first person to observe anything wrong? – I don't know.

Before you noticed anything wrong, had your attention been called to anyone else, or anything else? – No.

What was the first thing you observed? – I observed his hand move in a suspicious manner, but I could not see positively what it was doing.

When you first observed something wrong the second night, you were the first person to notice it? – So far as I know, I was.

Had you that night one of those carpenter's pencils? – No.

Was anyone else using them? – I cannot remember.

Was anything else on the table? Glasses? – I daresay, if anyone was drinking.

Were you smoking? – Yes. I should think so. Most certainly.

Were there ash-trays on the table? – I do not think there were. I cannot remember. There may have been.

Where was Lady Coventry sitting that evening? – Between General Williams and Sir William Gordon-Cumming. Then Mrs Lycett Green was next, and then myself.

You were round the corner? – Yes.

You could not see Lady Coventry's cards? – No.

Then at that time when, as you allege, you first saw, on the second evening, a hand come out and put a counter over the line, at that time you say you had not seen Lady Coventry's cards – No; but Sir William did not put the counter over the line until he knew she had won.

It was not a natural? – No, it was not.

So that the banker must have declared his points? – Yes, he must have done, and did too.

Were Lady Coventry's declared by her or by Sir William? – They merely said, 'we have won!' or Lady Coventry said so. As the banker's points were declared, as he said 'I have nothing,' the counter just went over the line.

Do you represent that it was a £10 counter? – Yes, I do.

Making it £15 instead of £5? – Yes.

You saw him do that, and have no doubt of it? – Absolutely no doubt.

All these other persons whose names have been mentioned were all sitting without any cards in their hands? – Of course.

Only having to see whether Lady Coventry had won in order that that might decide whether they had won or not? – Yes.

And with quite as good an opportunity as you had of seeing what the play was? – Certainly, if they liked.

Did you think they must have seen? – Yes, I did.

Why, then, did you not say at that moment, 'Sir William Gordon-Cumming, you only staked £5? – There were ladies at the table.

Well? – Well, I should think that was a sufficient reason for not doing so.

Why, sir, should the presence of ladies at the table prevent the immediate charge, when you yourself knew that that charge had been communicated to two ladies before you sat down to play? – As I have said before, it is not a natural thing to have a row over cards when not only one lady but half a dozen were present.

Why not? – It would not be a gentlemanly thing to do when ladies were present.

Would you if only your mother and sister were present? – No. I don't think I should even if there had been only one lady present.

You had no thought except the presence of the ladies? – My brother-in-law is rather hot-tempered, quicker tempered than I am.

Then you suggest your slow temper is the explanation of your seeing that, and then going on for an hour playing cards? – I have told you I don't think it would have been the right thing to do.

Not to call attention at once? – No, certainly not, when at the table.

Why not? – One does not have a scene over a game of cards when ladies are present.

Have you had so many scenes over card tables that you know what should be done? – No, I have not; but it is only natural.

And you did sit at that table for an hour afterwards? – I did.

Playing and staking your own money on the success of the cards which Sir William Gordon-Cumming was backing? – I did.

Very well. That's all I have to ask you.

Thereupon Sir Edward Clarke sat down, and the Lord Chief Justice showed that he had not got the right drift of the last piece of cross-examination by recalling young Wilson to the Associate's table and asking him, 'Do I understand that you took winnings which you obtained through the cheating you allege on the part of Sir William Gordon-Cumming? 'No, my lord,' said young Wilson hurriedly, and all over the Court there was a muttering of 'No, No.' (*Star*)

CLARKE: It is not suggested that Sir William Gordon-Cumming manipulated the cards at all so that other people could profit by it.

RUSSELL: He alone could profit by it.

COLERIDGE: I thought you stated you played for an hour afterwards and implied that you had put into your own pocket winnings which you had gained through his cheating. Can such a thing occur?

CLARKE: I do not suggest that, my lord.

COLERIDGE: I am glad I asked the question and cleared away a misunderstanding. Knowing something of the devices of lawyers, I thought the Solicitor-General's breaking off in the cross-examination was for the purpose of emphasising the point by going no further.

CLARKE: I stopped there because I had no further questions to put.

It was remarked that the Prince of Wales looked quite fresh although he had given a ball at Buckingham Palace the night before:

He sat quietly all day long in his chair to the left of Lord Coleridge, smiling to himself from time to time whenever a witness made an amusing remark or an advocate ventured on a joke. He seemed particularly delighted when someone alluded to the victory of one of his horses at Doncaster, and rendered timely assistance to the Lord Chief Justice when an avalanche of documents suddenly descended from that learned judge's desk upon the floor. Perhaps he was not quite so pleased when Mr Arthur Stanley Wilson told the Solicitor-General that the leather counters with which the game was played belonged to His Royal Highness who had brought them to the house with him and who, so the witness fancied, had drawn the chalk line on the table which was used on the second night. (*Morning Advertiser*)

It was now Mr Berkeley Levett's turn to give an account of himself. The Attorney-General had orginally been retained for him, but had returned the brief on the ground that he had to be present at, and advise, the

Committee of Privileges. The examination-in-chief was conducted by Mr
Charles Mathews.

Mr Levett is a young man of twenty-seven, though he looks several years
younger, with light hair and a slight moustache. He very aptly described
his position as an 'awkward' one, and he evidently felt somewhat uncom-
fortable. For he is a lieutenant in the Scots Guards, Sir William Gordon-
Cumming's regiment, and he seems to have had the greatest respect for
the plaintiff, who was at one time his superior officer. His examination was
conducted by Mr Charles Mathews, the well-known Old Bailey barrister,
who showed such conspicuous ability in the Turf Arbitration Case about
a year ago. Standing with his gown half falling off his back, as is his usual
custom, Mr Mathews addressed the witness in quiet tones while his wife,
who was seated on the bench, listened with evident interest as her husband
put his questions, emphasising them every now and again with a significant
gesture. (*Morning Advertiser*)

He didn't look like a guardsman. His long smooth hair gave him quite an
effeminate appearance especially as his small very light moustache was
invisible at a little distance. He spoke in a subdued voice which was rather
effective as expressing his great pain at appearing against a superior officer,
but which made a good deal of his evidence inaudible. (*Star*)

He had none of Mr Wilson's bland confidence, and grew a little confused
under cross-examination, but he gave his evidence modestly, and with a
certain air of reluctance. Apparently, however, he knew more of baccarat
than Mr 'Jack'. He told simply enough, but with no graphic power, the
story of what he saw, or thought he saw, on the first night after the
whispered talk with his friend. 'I saw him adding to his counters; he had
a £5 counter; when the banker declared his coup he added £5 counters
out of his hand; the hands were folded one over the other, and the lower
hand opened.' The witness illustrated all this with a pair of rather beefy
hands. 'Yes, he was ab-so-lute-ly certain.' (*Daily Chronicle*)

Mr Levett has that exceptionally well-groomed appearance all the young
men connected with the case wear. He is twenty-seven and has been a
brother officer of Sir W. Gordon-Cumming for two years. He added little
to the general story. He declared that he saw the cheating, that he was
painfully horrified and that he implored young Wilson to say nothing
of it. Of course, the greatest interest centres in the interview at barracks
between the two officers, when, it was insinuated by Sir Charles Russell,
Sir William asked Mr Levett to say he saw nothing on the eventful night.
This was very quickly reached after the recital of the familiar events at
Tranby Croft. And it proved to be of considerable importance, inasmuch
as it was an entire contradiction of the plaintiff's story. What actually
took place? This is Mr Levett's account of the conversation :-

When I entered, Sir William said, 'I suppose you know what has happened? It's all over the place.' I said, 'Yes, I know what you mean.' He then said, 'What do you propose to do? I don't ask you to withdraw, but can't you say you were mistaken?' I replied, 'I must believe my own eyes.' He then said, 'Could you not withdraw?' I said, 'I would if I could, for the honour of the regiment, but there is one man who would not.' He then said, 'What do you say you saw?' and I replied, 'I saw you adding counters.' He then asked me to go and see Mrs Wilson and see what could be done.

This was the whole of the statement, embellished by other contradictions of that of Sir William Gordon-Cumming; and the business of the locking of the door was very soon disposed of by the judge, who really attached no importance to it. (*Echo*)

Then, led by his counsel's questions, he told of the scene in his bedroom with Stanley Wilson and his conversation with him which must have lasted, he thought, about an hour, but he was so horrified at what had happened, he said, that he couldn't remember exactly what the conversation was, but he had begged Stanley Wilson, 'For God's sake don't say anything about it.' He claimed also that on the second night he had purposely abstained from looking at Sir William's play, and that he had refused to discuss it when Lycett Green addressed him on the subject. He then described the scene with the Prince who had asked him, 'I believe, Mr Levett, you too saw it?' and he had replied that he was in the same regiment and wished to be left out of it. (This contradicted Stanley Wilson who told the Court that Levett had replied to the Prince, 'Yes' – that he too saw the cheating.) Mathews asked;

Then in your hearing, did Mr Lycett Green make any statement to His Royal Highness? – Yes.

This statement having been made, did His Royal Highness put any question to Mr Lycett Green? – I cannot remember.

Do you remember His Royal Highness speaking to you . . . ?

CLARKE: I wish my learned friend would ask what took place. He is always asking, 'Do you remember?'

COLERIDGE: These occurrences took place months ago, and he may require some assistance, just to refresh his memory.

CLARKE: It is important to see what his unaided memory can do.

MATHEWS: I accede to my learned friend's request. (Then to the witness.)

What happened next? – After that I went to the smoking-room. I do not remember anything more transpiring that evening. I signed the undertaking next morning.

He was cross-examined by Clarke who first got him to confirm that he had seen no foul play whatsoever during the second night's play, and established that he had been, up until the Tranby Croft incident, the intimate friend of Gordon-Cumming and had liked him very much, as a subaltern to his colonel, but that they had met only at mess and regimental dinners, and so on. He asked for particulars of the alleged cheating on the first evening, whether he had been playing on any particular system, and then :

You noticed a sheet of paper was lying upon the table with one red counter on it? – Yes.

And this was upon the whist table? – Yes.

Were there other sheets of paper on the whist table? – There may have been. I don't remember.

Do you remember who were the persons playing there? I mean in the tableau? There were, I think, Mrs Arthur Wilson, yourself, Lord Edward Somerset, Sir William Gordon-Cumming, and I think, Captain Somerset? – I am not sure about Captain Somerset.

The others you remember? – Yes.

You cannot say whether any of these were playing with their stakes placed on white paper? – I don't remember.

We have heard from Mr Stanley Wilson the account of the system of staking one counter, and then, after winning on that, receiving a counter from the croupier, and adding another one in order to make the stake for the next coup. You have heard that explanation, and followed it? – Yes.

How much had Sir William staked on the coup before that which you described, and how much did he stake on the coup afterwards? – Which coup? Do you mean the one after the coup which I described?

Yes? – I cannot say.

So that, putting aside for the moment whether he had done anything improper, you cannot tell us whether at that time he was playing on the system described by Mr Wilson yesterday? – No.

COLERIDGE : On what principle or system would that be?

CLARKE : That which was described by Mr Stanley Wilson was, when you have taken up a counter of £5, the next stake will be £15, and the next £30, if you follow the three coups. (He turned again to the witness :)

At the time you saw what you have described, you repeated that you had made up your mind it was done dishonestly? – I had been told he was cheating.

Did what you saw, and that which you have described, make you come to the conclusion that it was dishonestly done, and not an accident? – It was that which I described.

Answer my question – It was not an accident.

Very well. There was nothing except the fact you had been told by Mr Wilson that the plaintiff was cheating, which would have led you to the conclusion that it was dishonesty and not an accident? – Only that.

I am not suggesting it was an accident at all. What I suggest is that you are sitting at a table playing cards with a gentleman you like very much and have reason to consider to be a perfectly honourable man, incapable of this conduct. You see something happening, something done or believe something was done. Do you mean to say you would jump at once to the conclusion that the man was intentionally cheating his friends at cards? – It all depends on what you saw done.

And what you saw done was one £5 counter upon that table before the coup was declared, and two £5 counters besides on the table after it? – I did.

Clarke passed to the second act of cheating that he alleged a few deals later. Again Levett could not remember what Gordon-Cumming had staked before or after the coup, or who had been handling the cards, whether it was Gordon-Cumming or another : his reply was always, 'I don't know' or 'I simply cannot remember' or 'all I can say is I cannot recollect,' but he admitted that if Gordon-Cumming was handling the cards he could not have done what was alleged.

. . . it resulted in an additional emphasis being placed upon the statement of the defence, for Mr Levett reasserted that he positively saw the addition of counters by Sir W. Gordon-Cumming, and that the counters were not pushed across the line by accident. Then the Solicitor-General made a point. Mr Levett had described the irregularities, and declared the fact that he saw counters representing money paid to Sir William. But had he noticed whether the stakes remained on the table, Sir William following what is known as the *coup de trois* system? No. He candidly confessed that he had not thought of watching as to whether the counters were taken from the table or not. This led up to a question as to the characteristics of the party – had they been partaking of various beverages, and were they smoking as the game went on? Of course, they were; and then Lord Coleridge interposed with a question as to whether the hospitality was 'a disturbing hospitality'? There was an outburst of laughter, which was accentuated when the Solicitor-General promptly replied, 'I imagine that is the inference, my lord.' (*Echo*)

Levett assented to Clarke's suggestion that 'There was late dinner every night, a pleasant party and great hospitality.' It is only too probable that this 'great hospitality' affected the defendants' judgement and behaviour. The *Daily Chronicle* took this up very strongly :

> No man of the world can suppose that the guests in this typically plutocratic family were altogether in their cool senses when one set of them engaged in a conspiracy to 'plant' Sir William Gordon-Cumming with a charge of cheating at cards. We can as easily bring ourselves to believe that they were capable of seeing clearly or reporting accurately what they say they saw when, with minds inflamed by exuberant bourgeois hospitality . . . they came to the conclusion that Sir William Gordon-Cumming was cheating the Prince of Wales, who, though a keen and experienced gambler, who from evidence given did not pay with a pleasant face when he lost, never dreamt there was any cheating at all. (*Daily Chronical*)

The next witness to be called was the controversial Mr Lycett Green, the emotional force behind the accusations. It is surprising that General Owen Williams had not been asked outright, 'From whom was the ultimatum you spoke of in your letter to Gordon-Cumming?' and 'Who was going to denounce Gordon-Cumming next morning on Doncaster Racecourse?'

Mr Lewis provides the answer to this in his brief. Describing the scene in which Lord Coventry and General Williams bring Gordon-Cumming the undertaking to sign, he says, 'They presented him with this document as the only possible escape for himself, inasmuch as his accusers would otherwise allow the matter to become known the following morning.'

This could only mean that the Wilsons were going to denounce him themselves, as they were the only accusers, except Berkeley Levett; and that the ultimatum was also from them, or from Lycett Green as their spokesman, which meant that his role had been perilously close to that of a blackmailer. The ultimatum, of course, was directed also against the Prince, Lord Coventry and General Williams, all of whom had an interest in the scandal not being noised abroad, and Gordon-Cumming was to get them all out of trouble merely by signing the document. No wonder they exercised 'extreme pressure' !

However, because these two important questions had not been asked, an area for doubt and misunderstanding remained.

The much talked-of Mr Lycett Green succeeded Mr Levett. Mr Green did not look quite so terrible a fellow as his brother-in-law and his friend had described him. He has a smooth face with a thin, unremarkable nose; his manner is modest, his voice low, with a curious hesitant catch in it. (*Daily Chronicle*)

He was also tall and fair, and he wore a monocle. One reporter thought he looked the picture of a healthy English gentleman and seemed to bring with him a breath of fresh moorland air into the stuffy courtroom. The *Star* reporter thought he was, 'without any of the 'side' or aristocratic drawl of young Jack. 'He has a curious staccato style of speech amounting almost to a stammer.' Mr Asquith conducted the examination-in-chief.

> He said he was the son of Sir Ed. Green, MP. About six years ago he married one of Mr Arthur Wilson's daughters. He was a Master of Hounds, and lived at York. He was 31 years of age, and he and his wife were members of the party at Tranby Croft last September. On the evening of the 8th (Monday) he was in the room while baccarat was being played, but on the Monday he did not play. He had been out cub-hunting in the morning, and, having had a hard day, went to bed early. The next morning Mr A. S. Wilson came to him and said, 'An awful thing has happened. Sir William Gordon-Cumming cheated at cards last night.' Witness said, 'Impossible. You must be mistaken.' Mr Wilson, however said, 'I am sure. There is no doubt about it.' He also said, 'Berkeley Levett has seen him.' Witness said, 'What are you going to do?' and Wilson replied, 'I have arranged to have a table made so that he can't do it to-night.' Later in the day he spoke to his wife on the subject. No agreement was made between him and Mr Wilson as to watching Sir William . . . The Court at this point adjourned for luncheon. (*Echo*)

On the Court resuming, an usher was seen to hand a juryman a letter. 'Stay! What is that?' exclaimed Lord Coleridge. The usher took the letter from the juryman, who had already opened it, and handed it to Coleridge. His lordship read it, and explained to the Court, 'Oh, it is simply a letter to the jury, generally abusive of both sides.' (Laughter). 'I suppose I need hardly say I am totally uninfluenced by this letter.' Asquith continued :

> I want you to tell us now what you noticed, if anything, as to the plaintiff's play? – The first thing that drew my attention to Sir William Gordon-Cumming was the way in which he leaned over the table with his hands close together over the chalk line. I cannot say whether his hands were like this, (he held his hands together,) but they were together. That aroused my suspicion, associated with what my brother-in-law had told me, and I naturally watched him. I saw him push a

blue counter over the line with his hands after the cards had been declared favourable to him. On the next occasion I saw Lady Coventry holding the cards. She did not take a card, and Sir William Gordon-Cumming was looking over her hand. She was making no effort to conceal her hand. I then saw him first of all look round to see if anyone was looking, and he gradually got up a counter like that, covering it with his hands close to the line. When the stakes were paid, Sir William Gordon-Cumming said, 'There is £10 more to come here,' and I think His Royal Highness said to General Williams, 'Owen, give him another tenner,' or something to that effect. He was paid that stake, making altogether £15 that was paid.

Mr Asquith went on with his examination of Mr Lycett Green who produced a coin to show what he says he saw Sir William Gordon-Cumming do on the second night of the play. In his nervousness Mr Green dropped the coin on the floor of the witness-box, and he had very considerable difficulty in recovering it, much to the spectators' amusement. (*Echo*)

You have no doubt that the counter was pushed over the line after the card was seen to be favourable? – I have no doubt of it.

When you saw this, what did you do? – At first I was horrified. I cannot precisely express my feeling. My first impulse was, I must say, to jump up and expose him, and say, 'Sir William Gordon-Cumming, you are cheating at cards,' but I did not do so. On second thoughts I felt it would be a horrible thing in the presence of ladies and His Royal Highness to jump up and make a scene; therefore I got up from the table and left the room. I went into the next room, the smoking-room, and wrote a note to my mother-in-law, Mrs Wilson. The butler, I think, came in, and I asked him to take the note in quietly and hand it to Mrs Wilson. The note has been destroyed. I believe I said in it, 'I have distinctly seen Sir William Gordon-Cumming cheating at cards.' As far as I can remember, I said something ought to be done to stop the game, or words to that effect. I went back to the room and took my seat at the table again. I would be away about two minutes, I think, but I cannot say precisely. After I came back I continued to take part in the game. The next morning I went to Doncaster to the races.

(Witness was here requested by his counsel to speak a little louder, as he could not be heard.) 'On the next morning I went to the races in the same carriage with Lord Edward Somerset and Captain Arthur Somerset. On my return I went to see Lord Coventry by myself at first . . . I told

Lord Coventry that some of us had seen Sir W. G. Cumming cheating at cards. I impressed upon him that there was not the slightest doubt about it, and we were willing to repeat the same before anybody. (*Echo*)

'And,' he added, 'to be confronted with Sir William Gordon-Cumming, if it was thought desirable.' He said he had told the two courtiers that his wife and his mother-in-law were prepared to come forward and say what they had seen. After dinner he was taken into the presence of the Prince:

I cannot recollect whether I made a formal statement to the Prince, but I know we were individually asked what were the cases of cheating. I am not sure whether it was by the Prince of Wales. When I was asked I stated the cases of cheating, but I cannot recollect exactly what I did say, it was so long ago.

Do you remember whether the Prince of Wales put a question to Mr Berkeley Levett? – I remember something about Mr Levett saying to the Prince that he was in Sir William's regiment, and that he didn't like to speak. I cannot remember who asked him, but some remark was made. I cannot remember whether it was by the Prince or not.

COLERIDGE: What did Mr Levett say? – He told him he had seen the cheating.

That statement, like Stanley Wilson's, contradicted Berkeley Levett's evidence and it was highly suspect as Lycett Green had just said he didn't remember who was speaking, and had mentioned that Levett's reply was that he didn't like to speak. The examination continued.

Do you remember the subject being mooted of the signing of what we have called the undertaking? – I do not remember the document being there, but I remember something of the sort being said. During the interview I said that if there was any doubt in the matter I should ask to be confronted by Sir William Gordon-Cumming. I cannot recollect whether anything further was said upon that. As a matter of fact I was never brought into the presence of Sir William Gordon-Cumming. Later on in the evening the document which has just been referred to was produced to me by, I think, General Owen Williams, I am not sure. I was asked to sign it. I read the document over, and I objected to the document, because I said that at some time Sir William Gordon-Cumming, when some witness might be dead or away in a distant land, might turn round on us and take proceedings against us when we were not in the position to meet him that we were then. When I made the

Lord Russell of Killowen

Sir Charles Russell cross-examining Sir William Gordon-Cumming.

Sir Edward Clarke

Caricature of Sir George Lewis by 'Spy' of *Vanity Fair*.

Lord Coleridge

Mrs Wilson being cross-examined by Sir Edward Clarke

objection, General Williams, I think, said that the signing of the document would be an admission of the plaintiff's guilt. I signed it soon afterwards.

That was about the end of the examination. It is remarkable that he, the prime mover in the affair, seemed unable to say anything without qualifying it with some such remark as, 'I don't exactly remember,' or 'I can't recall precisely,' except the actual alleged instances of cheating which he had frequently discussed with the other members of his family. We cannot accept that he couldn't remember making a formal statement to the Prince. The hedging by the principal accuser certainly weakens the defendants' case.

The final question, put to all the defendants by their counsel, enabled him to state that he had never spoken to any human being of what he had seen or heard on the evening of 9th September, until these proceedings were instituted.

Mr Charles Gill, much younger and half a head taller than Clarke, began his cross-examination by commenting on Lycett Green's last answer :

And I suppose you at once dismissed it from your mind? – I could hardly do that.
    As much as you could? – Yes.

There was quite a stir in the court when Mr Gill rose, instead of Sir Edward Clarke, to interrogate this witness. Ever since the Marks and Butterfield case last December Mr Gill has been a popular favourite. His memorable conflict with Sir Charles Russell at the Old Bailey has almost doubled his practice. On the morning after he had won that verdict Mr Gill woke up, like Lord Byron, to find himself famous. His exploits were commemorated in the popular song at Drury Lane, his portrait appeared in the comic papers . . . It was not unnatural, then, that there should be a hum of excitement when Mr Gill took the place of his leader, and the audience instinctively felt that the proceedings would be more lively. (*Morning Advertiser*)

When this matter happened, did you make any kind of note or record of it? – No, I did not.
    So that what you are telling us to-day is entirely from memory on your part? – Yes.
    It never occurred to you to make any memorandum? – I considered the matter was at an end.
    What is your occupation? – I am a Master of Hounds. (He said this with such an ingenuous air that the audience laughed.)

Gill then turned to Russell, and said, 'I don't know why we've heard so much about this gentleman's father being a Member of Parliament,' as if he thought even less of a Member of Parliament than of a Master of Hounds. Russell muttered, but didn't say anything, so Gill tried again : 'We've heard a good deal about it from Sir Charles Russell . . .' But Russell was not to be drawn.

Gill then asked Lycett Green about General Williams's record of events, the *précis* : he replied that until he came to court he had never seen it or heard what its contents were. He thought his solicitor, Mr Lewis, might have said something to him about it, but not what was in it, or who made it, or that it had been submitted to Lord Coventry and the Prince, and admitted by them to be a true record :

For some purpose or other you either constituted yourself the leading person in this matter, or you were selected? – I am older than my brother-in-law. I don't know that I was selected, or anything of the sort.

Now, you have heard more than once in this case of the document that has been read out. You have heard it put to General Owen Williams as to whether it was an accurate account, as well as he could say, of your statements? – I have heard that, but I cannot remember what was in it.

You cannot?

Gill mentioned several details in the general's account of what Lycett Green had told him, and asked, 'Was that an accurate account of your statements?' The only result was the usual, 'I cannot remember exactly the statement I made,' 'I cannot recollect,' etc. He did say, however, that he was sure he had not accused Gordon-Cumming of withdrawing his stake.

You have noticed that in the statement which purports to be an account of what took place, it is said that on Mr Lycett Green and Mr Levett having also been made acquainted with the facts, it was agreed to watch the play? – There was no agreement of the kind.

Can you tell me how General Williams came to make that statement? Asquith : Is that admissible?

Coleridge : Certainly not. If you want to cross-examine General Williams, call him back and do it, but you cannot ask the witness how General Williams came to do anything. You have first to show that General Williams was correct in his statement, and you have no right to cross-examine this gentleman about what somebody else has stated he said.

Gill went on to test Lycett Green's knowledge of baccarat: it turned out to be extremely rudimentary.

Did you notice the play on the first night? – No. Nor did I notice what kind of play it was on the second night.

Do you know whether in baccarat it is the practice of the banker to say what the stakes are? – No.

I suppose baccarat is played at Tranby Croft as at any other place? There is nothing special about the play? – It is not played habitually at Tranby Croft.

Was it played there the same way as it is played anywhere else? – I saw no variation that I know of.

You are speaking about men cheating at cards. I want to learn what you know about it. Is it the practice to say what the stakes are? – I do not know. I have not had the bank myself.

Is your answer that you do not know enough of baccarat to say whether the banker does in fact say what the stakes are? – The man who is paying would naturally look what the stakes are. I do not know that there is any absolute rule.

Did you see who was playing highest? – I cannot say that I did.

On the second night, will you tell us how many people staked as much as £10, £15, or £20? – I cannot do so.

If the banker looked at any stake, it would be the stake of the person playing rather high? – I can only speak for myself. I do not know what he would do.

You cannot answer that question? – No.

Did Mr Stanley Wilson say he would stake his life that Sir William had cheated? – He said he had no doubt.

Did he tell you he would stake his life upon it? – I cannot say if he used those exact words.

He has told us that he did? – Well, I cannot recollect.

Do you remember the story of three £5 counters being put upon the white sheet of paper? – No.

You do not remember being told that? – No.

Was that the idea that was conveyed to your mind, that the stake had been trebled? – I have no recollection at all. I cannot remember.

Do you understand what I am asking you? You have no recollection of what the character of the cheating was? – I do not understand the question.

Have you any recollection of a specific case of cheating which your brother-in-law alleged Sir William Gordon-Cumming had committed? – When I sat down the second time?

Yes? – I cannot say.

You had no recollection, and you did not ask him? – What he had done?

Yes? – I will not say I did not, but I have no recollection.

Do you remember his telling you he would stake his life upon it? – No. I have no recollection.

You don't recollect? – No. I have no recollection at all. He may have.

Do I understand that you do not recollect what the cheating was that was alleged? – No.

You thought it was a very serious thing to charge a man with cheating? – I think so.

I suppose you would hesitate, having some knowledge of the game yourself. Would you not ask some question? – As to the cheating?

As to what happened with regard to the play at the game of baccarat? – If you saw a man, as soon as he had seen his card, increase his stake, you must know he is cheating.

Would it not be proper also to observe the banker and, at the same time, to observe the croupier? – (The answer was inaudible.)

Do you understand what the business of the croupier is? – He pays the stakes on one side or the other.

Does he, before the cards are dealt, ascertain what the stakes are? – I think he looks round.

Do you know whether, in fact, he does ascertain what the stake is at each side of the table? – I do not.

Do you know the banker is influenced upon the question whether he will stand or take another card by the stake on either side? – (The answer was inaudible.)

Do you know that it is of the greatest importance that he should know? – I can see when you point it out that he might want to know what was on each side if there was a heavy stake.

At the commencement of this innocent game of baccarat, the majority of the stakes were small ones? – Yes.

Was £10 a large stake? – Well, I cannot say whether it was a large stake or a small one. In some cases it might have been large and in some cases small.

What was the average stake? – I cannot tell.

Do you remember upon that night the question, of what the amount was on each side of the table, was being discussed? – No.

Do you remember the Prince of Wales saying, 'There is more money on one side than on the other'? – I have no distinct recollection about it.

You admit it would be a most natural thing to ascertain what the stakes were before the banker took another card? – He might go for both sides.

That is the kind of thing he would make up his mind upon, is it not? – I cannot tell you at all.

Did you mention to Lord Coventry, or General Williams, or the Prince of Wales, that you knew very little indeed about the game? – I have no recollection.

Would it not have some bearing on the subject, in your opinion, that fact of your being entirely ignorant of the game? Would not that influence your mind as to whether you were really able to form an opinion? – I have no doubt there was cheating.

He was asked whether he had said, when making his accusation, that the others would swear to it.

Again he was uncertain and would not swear he had done so, or that he had not done so.

Do you not know that the people who were there that night had frequently played before, when very large stakes were being played for? – Do you mean the people who were there that night?

I mean Sir William Gordon-Cumming, the Prince of Wales, and Mr Tyrwhitt Wilson? – I do not know.

What was to prevent these people seeing what you say you saw? – I do not know.

You did not say that they knew a great deal more about the game than you did? – Perhaps they did.

Have you any doubt about it? – I cannot tell, as I had never played with them before.

Is your answer that you suppose you knew as much about it as they did? – No.

Did you ever hear of anybody playing baccarat upon a system? – I cannot say.

Did you ever hear of what has been described as the *masse en avant*? Have you ever heard of a man putting down a counter, it may be for £5 or £10, and if that wins adding to that? – No.

When he puts a counter down and wins, he leaves that counter down and puts on another? – I never heard of that. I have heard of leaving the money down.

He was asked if he had helped to entertain the party at the races, and he answered, 'Yes.'

> Of course I don't know that people in society do at the races, but other people lunch on these occasions? – Yes we lunched.
>
> The lunch went on all the afternoon, I suppose? (The Court tittered, Russell snorted, the Prince laughed, Lycett Green flushed up angrily and replied,) – No, and if you insinuate I was drunk, I was not.
>
> We have heard of the profuse hospitality of the Wilsons, and I presume they were entertaining everybody at the races? – Oh, not anybody that liked to come.
>
> COLERIDGE: They might have been lunching and he not be there. I don't understand the object of your question.
>
> GILL: But the jury will. I am in hopes that the jury will understand many things that are not on the surface.

The cross-examination continued: He had difficulty in remembering what time they had dined, and how soon after dinner they had begun to play.

> Did you notice whether Sir William Gordon-Cumming was keeping a tableau? – No.
>
> Did you at that time know what I mean by that? – I cannot say. My idea is that it is putting down whether the set you are playing with wins, or the bank wins.
>
> Did you understand that point that night? – I have seen the putting down on a piece of paper which set wins.
>
> Did you see whether Sir William Gordon-Cumming did that? – I do not recollect whether he did or not.
>
> Can you say whether he had a pencil in his hand? – I cannot say.
>
> Can you say whether he had a sheet of paper? – No, I cannot be certain.
>
> Do you know whether he was smoking or not? – I do not.
>
> Do you know whether he had a tumbler in front of him or not? – No.
>
> Do I understand that from first to last you cannot tell me whether he had a sheet of paper and a pencil? – I cannot say.
>
> You did not observe him sufficiently well to notice that? – I cannot say.
>
> The people were smoking, I suppose? – I dare say they were. Were all the men smoking? – I cannot tell that; it is so long ago.

Asked if he had watched anyone else's staking except Sir William Gordon-

Cumming's, he replied, 'I cannot say. I must have seen others stake.'

You knew some months ago you would be asked to specify what the acts of cheating were? – Yes; when proceedings were taken against us, and we would have to appear in Court.

Did your solicitor tell you you would have to be prepared to say definitely what it was you alleged Sir William Gordon-Cumming did? – I was told to state it to the best of my recollection.

Is this your account of the matter? Having been asked what were the acts of cheating, you say, 'that upon two separate occasions you saw Sir William Gordon-Cumming add to his stake when the cards were in his favour? – I do not understand.

I daresay you all discussed together about your answers? – What do you mean? That we made them up, do you mean?

You seem to me . . . but I will not make any comment. Did you discuss together about these answers? – Yes; we talked the matter over.

And you said what your answer would be. Did you say, for instance, to your wife that 'I shall answer so and so?' – I told her to the best of my recollection what I had seen.

You knew, the four of you, your mother-in-law, your wife, your brother-in-law and yourself, that certain questions were to be asked which you were to answer? – I received the interrogatories.

Did you see your co-defendants with regard to that? – I spoke to my wife.

How many times have you been to Mr Lewis's office? – Three times. I was there with my wife, I forget whom else. I think I was there once with Mrs Wilson and Arthur Stanley Wilson.

I suppose you saw the statement of claim? – Mr Lewis read it to me. I do not remember the contents. It was rather a long thing.

When you saw the statement, did you notice that you were alleged to have said to Lord Coventry that Sir William Gordon-Cumming frequently withdrew a portion of his stake? – Mr Lewis called my attention to it.

That brought the cross-examination to an end. The questions had not been put to him: 'Were you going to denounce Gordon-Cumming on Doncaster Racecourse?' and 'What would you have done if he had refused to sign the undertaking?' Possibly he would have again answered, 'I cannot say, it was so long ago. . . .'

Mr Lewis had already warned Russell that Lycett Green knew very little about baccarat, that 'he was a hunting man and hardly ever played cards,' but it was impossible that he could have sat through the whole trial till then and still be entirely ignorant of the game, particularly as he had had several months in which to swat up the rules. Neither can we accept after General Williams's *précis* had been read out four times in court, and the complete text published in the papers, that Lycett Green couldn't remember what was in it : some of it, purporting to be what he had told the general, concerned him closely. His refusal to remember anything was obviously humbug, a deliberate policy. We are left with the impression that Mr Lewis must have advised him that his role had been so unsympathetic that the less he remembered about it the better.

An interesting fact to emerge was that when he was making his original accusation as spokesman for the group, he still did not know precisely what Stanley Wilson was accusing Gordon-Cumming of having done, and that he didn't ask. He demonstrated also, when the Court laughed about the lunch that had gone on all the afternoon, the suddenness with which he could lose his temper.

The defendants' prestige was immediately restored when the next witness, Ethel Lycett Green, stepped into the witness-box. As the first lady defendant she naturally attracted much attention : she was small, slender, neat in her movements and perfectly self-possessed. Dressed becomingly in black, in half-mourning, which showed off admirably her bright complexion and fair hair, the only touch of colour was a green spray in her little hat that was perched high and slanted forward and from which hung a very thin short veil. Guided by Russell as her counsel, she explained in a clear mellow voice in answer to his questions :

I am the daughter of Mr and Mrs Arthur Wilson, and I have been married to the last witness, Mr Lycett Green, for six years. We have three children. I had played the game of baccarat before the month of September last year. I had played at Tranby Croft, once in my own house and once at a party at Ascot. I may have played it on one or two other occasions, but I do not remember. The occasion on which we played it in our own house was on a night on which Sir William Gordon-Cumming came to town with us. It was Sir William Gordon-Cumming who taught me how to play it. That was about the year 1888. I had known Sir William Gordon-Cumming before that; I had met him before I was married, when he was staying at my mother's house. I was very intimate with a near relation of his who lived in Yorkshire. I had a great regard for that relation, and I still have. That relation has no children. On the 8th September I was at my father's house as one of the house party, and we played baccarat for about an hour that night. I was seated at the opposite side of the table to that on which the Prince of Wales and my mother were sitting. I think there were more than three persons between Sir William Gordon-Cumming and myself on my right hand.

Russell asked:

Did anything at all attract your attention on the first night in the course of the play? – I heard His Royal Highness ask Sir William Gordon-Cumming to place his counter so that he could see it, and in reply Sir William said, 'My stake is on the paper in front of me.' I heard this said more than once, or heard words to that effect.

Do you recollect anything else as to Sir William's play? – I thought he was rather lucky. I mean by that he seemed to be winning . . . I did not notice anything happen on the night of the 8th.

. . . The next day I went out for a walk with my husband in the garden before we went to the races, and he told me that my brother had seen Sir William Gordon-Cumming cheating at cards the previous night.

She described the seating arrangements on the 9th, how Gordon-Cumming had come in rather late, and finding only two places vacant, one of them obviously intended for Ethel's husband, he had asked Lady Coventry if he might take the place next to her: she assented. He sat down between her and Ethel. There had been no arrangement she said, between her and her husband or between her husband and Mr Stanley Wilson, to her knowledge, to watch Sir William Gordon-Cumming.

After the gentlemen joined the ladies in the drawing-room we had some music. I sang to them, and then we went into the other room. The first time I noticed anything about Sir William Gordon-Cumming's playing was when the cards were with Lady Coventry. I cannot say how long I had been seated at the table before I noticed that, but the cards had gone all round the table. There had been several coups. Lady Coventry was the last at our tableau to take the cards. Upon that occasion, before the cards were dealt by the dealer, I saw that Sir William Gordon-Cumming had staked £5, a red counter. It was placed three or four inches beyond the line.

Russell asked:

Was it upon the tablecloth, or was it upon the piece of notepaper? – It was upon the green baize. I saw Lady Coventry take up the cards; I could see the cards from where I was sitting as they were turned up. I was sitting next but one to her, Sir William Gordon-Cumming being between. I heard the banker make some declaration. I heard him say 'one', 'two', or some small point.

Will you describe how Sir William Gordon-Cumming's hands were placed when that announcement was made? (The witness here placed her left hand over the back of her right hand with the thumbs concealed.) – His left hand covered his right. The counters were in his hand before that. I then saw him distinctly push on a £10 brown counter.

Over the line? – It just got on the line.

What did he do with his hands when the counter got onto the line? – He withdrew his hands. I saw the counter left on the line.

Do you recollect what payment was made in that instance? – I saw he was paid £5 by His Royal Highness. Thereupon Sir William Gordon-Cumming said, 'There is a £10 counter more here, sir, which has not been paid,' and His Royal Highness said, 'I wish you would put your stakes in a more conspicuous place – I never saw that,' or words to that effect.

Do you recollect who it was who paid that additional £10? – No, I do not recollect. It would be General Owen Williams or His Royal Highness. I have no doubt whatever that I saw what I have described. When the additional £10 was paid the stake was withdrawn and put into the heap of counters, and they were all taken off.

How soon afterwards did you observe anything else? – Shortly afterwards, I cannot say how long, but a few coups afterwards when the cards were with Lady Coventry, for she passed on several occasions that night.

Just to make that clear. You say, 'She passed several times that night.' Does that mean she was lucky? – Yes, she won. She beat the bank on several occasions. She was the only one who was lucky on our side.

And so long as she was lucky she would continue to take the cards or, as you call it, 'pass'? – Yes. On this occasion Sir William's stake was £5, a red counter. It was well over the line. Sir William had a piece of paper, on which he was marking the tableau, in his left hand. In his right hand he had a large pencil.

One moment. Was your tableau successful or not? – Oh yes, we were.

Did you hear the banker make any declaration? – No, but I knew we had won. I heard Sir William say that we had won. At any rate I know that our tableau had won.

Upon that did you see what Sir William Gordon-Cumming did then? – Yes. (At this stage the witness illustrated the way in which she alleged Sir William Gordon-Cumming pushed over the additional counter.)

What then did you see him do? I saw him push out a £5 red counter with the end of his pencil, and he was paid. I am positively sure that his original stake in the instance I have just mentioned was only a £5 counter. I saw the addition of a £5 counter. He was paid £10. I am one of the defendants in this matter. I told my husband that night what I had seen. He also told me what he had seen. I did not sign the paper, but I heard of it. I have never mentioned the matter to anyone until these legal proceedings.

The case has been dramatic all through, but Mrs Lycett Green rendered it almost tragic by reason of the minute tracings of the path of the accused man by her own hand. It was not enough for her to give a verbal account of what she had seen. She asked for a sheet of paper and a pencil, half a dozen at least of which articles were immediately forthcoming from the jury box. Mrs Green then proceeded to illustrate the *poussette* by actual representation of the way in which it was alleged to have been done. For the first time the Court heard the whole story of the Prince's remonstrance as to Sir William's stake not being properly exposed upon the table. Taking the sheet of paper in one hand, and the pencil in the other, this lady went through the whole performance. Mrs Lycett Green, amid the breathless excitement of the jury, the Bar and the public, imitated exactly what she declared the plaintiff had done. The plaintiff, she said, had been keeping a tableau on a piece of paper which he held in his left hand : she took the sheet of paper and laid it over her hand which held the pencil and almost imperceptibly with the pencil pushed the supposed counter over the imaginary line. This pantomime, if it may be so called, was more eloquent than words. The spectators watched it spellbound. Then the silence was broken by the witness who, taking up the snapped thread of the story, said that it was at the conclusion of that manouevre that the Prince of Wales complained of the actions of Sir William Gordon-Cumming. (*Daily News*)

It is perhaps a pity that no one asked the lady to give her demonstration again, this time showing the Court how the manoeuvre could have been performed without the other players seeing it.

Sir Edward Clarke now rose to cross-examine her. She showed not the least concern. He asked :

Have you told us all you saw? – Yes, of that there is no doubt.

How often had you played baccarat before that night? – Perhaps on six occasions.

Where? – At Tranby Croft, at Ascot, once at my own house, and perhaps I may have played on one or two other occasions.

On the first night, nobody was assisting you in your play? – No.

You thought you knew enough about it to play your own hand? – Yes.

Did you buy your own counters? – My husband did.

How much? – I had £5.

On the first night? – Yes.

Did you have to go to Mr Sassoon for more counters in the course of the evening? – No.

Did you win? – I don't think I did. I really don't remember.

Starting with £5 in counters the first night and not having to go for more, your stakes would be very small? – Very. 5/- or 10/-. Never more than 10/-.

At the first night, did you happen to be in the same tableau with Sir William Gordon-Cumming? – I think I was not, but I could not swear to it. I fancy I was not.

Did you see anybody at the other tableau use paper to put his stakes on? – No.

Did you see any stake put upon your tableau on white paper? – No.

But I understand on the first night His Royal Highness said something about seeing the stakes? – Sir William said, 'I put my stakes on the white paper.'

So far as you know, on this first night, Sir William Gordon-Cumming's on white paper was at least as conpicuous as any stake on the table? – I should say so.

More conspicuous undoubtedly than a dark counter would be on a coloured cloth? – Not necessarily.

What was the colour of the tablecloth? – I can't say. It was an indescribable colour. It was a tapestry tablecloth.

Can you tell me what was its tone, was it brown, or blue, or white? – It was all sorts of colours. I can hardly describe it. The colours were mixed.

The next morning, you were told by your husband something that your brother and Mr Berkeley Levett had seen on the previous night? – I was told my brother had seen something. I never asked what it was he had seen. It was too horrible.

You were shocked at the thought? – Yes, dreadfully.

Excited? – Not excited.

Only shocked? – Yes.

You thought it a very dreadful thing that such a discovery should be made at the table? – Dreadful.

Did you suggest that you should not play baccarat again the next night? – No. It was not for me to suggest anything.

You are quite right. Did your husband suggest anything of the kind? – I don't know.

Did he mention it to you? – No.

Did he not even suggest that your father should be told? – I understand my mother had been told, and if she had thought fit she would have told my father. . . .

On the evening of the 9th you spent some time in the drawing-room. After music the party moved to the billiard-room. Did the ladies go to the billiard-room first? – I think they did, but some of the men had gone before.

To the best of your recollection, the ladies did not seat themselves at the table until His Royal Highness had taken his place? – I cannot swear.

Did Sir William Gordon-Cumming come in with His Royal Highness that evening? – I cannot say. I think he came in some time afterwards.

When practically all the party had seated themselves? – Yes, at our tableau they were all seated.

You were not looking at the other tableau? – No.

At your tableau was there any vacant seat left, except one? – There was that vacant seat in which my husband afterwards sat.

Had your husband taken his place by putting counters there? – No.

If he had taken his seat where your husband eventually sat, he would have had your brother and yourself on his right, and your husband would have sat next to Lady Coventry? – Yes, but my husband would hardly have sat next to her. (Laughter)

No, not when you were there. (Renewed laughter.)

Sir William Gordon-Cumming took the seat next but one to the croupier, opposite the banker? – Yes.

COLERIDGE : Will you be much longer, Sir Edward?

CLARKE : I am afraid I must be some time, your lordship.

COLERIDGE : Then we will adjourn.

The Court adjourned at twenty-five minutes past four. Ethel Lycett Green had greatly impressed the jury, and also the public and the press, although she had given yet another different version of how Gordon-Cumming was supposed to have held his hands. The journalist who had written that Stanley Wilson told his story with inimitable aplomb and curious sense of dramatic effect, himself showing no emotion whatever, commented :

> Equally clear, cold and simply dramatic was Mrs Lycett Green, Mrs Wilson's daughter, a slight woman with a very young look, small features, tightly compressed lips, and an air of perfect decision . . . No one meeting her in the street would turn the eye a second time, but who met the Solicitor-General's sharpest enquiries with bland self-possession. (*Illustrated London News*)

Clarke, however, had made an important point of which she was hardly aware – that her husband had profoundly shocked her by telling her that Gordon-Cumming had cheated, and therefore when she came to the table she was in a condition expecting to see him cheat again.

CHAPTER NINE

A Star Performer

On the fifth day of the trial there was summer weather again, with bright hats, bright dresses and pretty faces everywhere. As usual the doors were besieged by people who were refused admittance. Some went disconsolately away, some hung around hoping for 'just a peep' into the courtroom, but the doorkeepers were obdurate. A small group of members of the junior Bar tried to push their way in, but reinforcements of attendants managed to close the doors on them.

The Wilsons were early arrivals. They consulted, according to the *Echo*, 'very vigorously' with Mr George Lewis. Lord Middleton, Gordon-Cumming's brother-in-law, came in with him and sat beside him. Just before the Court opened, Mr George Lewis was summoned to the Lord Chief Justice's room.

> The first two rows of the barristers' seats, which are assigned to the counsel engaged in the case, were conspicuous for the piles of papers which have accumulated since the action commenced. The little green handbooks on baccarat, which were strapped to several of the briefs, showed that the learned counsel for the plaintiff and for the defendants had been 'getting up' the subject. . . . (*Morning Advertiser*)

His lordship took his seat at twenty-five minutes to eleven. The Prince of Wales followed ten minutes later. On the entry of the learned judge, Russell asked whether he proposed to sit next day, which was Saturday. Coleridge replied that he would not, but that he would sit as usual at eleven o'clock on Monday. A juror asked for the counters that had been used at Tranby Croft. They were handed to the Foreman.

Ethel Lycett Green, still in black with a spray of green in her hat, again entered the witness-box. Clarke continued his cross-examination. She told him she had a clear recollection of the two incidents of cheating she had alleged, but she didn't remember who had paid out the money or who was handling the cards.

The croupier does not play in the game? – No.

And his only duty is to see what the stakes are, and to pay and receive? – I suppose so.

161

You do not know much about the game, do you? – Oh yes, I do. (Laughter.)

Now, on that occasion you said, 'I saw him', that is, Sir William Gordon-Cumming, 'distinctly push on a red £10 counter.' It just dropped on the line? – Yes, but the £10 counters were brown. (Laughter.)

COLERIDGE : I thought in my notes I had it, 'I saw him *drop* a £10 counter.' I thought you said that.

ETHEL : I think I said 'push.'

RUSSELL : That is what the shorthand notes say.

Coleridge graciously deferred to the lady, and altered his notes accordingly. Clarke continued :

The plaintiff said, 'There is £10 more here owing,' and His Royal Highness said, 'I wish you would put your counters where they could be seen. . . .

COLERIDGE : I have it, 'There is £10 more here, Owen.' (Laughter.)

Russell got out the shorthand notes and read the passage from Ethel's evidence of the day before. Coleridge again amended his notes. The cross-examination continued :

It was put to Sir William Gordon-Cumming in cross-examination that the words were, 'There is £15 more to come to me.' You don't suggest that on two occasions something was said about more being paid to Sir William Gordon-Cumming? – No.

CLARKE to COLERIDGE : If it is suggested that there were two occasions on which more money was asked for and any observation was made as to the manner of staking the counters, I will deal with it. I did not know it was suggested twice.

COLERIDGE : I think so. My impression certainly was that it was said there were two occasions upon which Sir William Gordon-Cumming got more money than he ought to have got.

CLARKE : That there were two occasions when *it is said* he got more money than he ought to have been paid.

COLERIDGE : I mean asked for more. Two occasions when attention was drawn to the fact by him that more was to come to him, and more did come to him.

CLARKE : I did not know that it was suggested that it happened twice. At all events, Mrs Lycett Green, you don't remember this happening twice?

ETHEL : No.

COLERIDGE : My recollection is that the evidence is that Sir William Gordon-Cumming made a claim, which was paid at once without observation, and that on the other occasion the Prince said, 'I wish you would stake your money where it could be seen. That is my impression.

The cross-examination continued :

You only remember one such incident of his asking for more money? – Only one.

And that was on the second night? – On the second night.

The argument being settled at last, Clarke went on to another subject :

Where did you play at Ascot? – At a house we had taken for the races. The game was only a small one. Shilling and half-crown stakes.

Do you remember it being observed that you did not know much about the game? – No, I do not. I do not remember anything about the game except that it was for very small points.

I suggest to you that a comment was made by one of the guests about your play, and that you said you had only played once or twice. I will mention the name of the gentleman who made the observation, if you like? – Will you do so?

Mr Bowles? – I do not know Mr Bowles. I never met him.

You remember the occasion to which I have referred? – Yes.

Do you remember who was there? – Not in the least.

Will you undertake to say that Mr Bowles was not there? – I never remember having seen him in my life.

That was the end of the cross-examination which had lasted only twenty minutes this time. Mrs Wilson followed her daughter into the witness-box. She was fashionably attired in black with white facings banded with gold-beaded lace : she wore a little hat with feathers, and a veil that just reached the tip of her nose. The examination-in-chief was conducted by Russell.

She was a clear, concise witness – cool, but not too cool. Her appearance, perhaps, was a trifle bourgeoise, but she was very well dressed. Her face had a certain matronly comeliness, as well as the sharp, clear look common to the Wilson family, and a slight action of expanding her hands in talk was not ungraceful. (*Daily Chronicle*)

Guided by her counsel's questions, she began by giving an explanation about Mr Bowles :

> . . . the year before last he came to our house for about an hour. He came in and played baccarat. I think my daughter had gone to bed. I do not in the least recollect any comment being made as to the want of knowledge on the part of my daughter as to the game of baccarat.
>
> I am myself one of the defendants in this case. I was the hostess at Tranby Croft on the occasion of the party. On the evening of Monday the 8th September, after dinner and music, the party went to have a game of baccarat. I sat near the Prince of Wales . . . I recollect noticing that my son, Mr Arthur Stanley Wilson, had a rather surprised air. I could not make it out. I thought he was puzzled about something. He caught my eye and then looked down to Sir William Gordon-Cumming. . . .
>
> That night he came to my dressing-room to see me, and he there made a communication to me, a very painful one : it was to the effect that he had seen Sir William Gordon-Cumming cheating during the game of baccarat. He asked me what he should do. I said (the witness spoke in an agitated voice) 'I cannot let you speak about it. Oh, you must not speak. We cannot have a scandal in our house.'
>
> My daughter and I were very intimate with one of Sir William Gordon-Cumming's relations, a neighbour of ours and a very dear friend of mine, and he was a very near friend of ours. I did not at the time make any communication to my husband. He came to bed rather late, and I did not wish to trouble him.

> Mrs Wilson . . . spoke with evident emotion of the grievous trouble which the events of last September had caused her. The incidents alleged to have happened under her roof, coupled with the domestic affliction which fell upon her simultaneously by the death of one of her relations, must have been a sore trial, and her voice quivered occasionally as she answered Sir Charles Russell's courteous questions. She . . . held a handkerchief in her hands which she applied from time to time to her eyes. (*Morning Advertiser*)

She continued her story :

> The next night . . . after we had dinner and some music, we again formed a party for baccarat. My son came to me in the drawing-room and whispered into my ear that he had made it impossible for him to cheat that night, as a chalk line had been drawn all round the table.

He said, 'It is virtually impossible.' The game was played in a different room that night, and at a different table. There was no agreement by me with anyone, or by anyone to my knowledge, to watch Sir William Gordon-Cumming; or as to the position that anyone should occupy at the table during play. It was purely accidental how they sat. His Royal Highness asked me to come and sit beside him. Until I received a communication from Mr Lycett Green the whole matter of Sir William Gordon-Cumming had entirely passed out of my mind. I had not noticed, or attempted to take any notice, of his play. I do not think I saw Mr Lycett Green leave the room, but in the course of the evening I received a written communication from him, brought to me by a servant. I have been in Court, and I heard Mr Lycett Green's recollection of the contents of that communication. I think it was to this effect, 'I have already seen Sir William Gordon-Cumming cheating twice. What can be done? It is perfectly horrible.' I shook my head at him. He had come back into the room by that time and was standing up. I do not know whether Sir William Gordon-Cumming saw me shake my head or not. I should say we had been playing rather more than half an hour when this incident occurred of the note being brought to me. I do not know how long after the incident the play continued; it might have been three quarters of an hour. Having got this communication, I looked to see what Sir William Gordon-Cumming was doing. I was sitting on the left of the Prince of Wales, on the left tableau, and Sir William Gordon-Cumming was next to Lady Coventry on the opposite side of the table, on the right-hand tableau, so that I was looking across at him. It was the second time round to Lady Coventry that I noticed anything.

Russell asked:

Then you had not noticed any of the incidents spoken to by any of the other witnesses in the first round? – I remember Sir William Gordon-Cumming asking for £10 to be paid, but I had no idea of his cheating. I remember the Prince seeming annoyed, and saying, 'I wish you would let me see your stakes.' When the cards came round to Lady Coventry the second time I noticed that Sir William Gordon-Cumming had staked £5. I recollect that his tableau won. The banker had declared that they had won, that he was either nothing or very small. I am perfectly sure that Sir William Gordon-Cumming's stake was £5.

Did you see him do anything? – Yes. He had his hands over the line, and when he saw who had won the coup he dropped the £10 counter out of his hand on to the table. He was paid £15.

You know this is a serious matter, Mrs Wilson? – I do indeed.

Have you any doubt that you saw that occur which you have described? – I have no doubt. I do not recollect how long it was, or how many coups had taken place, after I got the communication that I noticed this act. I think it was about twenty minutes after I received the letter.

Two coups had taken place before I noticed anything else. I observed that Lady Coventry was taking the cards at this time. She had a run. She 'passed' several times. I recollect that Sir William Gordon-Cumming's stake on that occasion was again £5. On this occasion Lady Coventry had a natural, and the cards were thrown down. I saw Sir William Gordon-Cumming looking at the cards, and I saw him with his pencil push on a £10 counter straight before him, so openly that I wondered others did not see it. I am perfectly sure that before the natural was declared his stake was only £5. He was paid the £15. No question whatever was raised as to his right to payment.

I recollect making a very short statement to the Prince of Wales on the morning of the 11th. I was then in domestic trouble. The interview was a very brief one; it was a leave-taking interview, I simply told him that I had seen Sir William Gordon-Cumming cheating. The only words I remember were that I feared my son would suffer. The Prince said, 'Oh no, nothing of the kind.'

. . . I was not a party to the signing of the agreement of secrecy. On my oath I have never mentioned the matter to anyone from the 10th September until these legal proceedings began. It was too much to my interest to keep quiet. . . . (The last remark was almost inaudible.)

The cross-examination was conducted by Sir Edward Clarke. He picked up her last remark :

You were asked just now whether you had mentioned this matter to anyone before the action began, and you said, 'No, I had not. It was too much to my interest to keep quiet?' – Certainly.

What do you mean by its being to your interest to keep quiet? – Well, I had not signed the paper, but I had promised.

When? – The Prince asked me not to say anything about it, and I said, 'Certainly not.'

Was the reason that it was to your interest, or that you had promised not to tell? – Both.

Having promised the Prince that you would keep quiet, interest or no interest had nothing to do with it? – I should think it had.

How? If you promised the Prince, there was an end to the matter. Whether it was to your interest or not, you would not have said anything about it, would you? – Probably not.

Probably not? Well, I won't reason with you about it. . . .

I understand that a communication was made to you on the evening of the 8th by your son? – Yes.

Why did you not tell Mr Wilson, your husband? – In the first instance he did not come to bed till very late. (Stanley Wilson said he had already gone to bed.) The next morning I thought it better not to talk to him about it.

Why not? – Because I hoped there would be no recurrence of it.

What is Mr Wilson by occupation? – A merchant.

And shipowner? – Yes.

He has been in Court? – Yes.

He is a man having experience in the business world? – Yes.

Sir Edward Clarke's chief point was made a few moments later. The impression has been that the table used on the second night was made purposely to prevent a recurrence of the irregularities. But Mrs Wilson removed this somewhat, and asserted that before the play commenced on the first night the Prince expressed the hope that a proper table would be provided on the second night . . . Sir Edward Clarke traversed several of the statements made by Mrs Wilson in affidavits in which were, she admitted, some slight inaccuracies. (*Echo*)

And although your son and Mr Levett had told you that one of the guests had cheated at cards at your table, you sat down at the table in company with the same gentleman on the following night, played for more than an hour and a half, and had forgotten the incident? – I had put it out of my mind.

Why, Mrs Wilson, your son had reminded you of it in the drawing room just before you went into the billiard-room? – Yes. He told me that it was practically impossible for him to cheat.

And your son having brought the incident back to your mind, you straightway went into the billiard-room and played without the incident recurring to your mind? – I was the hostess, you see.

So you were? – And I had plenty to think about.

Upon the second night, Mr Lycett Green sent in a note to you, saying that he had seen Sir William Gordon-Cumming cheat twice? – Yes.

Why did you not make an excuse and break up the party? – I did as soon as I could.

But actually they played on the second evening for just as long as they had played on the first.

> Sir Edward Clarke went at some length into the ethics of the continued play on the second night, both after cheating had been reported to Mrs Wilson and she herself witnessed it. Why did she allow the game to go on? Because to have stopped the game would have been an imputation on all her guests. Then came another little side-light. Why play at all? pressed Sir Edward. Why not have told the Prince (who one gathered suggested the game) that the host objected? Well, said Mrs Wilson frankly, and amid a little stir of surprise in the Court, she had mentioned the matter to His Royal Highness, but she had added they were such a staid party that she thought there could be no harm in it. (*Daily Chronicle*)

She admitted that General Owen Williams as croupier had nothing whatever to do but watch the stakes, to see they were properly placed and to determine whether the stakes on the table came to more or to less than the amount in the bank. It was obvious that, if he had done what he was supposed to do, he could not have failed to notice the difference if he had been called upon to pay out £15 when the original stake had called for only £5.

Clarke made the point also that the other players too would have noticed any irregularity, considering that Gordon-Cumming was talking to Lady Coventry at the time, and helping her, and she was having a run of luck that aroused comment and focused their attention on them, and the attention of the banker and croupier. Then came a surprise:

> If General Williams had seen £15 on the table as the stake before Sir William, he would notice it, perhaps, as an exceptional thing? – I don't think he did.
>
> But it would be an exceptional thing – There were others playing the same.

This was not true, as her next answer showed:

> Who was playing stakes of £15 at the table at which Sir William was playing? – I don't think anyone till my husband played.
>
> Did he play the first night? – I think so.

All this was pure invention. Apart form Mr Arthur Wilson's known dislike of the game, and dislike of high stakes, none of the party had mentioned him as having been among the players or allowed for his presence in their repeated descriptions of where each of them had been seated.

It is rather shocking really, considering that she had sworn to tell the truth, the whole truth, etc., to find her coming out with this big whopping lie spoken, apparently, with the same complete self-assurance that the other members of her family had shown.

You say Lady Coventry's good fortune had been commented upon at the table? – Yes.

So that the attention of the players would be attracted to her and to that part of the table? – Yes, to her cards.

And, of course, with a run of luck going in favour of the tableau, the attention of the banker and croupier would be directed to that part also? – Yes.

Do you say that you saw the counter drop after Lady Coventry had laid down her cards and shown a natural? – I don't think I said so.

Do you say that after the banker said what he had, you saw the £10 counter dropped? – Yes. After.

Was anything said on that occasion about the money that was to be paid? – I don't remember anything being said.

Who paid the money? – I think it was the Prince.

And he could see the £5 counter well out, as you describe it? – He could have seen it.

And, according to your impression, must have seen it? – He might not have noticed it. Everyone might have seen it.

Asked whether she had made a statement to His Royal Highness, she replied, 'On the morning of the 11th.' Some discussion followed as to whether she had seen him on the 10th or the 11th, and the cross-examination came to an end.

She gave the evidence both in chief and under cross-examination with as much coolness and aplomb as had characterised that of Mrs Lycett Green, but she spoke in so low a tone that it was difficult at times to hear what she said. (*Daily News*)

That was the end of the evidence for the defence. Some of the commentators found it unconvincing. The *Daily Chronicle* spoke of 'the obvious doubts which tainted the accusations of the defendants,' and continued :

They and the Prince's aristocratic flunkeys all contradicted each other on material points. From their muddled and conflicting statements given in evidence, and in the documentary record of the shameful, and we hold criminal, compact which they made with Sir William Gordon-Cumming, we confess our inability to construct a clear coherent story . . . Everybody who knows baccarat knows that it is quite possible for a man who plays on Sir William Gordon-Cumming's system of 'following his luck' to add counters to his stakes quite legitimately. No additions thus made by Sir William Gordon-Cumming, when we look at them in connection with the automatic regularity with which his winnings were represented every time by three £5 counters, were inconsistent with the hypothesis that he was only playing the well known *coup de trois*. But, of course, if, as the Prince was told, his accusers were ready to 'stake their lives' on the charge that Sir William Gordon-Cumming also withdrew counters when to do so enabled him to cheat, then the probabilities would be in favour of his guilt. But, after having, with the melodramatic effusiveness of their class, vapoured before the Prince of Wales about their willingness to 'stake their lives' on their charge of the withdrawal of the counters, Sir William's accusers when taken into court withdrew it. (*Daily Chronicle*)

When Mrs Wilson left the box at five minutes past twelve, Russell intimated that the evidence for the defence had now closed; but that if his learned friends on the other side wished to interrogate Lord Coventry, he would be called. Clarke said that Russell must choose his own witnesses, but if Lord Coventry was called, he would cross-examine him. 'You've had five witnesses to cross-examine already,' Russell replied somewhat ungraciously, 'with what result it is not for me to say.' Nevertheless, he called Lord Coventry, and proceeded to examine him.

There was some little doubt as to calling Lord Coventry. Sir Charles said he would if Sir Edward wished : and Sir Edward, not to be caught out on a point of tactics, indicated decidedly that he did wish. Lord Coventry's appearance was also familiar to Court *habitués* – a stout, solid, good-humoured, banker-looking gentleman, with slight grey whiskers, and thin, firm lips, courtly in manner, speaking with admirable elocution, and with a singular gift of clear expression, and a trifle deaf. He gave a somewhat new reason for the appeal to the Prince of Wales. He and General Williams felt they couldn't allow the friendship to continue without informing his Royal Highness of what had occurred. He also varied the report of the first conversation with Sir William Cumming by some dramatic touches. It seems that Sir William had been rather more explicit than he had suggested in his examination. He did, according to Lord Coventry, ask who were his accusers, and when he had been furnished with the names of young Mr Wilson and tolerably-young Mr Green, 'Do you believe statements of inexperienced boys?' was Sir William's next remark. Before the Prince Sir William protested his innocence, and the answer was, 'There are five witnesses against you.' It seems too that the Duke of Cambridge was mentioned, Sir William hinting at a reference to him. General Williams replied, 'By all means, but I don't think the Duke of Cambridge will take so lenient a view as we have done.' That phrase came two or three times, once with rather comic iteration. The witness denied that when asked what Sir William's accusers said they had seen, he replied, 'I don't know.' As to Mr Levett, that simple young Guardsman expressed his sorrow at having been mixed up in the concern, but corroborated the other witnesses. (*Daily Chronicle*)

(Berkeley Levett had not admitted in his evidence that he corroborated the evidence to the Prince.) Concerning Mr Lycett Green's alleged desire to be confronted with the plaintiff, Lord Coventry said yes, he had said so, before dinner and he said it later on. Russell asked :

Did you or General Williams communicate that to Sir William Gordon-Cumming – I believe we did.

Did Sir William Gordon-Cumming ever express the desire to you or to General Williams in your presence to be confronted with Mr Lycett Green ? – He did not.

After the interview with the Prince, did you and General Williams prepare the paper that was signed ? – We did.

Clarke objected to Russell asking the witness whether there had been anything in the plaintiff's demeanour to suggest that he had lost his head. Coleridge allowed the question.

Lord Coventry then described the scene in which they had persuaded Gordon-Cumming to sign the paper, how he had again said he wished to refer the matter to his commanding officer, how he had appealed to them as his old friends to advise him, how they had both said that if they had been in his place they would sign, and that he finally did so.

. . . a new document was produced in the shape of Lord Coventry's neatly-bound diary. Sir Edward proposed to get a copy of this, when Lord Coleridge mildly suggested that Lord Coventry might object to having his diary shown to any man. 'Not even to me?' cooed Sir Edward, with the note of a wounded dove, and there was a burst of merry laughter. The diary when read had one delicious touch. At the end of it Lord Coventry had recorded in brief the whole episode, the story winding up with the pious note, 'We have done our duty to society.' (*Daily Chronicle*)

A small cloth-covered diary was handed to Lord Coventry who found the entry in it, made on the Thursday, the day after the events at Tranby Croft. It was taken to Russell, who read aloud,

On my return to Tranby from the races, 10th September, 1890, Lycett Green came to my room and asked my advice in the following circumstances It appears that on the night of Monday the 8th, his brother-in-law J. Wilson, had seen a member of the party cheating at baccarat, his *modus operandi* being to slip counters surreptitiously on the table when the cards were shown. He communicated this to Lycett Green, who determined to watch the person on the following night. Then he, his wife, Mrs Wilson, and young Levett distinctly saw cheating on the part of Sir William Gordon-Cumming. I asked that I might mention the matter to General Owen Williams, and take counsel with him as to the best way of proceeding, and accordingly we summoned him to assist in dealing with the case. We determined to lay the matter before the Prince of Wales, which we did, and at the same time suggested the course to be followed of which His Royal Highness approved, and General Williams and myself then saw Sir William Gordon-Cumming and communicated to him what we had heard. He strongly denied the accusation, but, perceiving that the evidence against him was of an overwhelming character, he placed himself unreservedly in our hands, agreeing to do as we should advise. We decided that he should sign a paper promising never to play cards again, in considera-tion of the witnesses undertaking to preserve silence with respect to his conduct; and this was done. [He then gave the text of the under-taking.]

We were induced to recommend this course because we desired, if possible, to avoid a scandal which would naturally attach to the publication of the circumstances, and to keep the name of the Prince of Wales out of it, and also out of consideration for our hosts, Mr and Mrs Wilson, who are at this moment in domestic affliction. We believe that we have done our duty to society, so far as the circumstances permit, by insisting that the accused should never play cards again, but at the same time feel that the accused has been very leniently treated.

There were two very important statements in this account, written immediately after the event: first, it confirmed the general's *précis* in contradicting what all the Wilsons had sworn to – that they did not agree to watch Sir William Gordon-Cumming's play. Second, it stated that the purpose of making him sign the undertaking was 'to avoid a scandal . . . and keep the Prince's name out of it.' This showed up the general's pretence, so painstakingly developed by Russell and Asquith in accordance with their brief, that when the two courtiers used 'the strongest pressure' backed by an 'ultimatum' to make him sign, it was purely in his own interest and they were acting as his friends.

Further questioned by Russell, Lord Coventry explained that in order not to arouse any suspicion they had agreed to acknowledge Gordon-Cumming in the ordinary way whenever they met.

Have you ever mentioned this matter to any person before this litigation arose? – To nobody. I recollect, after hearing that proceedings had begun, seeing Sir William at the Carlton Club, but I cannot recollect that we had any conversation at all. We met in the hall of the Carlton Club once, and he said to me then, as far as I can recollect, that he wished to have a copy of the *précis*. I applied to the Prince for it, got it, showed it to him, and furnished him with a copy.

Do you recollect whether you offered to send the paper, if he wished it, to Colonel Stracey? – I believe I did, so far as I can recollect.

And what did he say?

CLARKE: I think he ought to be asked what he said about it.

Upon this, Russell resumed his seat. Clarke began the cross-examination of the witness:

I don't want to prevent any account being given of what took place, so I will ask you the question. Do you remember on one occasion something being said about that being sent to Colonel Stracey? – I do.

Will you kindly tell me where and when it was, and what was said? – I believe it was in the house of General Williams.

And when? – Sometime about the end of January.

And to the best of your recollection, Lord Coventry, what was it you said? – May I explain what happened in the first place?

Yes, certainly. – We read over the *précis* to Sir William, and after it had been read I believe I said something: 'Would you wish me to send it to Colonel Stracey?' or 'Would you like Colonel Stracey to see it?' I believe I said, although I won't swear it; and I understood him to disapprove of that course. He had taken objection to one passage in the *précis*, and the matter was not pursued.

You say he had taken exception to one passage in the *précis*? – The passage, I think, he had taken exception to was this: 'At the same time they clearly pointed out that his signature would be a distinct admission of his guilt.' That was the paragraph.

And he said *he* had said, when it was put before him, that it was an admission of guilt, and you agreed with it? – He did.

The difference was not, perhaps, very important, but that was the point of it? – It was. He said on the whole that he thought it was a very accurate description of what had taken place. The only thing he disagreed with was that particular paragraph.

And it was in consequence of his pointing that out, I think, that the letter of the 28th was written by General Williams. Do you remember that a letter was afterwards written, 'You are quite at liberty to tell Stracey you signed the document under extreme pressure'? – I do not know whether that was in consequence of the interview.

Well now, at the interview at which the *précis* was shown to him, and that discussion took place, he told you he had already been to Colonel Stracey? – Yes, I think he did. If not then, he told me so in writing.

You knew? – Not that he had been, but that his intention was to go, and I concluded that he had been.

You mean you heard some time before that it was his intention to go to Colonel Stracey, and when you saw him and read over the *précis*, you understood he had been to Colonel Stracey? – Yes, I did.

He was asked if he shook hands with Gordon-Cumming after he had signed the undertaking :

– We shook hands with him once during the evening. My impression is that it occurred when we were taking leave of him. And you and General Williams intended that neither by your speaking of it, nor by your behaviour in any respect, should any indication be given of what had taken place? – Certainly that was my intention.

If that intention had been maintained and acted upon by all the parties who knew of this transaction, of course no knowledge of it would ever have got about? – I cannot say. Probably.

Did you, at the time you left him on the evening of the 10th believe that this matter would remain an undisclosed and unsuspected secret? – Certainly I did.

In any event, Sir William Gordon-Cumming would have retained his rank in the army if he chose? – He would.

And would have retained, as he has retained, his membership of his clubs? – He would.

And that consequence, that hoped for consequence, of the arrangement was in your mind at the time? – It was not. I thought the whole thing would have been preserved a secret.

That is precisely what I am putting to you. You thought the whole thing would be preserved a secret, and that he would go on in the army and clubs as if nothing had happened? – Of course he would.

Did you look forward to that, in respect to a man whom you believed to be a cheat? – I did not look forward to it, but it was inevitable.

As the result of the course you had taken? – Certainly.

The course originally suggested by yourself and General Williams? – Yes.

A course suggested and determined upon by yourself before you had even spoken to Sir William Gordon-Cumming on the matter? – No; I don't think so.

The suggestion had been made that this arrangement should be come to, and the document afterwards signed. That suggestion had been made before you saw Sir William Gordon-Cumming at all? – I won't undertake to say it was not. I can't remember it having been made.

Did you hear of it? – We could not tell what Sir William's attitude might have been. He might have wished to be confronted with his accusers.

Did you hear General Owen Williams say in his cross-examination that statements were made, and you had determined on the suggestion to the Prince of Wales that the matter should be hushed up, before Sir William Gordon-Cumming had been seen at all? – I did not hear it said at all.

Does not your memory serve you to this extent; that before you saw Sir William at all, the suggestion of the hushing-up by the document had already been made? – The suggestion might have been made.

Lord Coventry was a much respected figure – he had won the Grand National on two successive years, or his horses had – but his testimony in the witness-box was a great deal less than candid. Many of his answers were evasive, obscuring the issue, and like a good courtier he had a habit of prefacing his statements with, 'I believe we did, 'I think it was,' 'I may have missed something but to the best of my recollection,' and so on, so that he could always shift his ground if he had to.

He was questioned about the general's statement, the *précis*:

The last line of the statement declares it to be an accurate statement of all the facts of the case? – That is so.

Then I may take it that at the time, to the best of your knowledge, it was accurate? – I will not go so far as to say that. There were one or two particulars with which I did not agree, but I thought that possibly I might not have heard correctly what was said.

You don't mean to say that in a case of this gravity you put your name to the statement as an accurate representation of all the facts of the case when you did not believe it was accurate? – I thought it was substantially correct.

Was there no particular part of this statement which at the time you considered inaccurate? – Well, I must say that there was one part which I did not entirely recollect. I was not quite certain about that part of the statement referring to the withdrawing of a portion of the stakes by Sir William Gordon-Cumming, but I will not say it is inaccurate. I heard one of the witnesses say something about the withdrawal of the stakes, and, as I am rather deaf, I concluded that that had been said which General Owen Williams put down.

Well, but will you observe that the statement purports to report an interview between Mr Lycett Green and yourself, at which General Owen Williams was not present? – It purports to report the general impression of what took place.

But the point is this : the statement purports to report an interview between you and others, and goes on to say, 'Lord Coventry on hearing this consulted General Williams as to what steps should be taken.' So you see, it purports to be a statement made to you before you consulted General Williams. Did you observe that? – I did not observe that. General Owen Williams came to my room, and Mr Lycett Green told him in my presence the same story, word for word, as far as I remember, as he had told me.

And was the same statement made before His Royal Highness later on? – I think so. Different words may have been employed, but they were to the same effect.

And, no doubt, the threefold repetition had the effect of fixing it upon your mind ?– Yes.

Is there any other matter which you noticed in the *précis* in respect of which your memory did not serve you? – I think the name of one of the guests.

But so far as the record of events went, you had no doubt as to its accuracy? – No. I thought it was substantially accurate.

You stated that one of the persons said something about the withdrawal of the stake? Who was that? – I cannot say.

Asked about the entry in his diary, 'It was determined to watch the play on the following night, when Mr Lycett Green, Mrs Wilson, and young Levett saw cheating on the part of Sir William Gordon-Cumming,'

Are you aware now that Mr Levett did not see any cheating on the second night? – I heard him say he saw cheating on one night.

Did you hear him say so in Court? – I don't remember it.

Then your diary is inaccurate? – It may be so. It was my general impression of the case that I put in the diary.

The diary goes on to say that General Williams and you determined to lay the matter before the Prince of Wales, at the same time suggesting a course to be followed, of which His Royal Highness approved? – Yes.

And then 'General Williams and myself saw Sir William Gordon-Cumming'? – I may say that that is inaccurate. I did not set down everything in my diary in order, but that was the ultimate arrangement arrived at. I did not pretend to set things down in order, but to refresh my memory. The diary is wrong in stating that before we saw Sir William Gordon-Cumming we had agreed on the course to be followed. That is not so. That was later.

Are you sure the diary is inaccurate in that respect? – I am certain it is. Nothing was absolutely concluded until after the interview.

No, but that is not the point. The point is that you had determined on suggesting the signing of the document and the keeping it quiet before you saw Sir William Gordon-Cumming? – No doubt it was suggested that it was desirable to keep the thing as quiet as possible.

And had been suggested to His Royal Highness? – I do not think so.

That evidence conflicted not only with his diary but with the *précis* and with General Williams's evidence.

Now let me ask you, how came you and General Owen Williams with regard to a friend of yours of many years' standing to be talking about his signing a document which would be an admission of his guilt before you mentioned the matter to him at all? – The document had not been drawn up before we saw him.

That is not an answer to the question. How came you and General Williams, friends of the plaintiff's of many years' standing, to be talking about and suggesting the signing of a document which would be an admission of his guilt before you saw him? – We thought it was the only way out of the difficulty.

You did not know at the time whether he would deny or admit? – We did not.

And as a matter of fact, during the whole of that interview it received the most peremptory denial from him? – Yes.

Asked who had made the suggestion originally that Gordon-Cumming should be made to sign the document, he replied,

– I should not like to take it on myself to say, but General Owen Williams and I agreed that it would be better to have the matter hushed up.

Do you remember Mr Lycett Green saying that something must be signed as a protection to him? – Yes.

Do you remember at what interview he said that – I believe that that was when we produced the written undertaking and read it over to the witnesses, but I would not like to swear to it. I believe it was.

I suggest to you that Mr Lycett Green said something about the document being a protection to him? – Mr Lycett Green from the first wished to have the matter out at once, and we asked him if he would sign this condition to preserve secrecy. He at first demurred, and said that whilst the facts were fresh in memory and he had his witnesses there, he would rather have it settled then and there.

But there was a time when My Lycett Green said that something must be signed, or else Sir William Gordon-Cumming would bring an action against him at a time when he couldn't prove anything? – I don't remember him saying anything about the signing of the document.

But you remember something being said about Sir William bringing an action? – Yes. I think that was the interview when the undertaking was read over to the witnesses.

At that time, had Sir William Gordon-Cumming signed it? – No. He had not.

Had he seen it? – No.

Had it been mentioned to him? – I think not.

Asked if he was a party to the suggestion that Sir William should leave Tranby Croft the next morning early, he replied that he was.

Did it ever occur to your mind that that would cause enquiry? – No. We were all going to leave the next day in consequence of the death of Mrs Wilson's brother, and Sir William Gordon-Cumming would have left with the other guests.

But I thought in your examination-in-chief you said that he thought of going to the races next day with the party, and you said that under the circumstances it was quite impossible? – Yes, quite impossible.

Quite impossible after what had taken place he should remain in ordinary intercourse with the other members of the party? – With those who had accused him, certainly.

Did it not suggest itself to you that it would create suspicion and enquiry? – Well, I thought he would probably find some excuse.

He might tell some lie? – That he might say he was called away, or something of that kind.

Which would not be true? – I supposed that if he was forced to give a reason he would endeavour to find one.

As near the truth as he could get? – Yes.

COLERIDGE : In society you sometimes say you deeply regret to have to decline an invitation when you are very pleased and do not wish to accept it. (This remark was greeted with polite laughter.)

And now at last the end was approaching. At a quarter to three Lord Coventry's cross-examination ended, and Sir Charles Russell proceeded to address the jury. There was deep silence in the crowded court as the distinguished advocate rose to his feet and slowly and solemnly commenced his final speech. He spoke with great eloquence, now raising, now dropping his voice, now emphasising his meaning by bringing his clenched fist down on his other hand. (*Morning Advertiser*)

Russell began his speech for the defendants thus :

Gentlemen of the jury, I am sure you will rejoice, as certainly as I rejoice, that we are approaching the end of this very distressing and melancholy case. We all recognise, and I venture in this regard to speak for those who represent the plaintiff as well as those who represent the defendants, the close and anxious attention that in the discharge of your painful duty you have given to the evidence laid before you. My task is now a comparatively light and simple one. Something I must say about some collateral topics that have formed the great staple in the lengthy cross-examinations of the various witnesses by my learned friend, but my main purpose will be to direct your attention to the real question, namely whether it is established by evidence satisfactory to your minds and consciences that upon the nights of the 8th and 9th September of last year Sir William Gordon-Cumming cheated at cards. That is what the defendants have said, and if it be the fact that cheating is established it will be your duty to say so, however distressing the performance of that duty may be. I have said that collateral subjects have been introduced, and you cannot fail to have observed the altered tone pursued by the learned counsel who represent the plaintiff since the damning evidence given by and on behalf of the defendants has been put before you.

He recalled 'the careful and elaborate way' Clarke had put to the jury that he did not doubt that the Wilsons had no intention of saying anything they didn't believe to be true, and described his 'almost prayerful entreaty' to the Wilsons to say they had been mistaken, and continued :

> Gentlemen, it was impossible that such a course should be taken. Had it been possible that such a course could have been taken by honest and honourable persons, it would have been. I think I may claim as descriptive, not merely of the substance, but the manner in which one and all the defendants have given their evidence, that, although they have said hard, damning things of Sir William Gordon-Cumming, they have spoken 'rather in sorrow than in anger.'

He objected to the manner in which Mrs Wilson had been cross-examined, because the question was not of the complete wisdom or propriety of her conduct, but whether she had told the truth about what she had seen Gordon-Cumming do. He then turned to the defence of Lord Coventry and General Owen Williams against Clarke's statements, first, in his opening speech, that they could not have believed Gordon-Cumming guilty, second, after they had asserted that they did so believe him, that they had come to premature and improper conclusions of his guilt :

> Which of these inconsistent positions am I to examine? That they believed in his guilt is undoubted. That fact is established, not merely by the oath of these two gentlemen. That, my learned friend will not attempt to question. It seems to me that if they did not believe him guilty – a man who, in the case of General Williams, was a friend of long standing, and in the case of Lord Coventry of some years' standing – they could not have been parties to advising him, as unquestionably they did advise him, to sign a document which, from the position in which he was placed, was a dishonouring document – a document therefore which no man, not merely of high honour, but no man with a glimmering of honour and intelligence, could have advised a friend to sign unless he found it impossible to believe the story of five witnesses, conscientious – believed to be so – intelligent, and with every interest not to raise this cloud of suspicion. They could not believe – you cannot believe – that these five witnesses, in the position in which they were placed, who spoke of different times, some of them of different instances, and some of them from different standpoints, could concur in fastening this damning story of guilt upon Sir William Gordon-Cumming. But if there could have been any doubt remaining in their

minds, Sir William Gordon-Cumming's demeanor speedily removed that doubt.

He derided Clarke's suggestion that the Wilsons could have mistaken Gordon-Cumming's system of play for cheating, and promised to show that none of the theories put forward would explain the character of that action, and that it was impossible for Lord Coventry and General Williams to disbelieve the statements of three persons vouched for by two others. He asked who were the people face to face with him in his moment of trial and difficulty :

One of them his dearest and most intimate friend of long standing; another who had known him for years; the third the Prince who, to use my learned friend's language, had honoured him with his intimacy and his friendship. Surely it would have occurred to an innocent man, not how this thing could be kept from the rude knowledge of the world, but to have said, 'You are to me the world. You are the friends I am most intimate with, whose respect I prize most highly, whose good estimation I could not bear to forfeit.' Yet he, in the circumstances, when judgement of condemnation had been passed on him by each of these three men, he is content to sign that document so humiliating and degrading. We have heard a great deal about the motive impelling Lord Coventry and General Owen Williams to give this advice, and the words 'scandal' and 'horrible scandal' have more than once been used. I pointed out to you what that horrible scandal was. The horrible scandal was that a man of Sir William Gordon-Cumming's status was accused by five persons of cheating at cards. The suggestion is not with regard to Sir William's part at all, or the truth or falsity of the charge, but that these gentlemen wanted to hush it up for the purpose of preventing a scandal which would affect other people besides Sir William Gordon-Cumming.
CLARKE : I did not put it that way.

I understood that from the cross-examination, not from the opening of my learned friend. If I understood the cross-examination, that is the suggestion he is going to make in the pinch of dire necessity.

My learned friend used the expression that baccarat is an innocent and harmless or moderate game, and so it is. I am glad we have before us the memorandum of Lord Coventry, for it shows in what direction there was operating the consideration of the question of scandal. It was desired to consider the position of the Prince of Wales and the host and hostess, and then it said, 'We conceive that we have done our duty to society as far as the circumstances of the case admit by insisting that the accused should never play cards again, but at the same time we feel that the accused has been leniently treated.' It comes, therefore, to this, that the operation of the desire to avoid this so-called scandal was, and Lord Coventry records that, being more lenient to Sir William than they would otherwise have been. Both these men, believing him to be guilty, offered him the chance of shrouding the thing in secrecy. They pursued that course for the sake of their old friend, actuated by a desire to bring such a scandal to an end.

What does my learned friend next suggest? The Solicitor-General says to Lord Coventry, 'You allowed this man to go back to his regiment and to continue in the service of the Queen.' I hope it may never fall to the lot of any one of us in Court to-day to have to determine according to the hard, strict lines of justice what we ought to advise to be done in such circumstances as these. I suppose that severe purists will say that, once cheating is detected, and the fact established by evidence reliable, there should be no room for mercy or leniency, that the finger of scorn should be publicly pointed to the man, that he should be driven from his profession, and that all hope of redemption should be taken away from him. It may be. With that I do not hold. In the hard exercise of a duty exceedingly painful, no such course as that may be required. But is it not too much to suggest, and too much to be suggested by the counsel for the man whom they honestly believed, rightly or wrongly, that they were acting leniently with, that they should be treated now as coming into the Court and not believing at the same time this man was guilty, because they did not issue against him a verdict of irrevocable condemnation?

He pointed out that General Owen Williams and Lord Coventry were not his clients but, he might say, as their friend, that he challenged the verdict and judgement of these gentlemen of the jury whether their conduct, whether wise or not did not matter, had not been actuated by a sincere desire to do what they believed to be best under the circumstances of the case, and with the most lenient regard to the man concerned.

There are still one or two topics with which I must trouble you for a moment. It was suggested by my learned friend the Solicitor-General about taking a cue from 'a parcel of boys': that you could not rely upon evidence given by these three men because they were boys, or on the evidence of the ladies because they were described as inexperienced players. They were not inexperienced. They had played before. They were not, certainly, so far as we can judge, habitual players of the game, but they had played it frequently before, and, in the name of goodness, what has experience to do with the point we are discussing? It is known that you must put down your stake before the cards are dealt, and, therefore, of course, before the cards are known. You must not increase your stake after the cards have been taken up; certainly not after the cards are known. It does not need any experience of the game to tell whether or not they saw a particular player furtively and surreptitiously increase his stake when the card was declared in his favour. It does not need any experience of the game, or knowledge of the *coup de trois*, or of the *masse en avant*, to know that if a player, after a coup is declared, is seen under the part protection of a sheet of paper to push a counter over the line, or when his hands approach the line, and when the coup is declared, lay down an additional counter. Is that a matter on which it is necessary to bring experience to bear to decide whether that is not a matter of gross dishonesty? The Prince of Wales, in answer to my question, gave his explanation: the banker is busy dealing the cards. The players, especially at a friendly game like this, need not exercise extreme vigilance, and nobody thinks of looking to see whether anybody is cheating or not, unless something out of the ordinary occurs. My learned friend suggests that if conscientious persons and intelligent persons come and swear to have seen particular things happen, you are not to believe them because others did not see these things. Five swore positively they saw him; seven did not see them; therefore, disbelieve the five.

He then referred to Clarke's indication that the evidence of the witnesses for the defence was in some particulars at variance with the records made at, or soon after the events, of what they had said – the general's *précis* and Lord Coventry's diary. He maintained that the defendants were not responsible for those records, nor had they to justify what had been written there without their knowledge: the witnesses were there simply to testify to what they had said and seen – that Gordon-Cumming had deliberately and distinctly cheated on both nights.

Now I come at last to what is the real question of the case. What is the evidence the witnesses give? Does that evidence bear upon it the imprint of truth? Is it the evidence of witnesses who are without ill motive? Have they borne the brunt of cross-examination? Has anything been imputed to them as a reason which would lead you to think that they are other than perfectly credible witnesses? Can you recollect a case, under circumstances of so painful a character as this, where five witnesses have gone through a cross-examination, an able cross-examination, and have left the box so utterly and absolutely untouched by cross-examination?

He lent the weight of his authority to Mrs Wilson's *faux pas* in the witness-box by solemnly affirming that her husband had sat down and played (all danger of cross-examination being over), and that this signified his approval of the game. He characterised Lycett Green's pretence that he could remember practically nothing about what had happened, as 'the care he was taking not to commit himself absolutely even to the form of language which he used or heard used on various occasions,' in order not to exaggerate the charges against Gordon-Cumming.

The Solicitor-General opened his case by admitting these persons to be persons of the highest respectability, but who might possibly be labouring under a mistake. I was, therefore, a little surprised to hear the suggestion made that as to the arrangement of the chairs at the table on the night of the 9th there had been – if I am wrong I apologise for it, but I certainly did understand the cross-examination of one or more witnesses had been directed to show it – a kind of family compact. Am I to take as suggested, or am I not, that there was this family compact concerning Sir William Gordon-Cumming by people to watch him and to treat him as if he were a cheat? I should be glad to think that the learned counsel was labouring under that mental excitement, perhaps irritation, to which we are all subject, and which, Gods knows, I have often experienced. I should be glad to think that it was this that led him to make the suggestion.

What are we to think about the further and last suggestion – what I may call the luncheon and dinner explanation? I do not know in which direction that suggestion was pointed. Sir William Gordon-Cumming was asked nothing about it. General Owen Williams was not asked anything about it, and it is only when Mr Lycett Green is in the box that we have the first suggestion that the explanation of this case is to be found in the fact that there was luncheon at the Doncaster Races and dinner at Tranby Croft in the evening. I like things not to be obscurely hinted at. If weight is to be attached to them I like them to be mentioned plainly, openly, and straightforwardly. Are my friends going to suggest that Mr Lycett Green had lost his head, and because he had lunched too freely and dined too freely? Or that the other witnesses had lost their heads? This witness, Mr Lycett Green, is the last man who would be in a condition so that he could not give you an accurate account. No, there is no ground for it, and there is no ground for suggesting it. And yet such a suggestion was made, and when the man about whom it was made was in the witness-box, he was not even asked a single question upon it.

I am glad I have come at last by slow stages to call your attention to the evidence. . . .

At this point Russell broke off, and asked Lord Coleridge if he might be allowed to finish on Monday.

Altogether it was a pretty and fiery bit of forensic by-play which gave the junior Bar the pleasantest half-hour they have had since they undertook to watch it from the back benches. Sir Charles finishes on Monday, when he comes direct to the evidence, yesterday's sitting closing with a stately rebuke from the judge to Mr Gill *à propos* of his remark about the jury understanding more than was on the surface of the case. 'That,' said the judge, in his kind, sweet tones 'was not a remark which counsel should address to a judge, or one gentleman to another.' (*Daily Chronicle*)

GILL : I can assure your lordship that I had not the slightest intention of being in the smallest way disrespectful to your lordship.

Russell then asked his lordship if he would like for his further assistance the manuscript of the shorthand notes that had been taken. Lord Coleridge politely declined, saying that he had taken two papers, the *Morning Post* and the *Daily News*, the reports in which seemed to him to be accurate. The Court rose at five minutes to four.

During the week-end, the Prince wrote to his sister Victoria, the Princess Royal, Dowager Empress of Germany,

Dearest Vicky, – Many thanks for your letter of the 30th March which I have been unable to answer before owing to having been five days last month in the Court of Justice, besides having many other things to do and having been much worried. This unnecessary and abominable trial is approaching its close, and may be over to-morrow, or at latest on Tuesday. Plaintiff does not seem to have any chance of a favourable verdict as the confidence of the defendants is so conclusive, but the British jury are composed of a peculiar class of society and do not shine in intelligence or refinement of feeling. The Lord Chief Justice is very fair and calm (Lord Coleridge) but one cannot say at present what conclusion he has arrived at. . . .[1]

A resumé of each day's proceedings in Court had been telegraphed every evening to Queen Victoria at Balmoral. These two extracts from her letters, also to the Princess Royal, show her distress :

Balmoral Castle.   June 8th, 1891.
This horrible trial drags along and it is a fearful humiliation to see the future king of this country dragged, and for the second time, through the dirt just like anyone else in a Court of Justice. I feel it a terrible humiliation, so do all the people. It is very painful and must do him and his prestige great harm. Oh ! If only it is a lesson for the future ! It makes me very sad.[2]

Balmoral Castle.   June 9th, 1891.
This trial is indeed dreadful. I hope and think there is no doubt that the verdict will be given against Sir William G. Cumming as the evidence is perfectly clear, but even if it is not he will be turned out of the army and society. His lawyer, the Solicitor-General most unjustifiably attacked Bertie most unjustly and unfairly. The whole thing must do Bertie harm and I only pray it may be a warning.[3]

CHAPTER TEN

'This is not a Theatre!'

The trial was resumed on Monday, 8th June. Although it had now lasted for a week, large crowds collected outside the Law Courts, as on the previous days, to see the fashionable folk drive up in their carriages to the judges' entrance, and the demand for seats was as great as ever.

The Lord Chief Justice entered punctually at eleven, followed by the Prince of Wales. 'He means to see it through,' a journalist commented, 'he likes the oysters. . . .'

The Prince of Wales was there, and the Lady Chief Justice was there, and the usual anonymous letter was on the rail in front of the Foreman of the Jury. (*Star*)

THE FOREMAN : May I read it, my lord?
COLERIDGE : Certainly. (The Foreman read the letter and then handed it up to the bench. Coleridge read it, and said,) I can only say that it is the sort of thing that reaches me. I don't know whether it reaches other judges, but it is the sort of thing that reaches the Chief Justice, I may say, by the hundreds The Chief Justice endeavours to treat them with absolute disdain.

The proceedings . . . were of a very different character to those of the former days. There was none of the brisk dialogue between counsel and witnesses which marked the earlier stages of the trial, and the action was composed of two monologues, one spoken by Sir Charles Russell, the other pronounced by the Solicitor-General . . . and seldom has an audience listened with so much attention. (*Morning Advertiser*)

Russell picked up the thread of his speech where he had left off on Friday :

Gentlemen of the jury, I have a grateful recollection of the attention you were good enough to pay to the observations I addressed to you upon Friday, and I do not intend to repeat anything I then said. Indeed I hope that it will not be necessary for me to make a very lengthy demand upon your attention, although I feel that you will not grudge the necessary time for the elucidation of this matter. I therefore on this occasion go straight to the consideration of the direct evidence incriminating Sir William Gordon-Cumming, and you, I am sure, will be able to discriminate between the relative value of direct evidence such as has been given, and the suggestions which will be made, and which in the discharge of his duty must be made by my learned friend to induce you to come to a different conclusion. This evidence excludes the possibility of doubt. It must be dealt with not on the lines on which he has hitherto dealt with these witnesses, but on the lines on which Sir William Gordon-Cumming has dealt with these witnesses – as conscientious witnesses, honestly believing that they saw what they say they saw. The only course open to my learned friend, so far as I can see, if, indeed it is a course that it is possible for him to take, for a hopeless one it must be, is to pronounce the whole of this story an invention.

There are eleven unquestionable and undoubted acts of cheating : if the withdrawal of the hands was an act of cheating, twelve : if the first coup which Mr Wilson noticed was an act of cheating, thirteen. See the chain of evidence. Mr Stanley Wilson's attention drawn by a startling occurrence; he watches and sees cheating. Mr Levett's attention drawn; he repels the accusation with some indignation; he sees it. Mr Lycett Green sees it; walks out of the room; informs Mrs Wilson, his wife's mother, of what he saw; she sees it. Mrs Lycett Green also sees it.

Now I come to the next stage in the story – the conduct leading up to and resulting in Sir William Gordon-Cumming leaving the house on the early morning of the eleventh – a house to which he came as a friend, and apparently on the introduction of the Prince of Wales – a house which he left on the morning of the eleventh, seeing no one, but leaving it with the full knowledge that he was leaving behind him a blasted reputation. Attacks have been made, polite attacks I admit them to be, upon Lord Coventry and upon General Williams by my learned friend, but I think you now see that the judgement of condemnation at which these gentlemen arrived – you may have thought at one moment, precipitately arrived – was a judgement inevitable in view of the evidence. If confirmation were needed to bring the conviction of guilt to their minds, that confirmation came from the acts and from the conduct of Sir William Gordon-Cumming himself. He stood doubly condemned – condemned by the independent testimony of those witnesses who had no motive against him, but every motive to prevent a scandal in Mr Wilson's house; doubly condemned by his own conduct when he is brought face to face with the accusation.

With regard to the suggestion that before Gordon-Cumming had signed the paper, it had been decided what should be done, he pointed out that Lord Coventry had contradicted this in the witness-box and properly said that they couldn't determine anything until they had seen him; but that it was when Gordon-Cumming didn't accept the offer to be confronted with his accusers that they found it impossible any longer to doubt.

Here I beg to call your attention to the fact that Sir William Gordon-Cumming's evidence upon immaterial points, as well as on points that are material, is not shown before you to be reliable evidence. In the first instance, he has denied that he was informed that Mr Lycett Green desired to be confronted with him. It is proved by three witnesses that he was so informed. Sir William Gordon-Cumming does not accept that opportunity of meeting his accusers face to face. Gentlemen, is it conceivable that any man who was innocent should pursue such a course? He told you, forsooth, that he did not ask to be confronted with the evidence because he was not advised to seek to be confronted with them. Why, the first impulse, I suggest to your better judgement, of an innocent mind, would not be to wait for advice, but to insist upon his accusers being brought before him and telling their story, and to hear his explanation – if explanation there should be – to the charge so conveyed to him. Ay, and what more necessary, if there were any truth in the feeble suggestion now made about the confusion of these witnesses in mistaking the deliberate acts of cheating for evolutions of the coup known as *masse en avant*. There was not a syllable of a like suggestion in any of the intervening intervals from the 11th September down to the moment that Sir William Gordon-Cumming appears as a witness in this Court. He again is contradicted.

Another material point is that he denies he made any reference to the Duke of Cambridge or to his commanding officer. It is sworn by General Owen Williams, it is sworn by the Prince, that he did, and the answer was, 'By all means if you like, do so, but I do not think the Duke of Cambridge or your commanding officer will be so lenient to you as we propose to be, or as we have been.' And we have, finally, got in the memorandum of Lord Coventry the significant statement that, while consideration for the feelings of Mrs Wilson operated on the minds of General Williams and of Lord Coventry, the desire to avoid the scandal of a man of supposed good character being mixed up with so discreditable a transaction occurred to the minds of both, and Lord Coventry's memorandum shows that it operated upon their minds in the direction of making them deal more leniently with Sir William Gordon-Cumming than they otherwise would have done.

He commented once again on Gordon-Cumming's plea that he had lost his head when he signed the paper knowing that it would be taken as an admission of his guilt :

> We have up to this nine persons, including the plaintiff, taking part in this distressing story. We have five persons who believe he cheated, swearing unmistakenly they saw him cheat, and telling you how they saw him cheat. We have three others – the Prince of Wales, General Owen Williams, and Lord Coventry – friends of Sir William Gordon-Cumming, who heard the accusation against him, and who arrived at the conclusion that Sir William Gordon-Cumming was guilty. We have, therefore, eight out of the nine actors in the story who have come to this clear conclusion of guilt, and we have the ninth – Sir William Gordon-Cumming himself – admitting that he was told before he signed the document that it would be regarded as, and was, an admission of guilt. If any excuse or explanation was possible of his signing it on the night of the 10th, if on cooler reflection he came to the conclusion that he had done an unwise thing, why did he not say so ? And why did he not act as if he thought so ?

He turned to the subsequent correspondence : Gordon-Cumming's letter to General Williams expressing doubt whether he had been wise in signing, and the general's reply of 11th September that it would be useless to deny an accusation with so many against him.

> When he got this letter, why did he not then, cool and collected as he was; as, indeed, he was at the time he signed it; take his stand and say, 'I made a mistake. I will now do that which, if I am to be regarded as an honest gentleman and as an innocent man, I ought to have done before.' What is his answer? It is very significant, very significant. He acknowledged the letter on the 12th, and he says, 'I had hoped that you, at all events, would have seen your way to giving me the benefit of any doubt in the matter' – this, remember, is the language of a supposed innocent man – 'but it seems this is not to be. This secret is in the hands of far too many to remain one long, and I have little before me to make life worth living.' Why had not he? Why did he not then have the manhood to assert his innocence? When the memory of the fact was fresh, why did he take no further steps?

Russell repeated the statements he had made in his opening speech – that when the story had leaked out there had been nothing for Gordon-Cumming to do but fight it out to the bitter end – that he had had to tell Colonel Stracey about it and see whether he could not be allowed to retire on half-pay – but first he had appealed to Berkeley Levett to help him. He again described the scene between them, and concluded :

And so, gentlemen, we find this : that the plaintiff, Sir William Gordon-Cumming, was content in the eyes of his most intimate friends, to be regarded as a detected cheat. God knows, gentlemen, it is not pleasant for me to use these words, but they must be used. He was content to be regarded by these five accusers in the same category with detected cheats. He was content to live under that odious imputation so long as this was kept secret. Nay, more. He then makes an attempt to leave the army, and for that purpose prays the assistance of one of these very accusers; and it is only when he is told by Colonel Stracey that the signing of a confession of guilt was an unpardonable act that could not be overlooked, it is not until then that he embarks in this attempt to vindicate his character by seeking in this action to condemn these defendants as wilful and unjustifiable calumniators of his name. That is the story, and there is no need to say much more. His state of mind at that time was shown by a letter that he wrote to General Owen Williams, and in which he told the general that if nothing could be done there was nothing left for him to do but to vanish or cut his throat. Sir William denied that he wrote any such letter or used any such phrase to General Williams; but that is for you to judge. Then there is the interview with Mr Levett – Levett, who repelled the suggestion of his being mistaken, who would have been only too glad if he could have arrived at a conclusion of his innocence, and have been able even to soften down the accusation against him.

No doubt there will be topics of prejudice to which my learned friend will appeal. He may seek to appeal for prejudice against Mrs Arthur Wilson and against those who took part in this game. He may appeal to prejudice in pointing out that Mrs Wilson did not take the wisest course when this accusation was made against Sir William Gordon-Cumming, although I must say I myself don't see that Mrs Wilson has much to reproach herself for. He may, too, make an attack on Lord Coventry and General Owen Williams, who, in his letter of the 28th January, showed how far he was ready to go in order to help the man whom he had known for years, and in which he said, 'You may tell Colonel Stracey that you signed the document under pressure.' Yes, indeed; but General Williams has told us that the pressure under which Sir William Gordon-Cumming signed the document was that if he did not sign he would be denounced as a cheat on Doncaster Racecourse, and the difficulty was not in getting Sir William Gordon-Cumming to sign, but to get Mr Lycett Green, as representing these accusers, to accept that signature as closing this painful incident.

Now, these are topics of prejudice which may cloud the reason, but which certainly will not be intended to help you in this matter. Your judgement in this matter must be that of the evidence in the case, and to prove the facts of the case. How, then, stands the controversy? On the one side you have the oaths of five witnesses, unimpeached and unimpeachable, and on the other side you have the denial of a man whose own conduct deprives that denial, given as it is now given, of any real weight. That is the state of things. Sir William Gordon-Cumming is tied hand and foot by a chain of evidence from witnesses against whose fame and credit no suggestion has been made, and who have passed scatheless through the searching fire of cross-examination. Have you any doubt, can you have any doubt, where in this controversy the truth lies? I and my learned friends have done our best to discharge our duty, and to put the facts fully before you. We have been obliged by the necessities of the case to say hard things. We have tried to avoid saying those hard things, as far as it was possible to avoid it, in the language of offence. You must now do your duty. So far as I am concerned I leave the case in your hands with the fullest confidence that the truth will prevail, and that justice will be done.

He sat down amid dead silence. During all this, the Prince had leant back on his chair and studied the courtroom ceiling.

Sir Charles Russell is perhaps not at his best when he has to deal in delicate shades rather than in broad effects, and at all events, it is certain that the latter part of his address fell a little flat.

Here and there it was lit up by effective phrases. The description of Sir Gordon-Cumming's state of mind at the time of the signature of the document – 'the manhood would have been there if the innocence had been there' – the comparison of the evidence on the two sides – 'On the one hand the oaths of five witnesses, unimpeached and unimpeachable, on the other the denial of a man whose conduct deprives it of any value' – the assertion that 'the plaintiff was bound by a chain of evidence not one link of which had been broken,' were points that told. But the curious feature in the speech was the evident anxiety it showed to forewarn the jury against the change of tone on Sir Edward Clarke's part, which he clearly anticipated. Again and again he went back on his point, and besought the jury not to be led astray by it. (*Daily Chronicle*)

Another listener was more deeply impressed. The well-known K. C., Heber Hart, wrote years later :

I still remember, as if it were an incident of only a few weeks ago, the extraordinary fervour which Sir Charles Russell, who led for the defendants, displayed in his address to the jury in dealing with the question whether an innocent man would have acted as the plaintiff did when he heard of the accusation against him and have been induced to sign this document. The apparent intensity of feeling concentrated in the utterance of his words on this point seemed irresistible. This faculty of speaking on appropriate forsenic occasions with overmastering natural eloquence was really Russell's special gift. No other advocate in my experience has equalled him in this respect. Indeed, of all the masters of the art of impressive utterance in my time, Irving – and he alone – excelled him in this histrionic power. Before the tempestuous force of his emotional display it seemed to me that the polished eloquence of Clarke was overwhelmed.[1]

The *Star* informs us that 'With face immobile, eyes fixed steadily in front of him, Sir William Gordon-Cumming had listened to the terrible charges which were being dinned into his ears, for he sat between Sir Charles Russell and the jury. He now composed himself, recomposed himself, on his seat, and relaxed the muscles of his face, for his own counsel was about to borrow the ear of the jury.

Clarke, in his concluding speech for the plaintiff, had to overcome two serious difficulties : firstly, in his opening speech, he had been mild, conciliatory, expressive of his anxiety to give the Wilsons an opportunity to admit they been mistaken and withdraw their accusations : his hopes had not been fulfilled; they had rejected his overtures and refused to budge an inch from the position they had taken up. Secondly, he had said that the Prince of Wales and General Williams could not have believed, when they first heard the accusations, that Gordon-Cumming was guilty because, if they had, it would have been a breach of the military regulations not to report the matter to his commanding officer. Now both of them, and Lord Coventry as well, had said in the witness-box that they did believe it.

The plaintiff's case had, in the earlier stages, been very quietly – not to say tamely – conducted. But it strengthened – perhaps the right word would be 'hottened' – very remarkably towards the close. And in the concluding speech Mr 'Jack' Wilson and Mr Levett would probably have remarked that it was 'too hot altogether.' It was really a very brilliant, powerful, wily and courageous effort which now and then called one's mind back to famous State Trials in which the leading figure was an Erskine or a Brougham. The Court fairly shivered when the Tory Solicitor-

General – speaking, as he said, as a 'private English barrister' – took up his song against the gentleman whom he called 'the most illustrious of my fellow subjects,' and dealt with him as faithfully as a Cromwellian preacher with 'the man, Charles Stewart.' (*Daily Chronicle*)

He began by answering Russell's insinuations that he would 'appeal to topics of prejudice,' reassuring the jury as follows :

It is with a sense of personal responsibility in dealing with the gravest of issues that I am going now to ask you to give me your sustained and careful attention while, dismissing as I shall (and my recorded speech shall bear me witness of it hereafter) every topic which could be called a topic of prejudice alone, I take you through the facts of this case, and the evidence you have heard, and from the calmest judgement you are able to bring to bear upon the most serious issue on which it is your duty to pronounce, I shall ask for a verdict for Sir William Gordon-Cumming in this case.

Gentlemen, the responsibility is a grave one. I am spoken of in this Court by an official title, which it is the great honour of my life to have been allowed to bear, but in this case I am not the Solicitor-General, I am a private English barrister, bound by the obligation of the robe he wears to disregard private friendships, political associations, personal interests, in the discharge of his duty towards his client. No duty could have been more painful to me than to have to cross-examine and to have now to comment upon the conduct of one of the witnesses in this case, for whom I have always entertained, and do entertain, the greatest regard and respect; but these comments must be made. But my responsibility goes further, and here, in the Royal Courts, where justice is administered by the judges of the Queen, I shall speak freely even of the most illustrious of my fellow subjects.

The occasion was too clear to be misunderstood. The Prince of Wales, who had taken his seat in Court, set himself with an amused smile on his face to hear what might be said about himself in this connection.
Sir Edward Clarke said that whatever he might have to say had been forced upon him by the line of action taken by his learned friend, Sir Charles Russell – who by this time had left the Court . . . There was evidently something else to come out, and the crowded Court bent their heads forward in intense interest to hear what it would be. (*Daily News*)

It is not I who have sought the conflict in this case. My learned friend, Sir Charles Russell, has again and again commented upon the

From left to right, Lord Coleridge, The Prince of Wales, Sir William Gordon-Cumming
and Sir Francis Knollys

THE EARL OF COVENTRY

LORD COLERIDGE

MRS. E. LYCETT GRI

MRS. ARTHUR WILSON

THE PRINCE OF WALES IN THE WITNESS BOX

SIR CHARLES RUSS

THE SOLICITOR-GENERAL

SIR WILLIAM GORDON-CUMMING

MR. E. LYCETT GREEN

Sketches in court from the *Illustrated London News*, June 6th, 1891

MR. ARTHUR STANLEY WILSON

GENERAL OWEN WILLIAMS

LORD COVENTRY

MR. ASQUITH

A DARING JURYMAN

LORD EDWARD SOMERSET

MR. GILL CROSS-EXAMINING

MR. BERKELEY LEVETT

Sketches in court from the *Illustrated London News,* June 13th, 1891

A CONSULTATION IN COURT

(Left) Ethel Lycett Green counselled by three of the most eminent lawyers of the age, George Lewis, Sir Charles Russell and Herbert Asquith. A sketch in court by the *Pall Mall Budget* artist

(Below) Cartoon from the *Pall Mall Budget*, June 11th, 1891.

"WAITING FOR THE ACCUSED." (With all acknowledgments to the Hon J. Collier)

I confess that I attach very little importance to Sir William having signed a document which was tantamount to an admission of the truth of the charge. The scene reminds me of what must often have occurred in the dungeons of the Inquisition. "Recant, or——" And often the victim did recant. Suddenly they burst in upon him whilst he was dressing for dinner. He denied the charge indignantly. They used "utmost pressure" to force him to sign. They gave him to understand that, if only he would sign, the whole business would remain a secret for ever. — Mr. LABOUCHERE in *Truth*.

difference of tone that has come to me in conducting this case from that which I used when I made my speech last Monday. Gentlemen, I confess I am not sorry for it. Anyone who will read with care what I said last Monday will acknowledge that at that time, and having regard to what might be the course of the case, I was justified, and even bound to be as moderate as I was in observations on those who were parties to the case. I was mistaken in my estimate of the Wilson family. I thought that when that Scottish gentleman and soldier had, in the witness-box upon his oath before you, said that on neither of those nights had he been guilty of any act of cheating at cards, possibly they might feel it their duty to say, 'Against such a denial as that, we do not dare to place our recollections, our impressions, never then recorded, now recalled in consultation between us for the purpose of this case; we do not venture to put those impressions and recollections, when so grave an issue is before the jury as the ruin of that man's life and reputation,' I said then, and I think now, that they might have taken a perfectly honourable and a fair course in saying that, having heard the evidence, they distrusted their own untrained observation, and distrusted their own unaided recollection, unaided except by consultation with the other members of the family.

He spoke again of Gordon-Cumming's war record and of his twenty-three years of honourable service during which he had never done an act that diminished in the slightest degree the regard and esteem that was felt for him by the most honourable and the most illustrious men in the country : every one of those years was a witness against this family accusation.

Believing, as I did, that when his evidence had been given, it might have been possible that the defendants would have shrunk from this issue and have accepted this denial, I deliberately abstained from saying any word whatever about either the Wilson family, or about General Owen Williams or Lord Coventry, or about His Royal Highness the Prince of Wales, that could afterwards be quoted to distress or humiliate anyone . . . In that very speech I think you will remember I said that there might have to be comments made upon the conduct of the defendants before the case was closed, but if those comments had to be made, they could be made at a later time. The defendants insist upon having them, and I shall not hesitate to say what I have to say about any and all of the persons who have been called before the Court in this case.

He said he had to deal with the case in a very different fashion now, not only because the defendants had maintained their charges against Gordon-Cumming in spite of his denial on oath, but because, through their counsel, they had also denounced him as a man who had tried to slip out of the army on half-pay, for which there was not one fragment of support in the evidence.

He explained to the jury that he might have put the Wilsons in the witness-box first, in order to know all they had to say before calling upon Gordon-Cumming to answer; but he considered that when a man came into Court to defend his honour, his place was to stand in the witness-box as soon as possible, there to meet any suggestion or accusation that might be raised against him, and there by prompt conduct, and the prompt denial of a gentleman, to clear himself from the accusation made against him.

It is Sir William Gordon-Cumming's bitterest pain to-day that while he came to the witness-box at the beginning of the case, exposing himself to that which my learned friend rightly calls, an often illustrates, the severe fire of cross-examination . . . he has been told over and over again in words which must have wrung his heart to listen to, that he is condemned already, because he has signed a paper that two friends suggested and urged him to put his name to. The question is : is this accusation proved ?

. . . Now, gentlemen, the case against Sir William Gordon-Cumming is put in two ways. It is put first that the evidence against him is in itself conclusive, and my learned friend three times over on Friday used a strong epithet, rhetorically strong, when he said there was 'damning evidence' against Sir William Gordon-Cumming. The second point put against him is that his other friends, the Prince of Wales, General Owen Williams, and Lord Coventry, all believed him to be guilty, and my learned friend has, with ingenuity and with undoubted power, put before you this morning that, of these nine persons, eight are agreed as to the guilt of the ninth. I said, and I honestly said, at the beginning of this case, that I could not imagine that the Prince of Wales and General Owen Williams and Lord Coventry believed Sir William Gordon-Cumming guilty of that which was charged against him. I cannot say that now; for they have been in the witness-box, and General Williams and Lord Coventry have distinctly said that they believed him guilty.

But although they had said so, he continued, he would not retract a single syllable of the comments he had made on the impossibility of a man of honour who believed another to have been guilty of cheating at cards, allowing him to remain in the service of the Crown and to continue a member of the clubs at which they were meeting other friends from day to day : the comments were spoken earnestly and in good faith, and there they must remain.

But there is one point to which I do, at once, wish to refer. It is impossible not to see that, with regard to the signing of that document which was procured in order to protect Mr Lycett Green from insult or an action at law at the suit of Sir William Gordon-Cumming; it is impossible not to see that the suggestion of arranging the whole case by the signature of a document like that did not come from His Royal Highness the Prince of Wales, but came from two men older than himself, his trusted friends and counsellors, who brought to him for his adoption the suggestion which he, as I venture to think, unwisely accepted. But a word has been said by my learned friend, Sir Charles Russell, in the course of the last few minutes, of which I must take notice : he has referred to the signing of this document as being in itself, apart from the question of the guilt or innocence of Sir William Gordon-Cumming, an offence against military law so grave that it cannot be pardoned. I do not quite understand if that means that, even if your verdict goes in favour of Sir William Gordon-Cumming, the military authorities will continue the enquiry that was suspended because this action was brought, and that they will, even if your verdict declares him to be an innocent man, go on to punish him by removal from the Army List because he signed that document. . . .

The Court was very still while this was going on, and it grew stiller at the sentence which followed . . . (*Daily Chronicle*)

. . . if you find that Sir William Gordon-Cumming was not guilty of that which is charged against him, and if, as I trust he may, he goes forth from this Court justified by your verdict, I am bound to say that I think it is impossible that Sir William Gordon-Cumming's name should be removed from the Army List, and that the names of Field-Marshal the Prince of Wales and of Major-General Owen Williams should remain there.

Phew ! This was warm, and the gentle shock which ran through the Court, mixed as it was with a hum that was not a sound of disapproval, showed that the missile had struck its mark. From this point on, indeed, the Solicitor-General had his audience with him . . . (*Daily Chronicle*)

There was an extraordinary sensation at this very bold alternative thus suggested. There was that peculiar kind of rustling in Court when anything unusual has been said, and it was only the calm impassivity of the judge and the imperturbable coolness of the Prince of Wales that were absolutely unaffected by this stirring passage. (*Star*)

Now I desire to deal separately with these matters : the evidence, the inference to be drawn from the belief of General Owen Williams and Lord Coventry, and also with the conduct of Sir William Gordon-Cumming. But I would first make an observation or two to you with regard to the character and value of the evidence which is before you in this case. Gentlemen, you are asked to investigate events which took place on the evenings of the 8th and 9th and 10th September last year, 1890, and you are asked to deal with those events upon the evidence of eight witnesses who have been mentioned, five of whom made no record whatsoever of what took place on that occasion until after the 27th of January this year, when a solicitor's letter was written to tell them that an action was about to be brought.

Let me just ask you to consider for yourselves this question – I am content to put it quite frankly to you and take your judgement at once upon the answer. If you were going to investigate circumstances which took place six or nine months ago, would not the first question you asked be, did anyone make a record of the transaction? And if you found that the persons who felt most deeply their responsibility in the matter had between them set down on paper what they declared was an accurate record of all the circumstances of the case, would you not accept that record? Gentlemen, that question is of vital importance in this case. My learned friend, Sir Charles Russell, has felt it so, and on Friday devoted a considerable portion of his address to you to what he said was an irrelevant topic. To my astonishment, Sir Charles Russell on Friday said that he was dealing with irrelevant topics when he considered the accuracy or inaccuracy of the record which had been kept of these matters; and he went on to say that his witnesses had proved that those statements contained in that record were inaccurate statements. Is it not a most curious thing that after these people saw that record, knew the circumstances in which it had been made, knew the persons by whom it had been vouched for, knew the purpose for which it had been preserved and the way in which it had been preserved, that, after seeing that, they are so determined to force this matter into Court, so vindictive in their action towards Sir William Gordon-Cumming, that their counsel is instructed to say that the very men they appealed to themselves on the 10th September have altogether forgotten, nay, had in the following week forgotten, the statements which were made to them on that occasion?

He then dealt with what he called Russell's invitation 'to treat the Wilsons as if they had committed perjury.' It was not, and had never been part of his case to accuse the Wilsons of perjury. He did not doubt that they thought they had seen Gordon-Cumming cheating but that they were mistaken.

I shall show you that what my learned friend calls cumulative testimony is not cumulative at all. With the exception, as I make it out, and as my friend admitted might be the case, of one incident, an incident easily explained, and to which attention was called at the time, there are no two persons that allege that they saw any one of the acts complained of, and the different things they say they did see, things incredible as alleged to be done at such a time, at such a place, by a man of such character, those things are spoken of only by the people who went and took their seats at the table expecting to see what they now tell you they saw.

He left that subject to be dealt with later in detail, and asked the jury to consider the character of the circumstances at Tranby Croft and its large and generous hospitality. Russell, saying he liked to have things straight-forwardly in plain language, had asked if he had meant to suggest that the people there were drunk. No, he had not. But there were circumstances which should make them very careful of accepting the random recollections of inexperienced and youthful persons, and interested persons, as to what took place.

Altogether there were six discrepancies between Williams writing a week after the Tranby Croft sensation and the Wilsons in the witness-box nine months later; and Sir Edward did not make light of the point. The question was – and here the Court got to tittering again – what was the opportunity of the Wilsons for giving accurate evidence? The Solicitor-General's ironical conclusion was that the circumstances were not such as to make 'their observation very keen, their judgement very good, their recollection very accurate.' In other words we had a delicate version of Mr Gill's 'all-day luncheon' theory. On the whole the Solicitor-General's advice as between the two accounts was 'put your money on Williams and not on the Wilsons'. And then followed some openly scornful references to the defendants, emphasised now and then by a contemptuous jerk of the hand in their direction. (*Daily Chronicle*)

If you were depending upon recollection against recollection now, and you asked yourselves who was the more likely to be correct as to what took place at Tranby Croft on the 10th September, Lord Coventry or Mr Lycett Green, is there one of you who would hesitate to say that where memory differed you would accept Lord Coventry's word? I would say the same with regard to General Owen Williams; I would say the same with regard to His Royal Highness: and here you have a cardinal fact of the case, one which my learned friend has tried to get over, but I venture to suggest has tried in vain to get over, that the three persons who, if they were speaking now from their recollection on oral evidence, you would accept as the witnesses of accuracy and truth against the younger people who have been called on the other side, you have not only their evidence, but you have the record which they made within a week after.

Yet these younger people, he continued, whose evidence had been represented as damning, as overwhelming, against Sir William Gordon-Cumming, had now come into the witness-box and sworn there were six definite misstatements of fact in that record – and the jury had been asked to believe the evidence of these witnesses against Sir William Gordon-Cumming!

I ask you to note what the statement was that Mr Lycett Green made on that evening, the statement as these gentlemen understood it and set it down : 'His brother-in-law, Mr J. Wilson, told him on the evening of the 8th that Sir William Gordon-Cumming systematically placed a larger stake upon the table, after the cards had been declared in his favour, than he had originally laid down; and when the cards were against him he frequently withdrew a portion of the stake, by this means defrauding the bank. This conduct had also been noticed by Mrs Arthur Wilson' – still referring to the 8th – 'who informed her husband of what she had seen. Mrs Lycett Green and Mr Levett, having also been made acquainted with the facts, it was agreed they should all carefully watch the play on the following night, when, again Sir William Gordon-Cumming was observed most distinctly to repeat the same practice. On hearing this, Lord Coventry consulted General Owen Williams.'

Now, gentlemen, that sentence that I have read to you is the accusation which was made by Mr Lycett Green on that evening, according to the evidence of the document which is signed by these gentlemen as an accurate record. He says it is not what he said on that evening; that he said nothing about withdrawing the stakes, that he said nothing about agreeing to watch. Which do you believe? That document which General Owen Williams, Lord Coventry and Prince of Wales are jointly responsible for, or do you believe Mr Lycett Green? Ask yourselves the question, and answer it.

. . . My learned friend says, 'I call five witnesses before you as to facts; they could see, and did see, and are honest, and you must believe them.' He spent more of his time in pressing upon you that which I feel to be a very grave and serious matter in this case, that the Prince of Wales and General Owen Williams and Lord Coventry had formed an opinion hostile to Sir William Gordon-Cumming. Yes, gentlemen, but the opinion that was formed against Sir William Gordon-Cumming was formed upon what they believed had been told them by the defendants . . . they accepted a statement against him which his accusers now say they never made at all.

To the evidence of the *précis* and of General Williams in the witness-box, Clarke added the evidence of Lord Coventry in the witness-box, and also quoted his diary, written on the morning after these events, that Mr Lycett Green 'determined to watch the person on the following night.'

Now here again we are at a vital point of the case. Did they or did they not agree to watch Sir William Gordon-Cumming on that second night? If they did, there is no escape from the conclusion that they, to avoid acknowledging conduct which everybody feels would be disgraceful, denied upon oath that which did in fact take place. There is no escape from that conclusion at all. Now pray decide, for it is for you to decide, did they or did they not agree to watch? Here is the record – and General Owen Williams and Lord Coventry do not minimise or modify upon this point in the way they did with regard to the withdrawal.

He mentioned in passing that one or two of the alleged mis-statements were not of great importance : the authors could not have known whether Mr Arthur Stanley Wilson had told his brother-in-law on the evening of the 8th or on the morning of the 9th : and they were not aware that Mr Arthur Wilson, the host of the Prince of Wales and of all these gentlemen, a man of mature age, capable of dealing with affairs of business and affairs of the world, had been studiously kept in ignorance of the whole plot and contrivance that was going on under his roof to entrap and detect one of his guests. There were reasons, of course, why he might have been extremely angry that the game of baccarat, played at that house against his wish, should have led to a scandal like this.

Poor Mr Wilson senior, who sat hand to ear, patiently receptive of Sir Edward's vitriol, was a special mark for these legal arrows. 'The ornamental position' this gentleman seemed to occupy in his own house, the fact that he was 'studiously kept in ignorance of the plot to ensnare a guest,' were skilfully contrasted with the malign activity of the other members of the Wilson household. As to the agreement to watch, Sir Edward boldly declared it to be proved – 'proved against their oaths,' he declared; while Mrs Wilson bit her lip angrily. (*Daily Chronicle*)

You are aware that when any citizen makes a complaint that he has been maligned, and his accusers say that they are prepared in Court to prove the truth of their accusations, he is entitled to know what it is substantially that they allege against him; and so in due course interrogatories are applied. We asked them what accusation they made against Sir William Gordon-Cumming. Gentlemen, the interrogatories, all drawn up by the same solicitor, who appears for all the defendants in this case, agree in their words; that is to say, one of them will do for all. And the answer is this – it is the answer in this case of Mr Lycett Green :– 'I saw the plaintiff cheat at baccarat by placing a larger stake on the table after the cards had been declared in his favour than he had originally laid down;' and the only information I had, or could have at the time I made my opening speech to you, was that each of the five defendants said that that was the accusation they made against Sir William Gordon-Cumming, that after the card had been declared in his favour, that is, after everybody at the table knew he must win, he had increased the stake which he had put upon the table. Now, I think you will follow me – I am sure you can – in the observations which I am going to ask you to consider. . . .
COLERIDGE : Is it not more absolutely correct to say, when everybody must have known his tableau would win? It makes some difference.

The correction made no difference at all. The interruption was obviously intended merely to distract the attention of the jury and to break the chain of Clarke's reasoning.

As your lordship pleases . . . When everybody must have known that the tableau on which he was playing would win. I am very much obliged to my lord. There is nothing I am more grateful for, in the course of perhaps the most responsible and anxious case I have ever had in my life, than that my lord should keep me exact as to matters which I am putting to you.

COLERIDGE : Sir Edward, you do not need it, but I hope you understand I really only interfere, whenever I do interfere, simply to help you.
I am sure of that, my lord. That is why I express my gratitude. (He turned again to the jury.) Gentlemen . . . I only knew that that was their allegation, that he had added counters after the cards were declared, whether by the banker or by the person who for the moment was representing the table at which they played. But do you remember what I said to you, and proved in examination-in-chief, about Sir William Gordon-Cumming's play? Knowing from the information which one had to get for the purpose of this case, what the system of play was with many players in the game of baccarat, I could see at once that there were points in the game at which that might happen which an inexperienced and careless or prejudiced observer might take to be cheating, and I explained to you in my opening, and Sir William Gordon-Cumming proved in his evidence-in-chief, what his system of play was.

He reminded the jury that Gordon-Cumming's system of play was to stake a £5 counter : if he won he would be paid £5 which he would leave on the table with his original stake, and add a further £5 to it, making his stake for the next coup £15 – the *coup de trois*.

In every case Sir William Gordon-Cumming staked a £5 counter, and in all the cases but one, I think, £15 was the amount which they thought they saw paid to him. Now, gentlemen, just let me ask your attention to this. We have to consider the recollection and observation of people upon two nights of baccarat play. Nobody except Stanley Wilson saw any foul play except a person who was expecting to see it. I beg you to note that observation, and I think you will see the importance of it. It has been truly said that the eye sees what the eye brings the power of seeing. It might with even more truth be said, if there be gradations of truth, it might with as much truth be said that the eye sees what it brings the expectation of seeing. The explanation of every conjuror's success, the explanation of every theosophist's séance, is that the people are brought into a state of mind in which they expect to see a thing, and they see it. You know well the old story of the humorist who stopped at the end of the Strand, and pointed to the lion which then stood upon Northumberland House, and declared that its tail wagged. You will remember that a crowd was assembled round him in two minutes ,and before three minutes half the crowd was declaring that they had seen the tail move, though it was a stone one. You have yourselves seen a conjuror's performance; you have seen him fix your attention on one particular thing and tell you that something else is going to happen, and you know you have been deceived, and the thing has never happened, although you have seen it, apparently, and would declare it had, though it was in defiance of all the laws of nature that you ever learned or heard of. All of us know that the eye sees what the eye brings the expectation of seeing. That is a true axiom and, applying it here, there is only one witness who saw anything wrong, or says he saw anything wrong, in Sir William Gordon-Cumming's play, without having been told beforehand that he was going to see him cheat. And if you examine with your intelligence the particular acts alleged against him, you will see, with regard to Mr Berkeley Levett, and especially with regard to Mrs Wilson, what singular prominence comes into that consideration.

He described the play on the first night on the improvised table. They had been asked to believe, he said, that at the very first coup something happened that might be interpreted as cheating. Mr Stanley Wilson had seen that Gordon-Cumming placed a £5 counter on his white paper, and then saw that he had three £5 counters on the paper, for which he was paid £15.

The evidence with regard to it is as complete as the evidence with regard to any act that is alleged – the one £5, the three £5 counters, and the £15 paid. But when I came to cross-examine Mr Stanley Wilson with regard to this, and asked him whether he imputed cheating to Sir William Gordon-Cumming on that occasion, he said 'No.' well, gentlemen, just let me ask you to remember this. Supposing I had not cross-examined Mr Stanley Wilson at all, but had left that unchallenged, my learned friend might have said, 'There is a clear act of cheating, as to which Sir Edward Clarke has asked no question.' I did ask that question, and I put this question to him :

QUESTION : Am I to understand that you do not suggest that you saw any cheating on the first coup?

ANSWER : No, certainly not. I do not suggest anything of the sort – not the first coup.

Gentlemen, in the face of that answer, given by Mr Stanley Wilson, my learned friend has this morning, in his speech to you, said that in the light of the evidence which has now been given, you may well think that that was an act of cheating. By what rules, but what canons of evidence, in the light of what judgement, is a man to hold his honour before a jury on a charge of cheating at cards if this is the way in which evidence is to be treated; evidence given by a witness, which, if not cross-examined to, would have appeared to be an act of cheating, whereas when cross-examined to he says : 'I suggest no act of cheating at all – not the least,' and then his counsel, after he has left the witness-box, says : 'In the light of the evidence that you now here, you may take a different view of it' ?

It is hard to deal, and to deal patiently, with some of the suggestions that have been made in this case, and some of the attacks made on the client with whom at this moment my interests are bound up, but why this suggestion should be made to you when the witness himself has distinctly refused to make it at all, I am at a loss to understand. Gentlemen, that incident, if you watch it carefully, is the key to the whole matter.

I will show you that Mr Berkeley Levett, of whom I will not now, or at any time, speak with harshness – I will show you that Mr Berkeley Levett, as far as he tells you what he saw, saw that and nothing else, and that is exactly what I told you would happen. I told you in my opening that Sir William Gordon-Cumming staking the £5, the system of play would be that for the next coup there would be £15 on the paper – the £5 he staked orignally, the £5 he took from the croupier, and the £5 which he added himself. And you will notice this, for it is very remarkable, in all these instances which the defendants' witnesses refer to as proving his cheating, the stake which they saw upon the paper originally was a £5 stake. Now, gentlemen, do just imagine. Supposing for one moment that this extraordinary event had happened; that Sir William Gordon-Cumming, who for twenty-three years had passed the life of which I have spoken to you, who had no conceivable reason in his own private circumstances to try and get dishonest winnings from his friend the Prince of Wales, supposing for the moment that he condescended to acts of this kind, what do you think he would have done? Do you think that, intending to cheat, he would have said to the Prince of Wales, as it is proved by the defendants' witnesses he did say, 'My stakes are on the white paper'? Do you think that if he had intended to cheat he would have chosen as the counter which was to be the instrument of his cheating precisely that which is most easy to see, whether on white paper, or on tapestry tablecloth, or on the green baize that covered this improvised baccarat table of the second night? There is no counter among these counters – all the denominations of which I hope you will look at and examine – there is no counter so obvious and so clear to sight, at any distance you like to name, as the £5 red counter, trying it on any cloth you will. On the tapestry cloth, if you take the brown counter, or the yellowish counter, it might be very difficult to see – such a table was used the first night; but on that night, at the very first coup, he is putting his £5 counters upon a white paper, when, as you see for yourselves, it is about the most conspicuous combination that could possibly be invented . . . Gentlemen, just consider what you are asked to believe. The man who is supposed to be intending to cheat some of the keenest eyes in Europe selects the most conspicuous counter as the instrument of his cheating, puts it on a white paper, which makes it more conspicuous than any other object on the table could be, and continues during the evening to stake the £5 counter, when the very fact that it was his habitual stake would call the attention of the croupier and of the banker to the change, if there had been a change, in the amount they were called upon to pay.

He reminded the jury that in the game of baccarat there were only three people of the whole number sitting at the table who were handling cards, and that the others had nothing in the world to do but to put down the stake which they intended to risk and to observe what other people were staking; that the banker and the croupier had three necessary reasons, the croupier to see what he will have to pay and receive, the banker in order to decide whether to take another card or not, and both of them to see that the stakes do not collectively exceed the amount remaining in the bank.

Gentlemen, my learned friend quotes against me the very reasonable suggestion that . . . if it is said a thing has happened and three men are called who saw it, it is no answer to call half a dozen who did not see it. No. If you call three men, and they say, 'I was going down Fleet Street and I saw something in a window,' and to contradict that you call six men who were walking down the other side of Fleet Street and did not see the window at all, the contradiction is idle, I agree; but if you have got a party of players sitting at a table so small as that which is described, the size of an ordinary whist table, two on either side, and the banker and croupier sitting possibly a little higher, but at all events looking down from their table to that table, and the experienced players, and the inexperienced players until they were told what to look for, did not see it, what is the conclusion? Why, that these inexperienced players had blundered and were mistaken, and attacked the character of an honourable gentleman for acts not investigated at the time, not capable of being recalled now – except by those who have had the happiness of frequent interviews with Mr George Lewis for the purpose of preparing their evidence in this case – now distinctly remembered!

But actions which, when they are examined, are perfectly consistent with honourable dealing on the part of the man who is accused.

He proceeded to analyse the evidence, and reached the incident where Stanley Wilson stated he had seen something red in Gordon-Cumming's hand, and that after the card was 'virtually declared' he had dropped three more red counters onto his stake. He invited the jury to try it for themselves : they would find it practically impossible to arrange red counters in their hands in such a way that other people would see them, and yet they could drop them :

His account is this, that there had been a counter placed upon white paper, and . . . after the card was declared, he said Sir William Gordon-Cumming dropped out of his hands three more red counters, so as to make £20. Gentlemen, £20 on that night was a perfectly phenomenal exceptional stake. It would have been noticed directly . . . Mr Arthur Stanley Wilson is the only person who sees it, and suggests to you that whereas right out upon the table, on the white paper, in the view of the Prince, of the Somersets, of everybody else, one counter had been staked, that after the cards were declared Sir William Gordon-Cumming dropped three more red counters upon that same piece of white paper, and that they were paid without any demur at all. Gentlemen, this is the only incident of cheating alleged to have been seen by any person before the idea of cheating got into his mind, and that rests upon the evidence of Mr Stanley Wilson only. But now, what did Mr Stanley Wilson do? Mr Stanley Wilson, when he sees this, tells Mr Levett. . . .
ASQUITH : There is another incident first. He saw it withdrawn.
CLARKE : My friend is harping on the withdrawal. I do not understand the way this case is being fought. My friend interrupts me to say that there was another incident of cheating.
ASQUITH : No. My learned friend must not say that. I am only correcting him in his sequence of events.
CLARKE : I am dealing with incidents of cheating. Does my learned friend mean to say that there was another before?
ASQUITH : No.
CLARKE : Then I am right, and I am going straight on.

He analysed what Berkeley Levett claimed to have seen as an act of cheating, and showed that he had described it in exactly the same language, with the same inference, as the first incident of which Stanley

Wilson had spoken and who did not suggest that it was an act of cheating : he saw one £5 counter staked; the coup was declared; he looked away for some other purpose, and when he looked again there were three on the table. It was precisely what Gordon-Cumming had told them : there would be three on the paper; the one that was first staked, the one which was paid and the one he had contributed from his own stock – the system of the *coup de trois*. In cross-examination, Berkeley Levett had been asked, 'At the time you saw what you have described, do you suggest that you made up your mind that it was done dishonestly?' What was his reply? 'I had been told he had been cheating.' No witness could have more unconsciously given in evidence the current of his thoughts. There was the revelation of the whole thing. These were the two youngest men at the table. They had exchanged their observations to an extent that would have put Gordon-Cumming on his guard had he been an experienced and intentional cheat : 'This fellow next me is cheating,' 'This is too hot . . .' etc.

I beg you to observe it is impossible to suggest that there is anything which might not be reasonably and fairly and honestly explained by the system of the *coup de trois* which was being played by Sir William Gordon-Cumming on that occasion. I agree there is one incident alleged on the 8th which this will not explain : Mr Stanley Wilson says there was £5 upon the paper, and that with a pencil Sir William Gordon-Cumming pushed a £2 counter on to the paper. Gentlemen, everyone could have seen it, if it was done. Mr Berkeley Levett at that time was looking, and had been warned, and was noticing what was done, and he never saw it at all; and when one suggests that upon such a cloth as has been described, a tapestry cloth, you can push a counter on to the top of a piece of paper that is lying on the table, I do not know whether you, gentlemen, have tried it or not, but it is a thing which might be done perhaps once in a few times, but if it were done it would certainly, as I submit to you, attract attention.

He reminded the jury that Gordon-Cumming, until he had the misfortune to sit down at a card table with Stanley Wilson, had been absolutely unimpeached in his honour, had been accepted as a friend for years by His Royal Highness, for whom he felt, and showed by his actions that he felt, a sincere and loyal attachment.

As to what was noticed on the second night, I do not wonder at anything being said when we know what happened before. Mr Stanley

Wilson and Mr Berkeley Levett with their great secret, go up and discuss the matter in their bedroom. 'Sir William Gordon-Cumming, Bart., cheating at cards!' 'Dear old chappie, what is to be done?' 'My God, what are we going to do?' and all the rest of it, and these two boys have to come to the conclusion, I do not doubt honestly – God forbid that I should say a word that to the end of their lives would be remembered by them as having been a suggestion that they were saying what they knew to be untrue – but here these two think they have seen this gentleman cheating at cards. Well, what do they do?

. . . they seek an experienced counsellor, a man of the ripe age, I think, thirty-one, or something of that kind, Mr Lycett Green, whose capacity is that of a Master of Hounds who hunts four days a week; and Mr Lycett Green promptly takes it up. He feels that the whole reputation of the family has been committed to him; and instead of going to Mr Wilson, who was entitled to know, he goes and tells his father, who is not entitled to know; a Member of Parliament it is true, but there are Members of Parliament whose advice one would not desire to ask in matters of this kind. He goes and tells his father, takes his father's advice, and then, for the most foolish of all reasons, tells his wife. Why should he tell Mrs Lycett Green? He says proudly in the witness-box that he has no secrets from his wife; and he went and told his wife, Mrs Lycett Green, the daughter of the house, that Sir William Gordon-Cumming was accused of cheating at cards. He had no sort of right to tell her, and to set about to her, and through her, the story on this occasion. But they had the most charming family party that ever was known. The Wilsons were told, Mr Berkeley Levett is told, Jack Wilson tells Lycett Green and Mrs Wilson, his mother; Mr Lycett Green tells Mrs Lycett Green, and there are five of them all agog to know whether Sir William Gordon-Cumming will or will not cheat the following night.

He commented on the curious behaviour of Mrs Wilson, who said in the witness-box that when they sat down to play that night at the specially prepared table, she had completely forgotten not only that twenty-four hours ago she had been told that Gordon-Cumming had cheated at cards, but that just before she came into the room her son had come to her and whispered it was all right, because he could not cheat that night as there was a chalk line on the table.

Is it not ridiculous? I say one cannot accept such a story. Surely no jury can accept it for a moment against the witness of an honourable life!

Now, the second night they sit down. This time there is a table all on one level. It appears, by some accident, that all the people who know that Sir William Gordon-Cumming has been accused of cheating are sitting very near him. You are told that that was an accident. You are told that two chairs were left vacant, which happened to put him next to Mrs Lycett Green. If he had taken the other he would have been at another part of the same family party. Sitting immediately opposite to them is Mr Berkeley Levett – within three feet. When I first heard that dimension mentioned I thought it must be a mistake, that you could not have got a table so narrow as three feet to play at, but it is so : the table has been measured, and therefore within a distance as near as that (he held up his hands and measured the distance) you have Mr Berkeley Levett sitting opposite Sir William Gordon-Cumming during an hour and a half of baccarat play, and he saw nothing wrong whatever in his play, and says, 'I looked away and did not observe.' Curious behaviour for an officer of the Scots Guards to sit down immediately opposite the lieutenant-colonel of that corps, knowing that that lieutenant-colonel was alleged to have been cheating, and, as he says himself, knowing that he had been cheating the night before, knowing that there were sitting at the table four persons at least to whom the secret had been confided, and that at any moment any one of those persons might put his hand down on the table and say, 'That was not the stake you had there when the cards were dealt.' I do not envy Mr Berkeley Levett's feelings during that hour and a half. It is a pity he had not the facility of Mrs Arthur Wilson who succeeded in forgetting it altogether.

But what goes on? Now there is a most interesting event, and the Master of the Hounds comes on the scene. Mr Lycett Green is the person who said he was going to watch. Now, there is no doubt about this at all. This is in Lord Coventry's diary, written the next day – it is not a question of even twenty-four hours interval – that Mr Lycett Green said he was going to watch, and that if they found him cheating they would denounce him. Quite right. That was the proper attitude. It is at the card-table, and nowhere else, that cheating at cards should be denounced and pointed out. To save up an accusation like that, to be in friendship with a man you are going to accuse, and then to bring the accusation against him in circumstances which would make it impossible for him to say anything but 'In the name of God, I am not guilty,' – that is not the conduct of an honourable man, and never has been.

He recalled that Lycett Green had said that when they sat down on the second night he saw Gordon-Cumming push a blue counter over the line, and that aroused his suspicions – but nobody else of the whole five saw this, and he himself did not consider it an act of cheating. Then there occurred the only incident claimed to have been seen by more than one witness: Mr Stanley Wilson said there was a £5 counter four inches beyond the line, then a brown counter was pushed, he said, just over the line: Lycett Green said just on the line.

> Then the banker loses and has to pay, and Sir William Gordon-Cumming says, 'There is another £10, sir, to come here.' That is, to the Prince of Wales, upon which the Prince says, 'Give him another tenner, Owen' (speaking to General Owen Williams), and 'I wish you would put your counters so that they can be seen better,' or something of that kind, in a more conspicuous place' or some observation of the kind. The moment Mr Lycett Green heard that said by His Royal Highness, his loyal heart was quite satisfied that there was something wrong. He jumped up from the table, and went away from the table. He felt that he had seen an act of cheating, and what was the course he took? The Master of the Hounds knew what ought to be done. He knew that if you think a man is going to cheat and you find him out at cheating, that then and there, on the spot, at any cost, you should make an accusation, or ever thereafter hold your peace about it; and so he had told Lord Coventry that if they found him out they would denounce him. He jumped up, full of valiant resolution, and he changed his mind. He went away, and – wrote to his mother-in-law!

> When Clarke went on in light and lively vein to sketch the scenes of the Wilson baccarat table, the strained feelings of the spectators relaxed, and the unwonted sound of laughter was heard in the Court. Hitherto everything had been sad and sombre. But when Sir Edward Clarke took Mr Lycett Green in hand he extracted some laughter from the subject. The bathos of Mr Lycett Green's explosion of indignation at the discovery of the alleged cheating was provocative of unrestricted mirth. (*Star*)

> It is not my fault, and it is not my wish, if the putting of these things in their close relationship appears a laughing matter. It is no laughing matter to the man I am defending here in this Court; but it is ridiculous to talk of the evidence of people like this as evidence upon which a life is to be ruined and a reputation wrecked. He gets up and goes into another room, writes the note, and sends it to Mrs Wilson. Do you remember that odd little incident that occurred when my learned

friend, Sir Charles Russell, was describing to you Mr Lycett Green's conscientious and high-minded conduct? Said my learned friend, in the most magnificent tones of elevated morality which he could use: 'Mr Green saw this. He got up from the table; he would not play again. He did not sit down to play;' and my learned friends behind began tugging at his gown, and told him he was making a mistake, and he said, 'Well, well, he did sit down, and played for the rest of the evening.'

Mr Lycett Green comes back to that room again, sits down at that table with the man he called a scoundrel in the letter he wrote to his mother-in-law, and goes on peacefully playing during the rest of the evening, this Master of Hounds, and bottles up the accusation until the night after the Leger, when probably he felt a little more valiant and thought he might make it and stick to it, and ask to be secured against an action, if Sir William Gordon-Cumming threatened one.

He pointed out that if Gordon-Cumming had been cheating, and deliberately cheating, these whisperings, the getting up from the table of one of the players, the sending of the note by the butler to the hostess, would have warned him and stopped it, nor was it conceivable that he would have called upon His Royal Highness to pay an extra £10, knowing that he had dishonestly pushed the counter forward to a place where its position would have attracted attention and comment....

... and now just that happens which you might expect. Up to that moment, on neither night, had Mrs Wilson seen any cheating at all, but when Mr Lycett Green wrote her a letter, and said Sir William Gordon-Cumming was a scoundrel and was cheating, she saw it at once, and saw it in such a manner that it is perfectly ridiculous to read the evidence, or hear the evidence, which she gave on Friday. Mrs Wilson was further off from Sir William Gordon-Cumming than the Prince of Wales, General Owen Williams, Lord Edward Somerset, Captain Somerset, Mr Berkeley Levett, and Lady Coventry – she was certainly farther off than all of these, and she says that she saw a £10 counter on one occasion dropped, and a £10 counter on another occasion pushed so openly over the line that she wondered the others didn't see it. She might well wonder the others didn't see it. There were three of them looking for it, Mr Lycett Green, Mrs Lycett Green, and Mr Stanley Wilson, and none of them saw it!

He again stressed the point that, except for one incident which, had it occurred, would have aroused the suspicions of His Royal Highness and General Williams, no two of these five witnesses claimed to have seen the same thing – and the jury were being asked to believe on their evidence that Gordon-Cumming, with all the resources and cleverness of a conjuror, was manipulating the counters, and flicking them, or pushing them, or dropping them, or withdrawing them, with such remarkable and discriminating skill that he could be seen by everybody who expected to see him, and by nobody else.

The only way of testing witnesses like these is to ask them what they know about other things. You will see at once that an accusation like this made against a gentleman – he cannot answer except by saying, 'I did not do it.' If he were playing honestly there is no coup out of the whole series that would attract his particular attention, and the only possible way of testing and gauging the evidence of people who come to make charges like this is by asking them to tell what else was happening, and to give particulars about other things. It is a most remarkable thing, and I dare say you noticed my asking the question, that when Mr Berkeley Levett and the other witnesses were speaking about this £5 coup and the £15 being received, I asked, I think in every case, 'What did he stake the next time? and they never could tell me. 'What did he stake the time before?' They could not tell me on any one occasion, and though, if these people were right, their attention must have been riveted to the table, and they would have watched, one would think, what happened immediately afterwards, there is not one of them who can tell me what he staked before or what he staked afterwards, though the answer to that would show you at once that he was playing upon the system which has been described to you by Stanley Wilson and, before we knew it was important, was described by Sir William Gordon-Cumming himself. Take an instance of their not being able to say what happened. My learned friend cross-examined Mr Lycett Green as to the state of things on that evening with regard to which one would have thought the recollection, even of a Master of Hounds, would be clear. He is asked this :

QUESTION : Had Sir William Gordon-Cumming a piece of paper before him?

ANSWER : I cannot say.

QUESTION : Was he using a pencil?

ANSWER : I cannot say.

QUESTION : Was he smoking?

ANSWER : I do not know.

QUESTION : Had he a tumbler in front of him?

ANSWER : I cannot say.

And the moment you get them off the particular point which was in their minds, and which they went to look for, something which would indicate the cheating; the moment you get off that they are all astray and can tell you nothing at all about it.

He explained that he had analysed and discussed the evidence because he did not want it said afterwards that the verdict in favour of Sir William Gordon-Cumming was obtained by an appeal to the sympathy or pity of the jury. He wanted to show them that there was no evidence upon which they could convict a gentleman of such an offence.

Dealing with Russell's argument that Gordon-Cumming must be guilty because his friends thought 'that the evidence was overwhelming :'

Two questions were asked by one of your number; and the second question was an important one, as to whether His Royal Highness believed in this accusation, and I think you noticed that His Royal Highness, with an expressive movement of the shoulders, said, 'They seemed so strongly supported – unanimously so – by those who brought them forward, that I felt no other course was open to me but to believe what I was told.' Now, these were the exact words of the answer, and I do not doubt that His Royal Highness had the impression on his mind that he had been, when he dealt with this accusation, in possession of the evidence of five witnesses. But, gentlemen, he had nothing of the kind. The unanimous story of the five witnesses was nothing but the statement of Mr Lycett Green, supported by answers to questions of His Royal Highness to Mr Stanley Wilson and by one answer of a most remarkable character from Mr Berkeley Levett . . . 'Well, it is a painful thing to me,' or some words of that sort, 'because he's an officer in my regiment, but I did.' That is all he said. The details of the accusation were not mentioned : the circumstances under which he had seen it were not mentioned . . . and, it is amazing to think of it, General Owen Williams and Lord Coventry, before they go to Sir William Gordon-Cumming, have made up their minds what could be the best thing to do. I do not say they had decided finally upon the course that they should adopt, but before they saw Sir William Gordon-Cumming they had suggested one to the other, 'Let us have a promise not to play cards again, and a promise of secrecy, and then it will all be at an end.' But how Lord Coventry and General Owen Williams ever persuaded themselves that they could honourably adopt that course, I cannot see.

This man had been their friend for years; they had been together as soldiers, they would have shared each other's perils, they would willingly have ventured life for each other had they been together, they very likely have done so travelling through the world; but the moment this accusation is made against him, made by people like this, meeting in this way, evidenced by this fragmentary statement, supported only by the confirmation of otherwise almost silent witnesses who agreed with what was being said at the moment, before they ask him whether there was any foundation for it or not, they suggest to each other, 'Suppose he signs a paper that he will not play cards again, and then we get a promise from these people that they will not take any further notice.'

Now, that is the course which they took. It is not for me to comment on them further. It is the most painful of duties to have to say as much as I have had to say. To me it is most painful, and I will not say a syllable more than I am compelled, but I cannot help pressing upon you the course which was taken with regard to Sir William Gordon-Cumming. If my learned friend, Sir Charles Russell, had not made so strong a point of this, I should gladly have abstained from commenting upon it, but he has made it the very point and front of his case, and he has said to you in your hearing, in indignant tones, 'Is it possible that a man of honour should sign that which he is told, and which he knows, will be read and accepted as an acknowledgement of his guilt, when he himself knows that he is innocent?' I retort the question, 'Is it possible that men of honour, after twenty or thirty years of friendship, applied to by their comrade to advise him in the circumstances of the time, could advise him to sign a document which would condemn him, as they believe, if ever the scandal comes to be discussed; a document which they have already told his accuser, Mr Lycett Green, will be a safeguard and protection to him in case Sir William Gordon-Cumming ever brings an action against him for slander?'

He turned now to their reason for thus advising him, and said it was to save the Prince from being involved in a scandal. He began by drawing attention to an incident in Gordon-Cumming's cross-examination when Russell had apparently scored an easy triumph :

QUESTION : Sir William, baccarat is an innocent game?
ANSWER : Certainly.
QUESTION : You do not see any scandal about playing baccarat?
ANSWER : None.
Of course not. He was playing baccarat himself. He thinks, as a great

many people think, that there is no harm whatever in the playing of baccarat ... but my friend would not have it. He insisted on it that there was no scandal affecting His Royal Highness – that the only possible reason for their suggestion this to Sir William Gordon-Cumming was that they felt that he was gone, that the evidence against him was so conclusive and overwhelming that he never again under any circumstances could hold up his head, and that it was in mercy to him that they suggested this writing and this statement. My learned friend would not admit that there was any question with regard to His Royal Highness the Prince of Wales. Now, let me quite frankly say what I have to say before I read what Lord Coventry had to say about the matter. Sir William Gordon-Cumming and those who share the society which he then enjoyed are entitled to choose their amusements, and they may not think that there is scandal attaching to the playing of a game like this. But there are the great masses of our people whose knowledge of gaming principally is that a club is visited and people prosecuted for playing baccarat there, or an innkeeper loses his licence because betting on horses is allowed on his premises; and in a great part of the community of which we are members, there must be, I am sorrowful to think, a keen and abiding feeling that this unhappy incident ought never to have been allowed to occur, because the circumstances were those which are at variance with the feeling and the consciences of the people.

We might not all, Clarke said, be able to understand the feelings of Lord Coventry and General Williams at that moment : they thought they would be doing good service to the Prince, whom they were bound to think of in circumstances of this kind, if they took a course which would allow the whole matter to pass into oblivion.

There is a strong and subtle influence of royalty – a personal influence, which has adorned our history with chivalrous deeds; and has perplexed the historian with unknightly and dishonouring deeds done by men of character, and done by them because they gave their honour as freely as they would have given their lives, to serve the interests of a dynasty or to conceal the foibles of a prince. That is what was in the minds of Lord Coventry and General Owen Williams.

And again the Court responded to the Radical sermon of the Tory Minister – a murmur, light as breath, but still with an ominous sound in it. (*Daily Chronicle*)

The Prince endeavoured to look unconscious during this straight talking, but he didn't succeed too well. He shifted uncomfortably in his seat and displayed a remarkable interest in the books on the Lord Chief Justice's desk, which quite fascinated him. (*Star*)

There is no room for controversy now. It does not rest on the speculation of an advocate, on the inference from the ambiguous answer to a question. Here in Lord Coventry's diary we find it, written the next day, contradicting every syllable of the speech which, in ignorance of the diary, my learned friend made when he was opening his case.

If Lord Coventry and General Williams were to be excused for persuading their old comrade to sign the paper because of their devotion to the Prince, whom they desired to serve, should not Gordon-Cumming, he asked, be given that credit too? Was there no loyalty to the Prince of Wales in the man who sacrificed himself, as his old friends were willing to sacrifice him, in order to save the reputation of one whose kindness during those years, whatever may happen here, will always be a recollection he is entitled to remember with pride?

'Two false friends,' was a description at which General Williams raised his brows and smiled not over-pleasantly. (*Daily Chronicle*)

Commenting on Russell's accusation that Gordon-Cumming had tried to slip out of the army without an investigation, he showed that this had been negatived by the evidence : he could have done so at any time before 25th January when he himself had gone to Colonel Stracey and told him of the accusations against him. That had made an enquiry inevitable.

> COLERIDGE : He applied to retire.
> CLARKE : Yes, on that day, telling Colonel Stracey.
> COLERIDGE : He applied at the same time to retire on half-pay.
> CLARKE : Yes. 'Simultaneously' was the word used. . . .

Now, observe what happens the next day. Up to that date, the 25th January, he had no knowledge of what had been said against him at all. He had asked Lord Coventry, 'What do they say?' and Lord Coventry did not know any detail, and could not have told him. He had asked Lord Coventry the names of his accusers, and he had been told of Mr Lycett Green and Arthur Stanley Wilson, and Lord Coventry does not know he had been told any other name. But on the 26th he went to the friends by whose advice he had signed the paper. He saw them in the morning; it was arranged they were to get the paper and see him in the afternoon. He came back in the afternoon; he read the *précis*; he took exception to that part of it which was indicated by Lord Coventry, and he then said to them, 'What do you advise?' They had no advice to give him. Their views had been bound and closed up by the idea of this never coming out at all. They had treated him as a friend afterwards. They had shaken hands with him after he had signed what they called a dishonouring document. They had met him at the clubs; General Owen Williams had written to him 'My Dear Bill;' Lord Coventry had written to him 'Dear Sir William,' and 'Yours truly, Coventry,' after this time; and then on the 26th, when they are face to face with that which they should always have foreseen, their capacity for advice is gone. They have no advice to give him at all. He took his own course. It is for you to vindicate that course by the verdict which you give in this case He determined on a public examination of these facts. He applied for a copy of the record. Until he got a copy of the record he could not tell who had actually made the statement against him. On the 5th February he got a copy of the record, and on the 6th of February a writ was issued against every person mentioned in it as having made a statement to his discredit. By every means that we have known, this trial has been hastened, in order that he should be able to come into Court to vindicate himself; and when the trial is called, on he goes into the witness-box first, to face that cross-examination which has terrors for men who have shameful secrets to conceal, or a disgraceful past to reveal to the world, but has no terrors for a man who could come into this or any Court, and face any cross-examination which envy or malice could suggest, knowing that 'whatever record leapt to light, he never should be shamed.' So he gave his statement and his evidence before you, and it is for you to decide upon it. I ask you, in his name, to clear him of this charge. It is too late to undo much of the mischief which, however this case was treated, could not but arise from this discussion. It may be too late to save the reputations of some of those who have been mentioned in the case; it is not too late for you to prevent the completion of the sacrifice of a gallant officer to the desire to keep a painful secret quiet. The motto of his race is 'Without fear'. He came without fear into the witness-box, for he had nothing to conceal. He sits without fear at this moment, for he believes, as I believe, that honesty is safe in the hands of a British jury, and that he has good reason to hope that the result will happen, which I believe will not be unwelcome to some of those upon whom I have been obliged to make sharp comments – that result which will assure the Prince, General Owen Williams and Lord Coventry that they made an honest but a sad mistake – that the man they had known and honoured was worthy of their friendship and their esteem – a result which will wipe a stain from a noble service and a gallant regiment, and will send Sir William Gordon-Cumming back, with that title-deed in his hand, to public service and private friendship, which will be written in the verdict given by you that clears him of this foul charge.

And then, having at least done well – supremely well – for his client, Sir Edward sat down. He was followed by a brief clatter of applause from all over the Court, which the judge suppresses – with a stern voice for so quiet a judge – by a fierce and angry cry of 'Silence! This is not a theatre!' (*Daily Chronicle*)

Another paper reports a voice from the back retorting, 'You have made it so!' Instead of starting on his address to the jury, he adjourned the Court until the following day. As soon as he had left the bench, and the Prince had followed him out in silence, 'the overcharged feelings of the spectators again broke out, and, unchecked this time, they gave way to their feelings. Then the assembly gradually broke up, and melted away.' (*Pall Mall Gazette*)

Sir Edward had amply redeemed the pledge which he gave at the commencement of his speech, to speak freely even before the most illustrious of his fellow subjects. Seldom indeed has a Prince sat by while an advocate spoke thus openly about him. But this trial is an exceptional occasion, and an honest advocate, who is anxious to do his duty to his client, cannot afford to be a respecter of persons, even though they be princes of the blood. (*Morning Advertiser*)

Heber Hart, KC, who had been so deeply moved by Russell's speech, wrote that Clarke's speech was 'probably the most conspicuous example of the moral courage and independence of the Bar that has occurred in modern times.'[2]

Clarke's allusion to the Prince of Wales has attracted a good deal of attention. It is not altogether favourable to Sir Edward. The line is admitted to have been attended by considerable social risk. The court is still an enormous social power. The Prince of Wales can raise or crush ambitious men with a nod or a frown. It was certainly what is sometimes known as 'a large order' to ask if Sir Gordon-Cumming be declared guilty the heir apparent should be drummed out of the army. (That really is what Sir Edward's deduction implied.) How the court will receive this extraordinary inference remains to be shown, but in the meantime a strong disapproval of the attack is expressed in a section of the Cabinet. Rumour last night pointed to a possible sensational *dénouement,* but this *dénouement* will not, I venture to think, go beyond a remarkable accession to Sir Edward's reputation at the Bar. (*Nottingham Daily Express*)

Clarke himself thought it was one of the best speeches he had ever made : 'It has sometimes happened to me when making a speech,' he wrote, '– on rare occasions – perhaps a dozen times in the course of my life – to have all the faculties so working together at the very height of their powers that there has ceased to be the slightest sense of effort, physical or intellectual. No choice of topics, no hesitation of thought, no selection of phrase. As the thought comes into the mind the perfectly apt word comes with it. The phrase has no ambiguity and no extravagance. And voice and gesture instinctively give melody and force to the flowing period.' He commented in his autobiography, 'Lord Coleridge's angry exclamation when the crowded court cheered my closing speech, 'Silence, this is not a theatre,' sounded in the circumstances rather amusing,' and he added, 'Lord Coleridge . . . told Lady Coleridge when he reached home that until he heard my reply he had never doubted what the result of the case would be. And he set to work that night to prepare, or perhaps to complete, the very fine specimen of judicial advocacy which he delivered the next morning.'[3]

CHAPTER ELEVEN

A Question of Honour

On the seventh and last day of the trial, Tuesday, 9th June, the Prince was not in his usual place : he had gone to Ascot. The *Star* commented that the racing there would be a very trivial affair compared to the struggle for life and honour which was now reaching its climax in the Royal Courts of Justice. Gordon-Cumming's bronzed face was 'expressionless, unmoved, sphinx-like as all through the trial.' The defendants were all in their places.

> Members of the Bar crowded the back of the Court, and among them Mr Bancroft and several other representatives of the drama, while Sir Robert Peel, wearing a frock coat and a gorgeous blue tie, was content to seek shelter there also. (*Echo*)

> As the judge entered, General Owen Williams, his face pale with excitement, threw himself full on Lord Coleridge's view, and as the Court was settling to its seat began to speak. There was an instant hush in the delightful prospect of another sensation. General Williams, getting his words out with difficulty and with great passion, pressed for the right to speak . . . but the judge calmly, almost regretfully, waved him down. . . . (*Daily Graphic*)

> O. WILLIAMS : (In a very loud voice) As one of the witnesses in this case I have to ask your lordship's protection. Yesterday the Solicitor-General in the course of his speech thought proper to accuse Lord Coventry and myself. . . .
> CLARKE : My lord, I ask your lordship that no statement of this kind should be allowed to be made in Court. General Williams has no privilege here.

Coleridge, however, ignored him, and asked the general :

> COLERIDGE : What do you want protection from ?
> O. WILLIAMS : We are accused of a crime, my lord, of an abominable crime.

COLERIDGE : I do not now recall the expression; but I'm afraid the law is inflexible.

'We are accused of sacrificing an innocent man,' said the general sternly, and labouring under great excitement. The Lord Chief Justice, speaking quietly and deliberately in order not to contribute to the excitement of what even he apparently felt to be a dramatic incident, said he had no control over counsel who spoke under the sanction and control of their professional duty, and he was afraid that if he consulted the authorities he would find that there was absolutely no restraint on the language of the counsel when it was relevant; and indeed it was very doubtful whether there was restraint when the language was not relevant.

'I only thought it due to myself, my lord, to apply to be put in the witness-box,' said General Williams, 'to refute that statement which counsel made without any evidence or justification.' The Lord Chief Justice assured him again that he could put absolutely no restraint on the language of responsible counsel, and, seeing that there was no hope for it, General Williams accepted the inevitable, bowed very formally to the Court, glowered at the Solicitor-General and returned to his place at the end of the Queen's Counsels' seats, glum and moody. (*Star*)

From this little scene, several points of interest arise – first, of course, that Coleridge while explaining that nothing could be done was in fact allowing him to make his protest.

The second point is even more significant : it was a revelation of the general's character. He was no longer 'a very proper general,' who had behaved with restraint and decorum in the witness-box, he was a man blazing with indignation because some plain speaking had offended him. The fact that he made his protest at all at this crucial moment when Gordon-Cumming was facing the decision that would clear him or plunge him into ruin and dishonour, proves that he had no friendship for him whatever when his own social position was touched upon. It is only too probable, therefore, that when he first heard the accusations of cheating and foresaw a scandal in which both the Prince and himself would be involved, he was equally regardless of what was due, in all fairness, to Gordon-Cumming. From this demonstration we can understand that it was not as a very proper general, but as a man labouring under violent emotion that he suddenly descended upon Gordon-Cumming with the accusations, and later with the ultimatum. His angry words, 'We are accused of sacrificing an innocent man,' spoken at that moment and before the jury, were calculated to prejudice them against Gordon-Cumming, and should not have been allowed. Both the fact and the timing of his protest greatly strengthen Clarke's contention that he sacrificed Gordon-Cumming, not perhaps knowing that he was an innocent man, but not caring whether he was innocent or not.

After this diversion, Coleridge began his summing-up – his address to the jury.

> The stately man in black robes edged his chair to the jury and began a long, and it must be confessed a discursive and rather formless talk, which lasted for just four hours. The steady drip of Lord Coleridge's speech acted effectually – as doubtless it was intended to act – as a cold water *douche* on the imflammable matter which Sir Edward's harangue had stirred into flames. From the beginning it was utterly – and notedly – hostile to the plaintiff's case . . . Here and there the scholar and stylist would peep out, and the easy shambling talk, spoken in a low but very sweet and clear voice, would take a statelier note, and a line of Shakespeare or a classic maxim would be spoken so that the ear heard it with delight. (*Daily Chronicle*)

He told the jury he was thankful he had allowed the night to intervene because he could not help feeling that they had been subjected yesterday to influences of unusual power and ability. The learned counsel whom they had heard were certainly, if not the foremost, among the foremost men of which the English Bar could boast. They had used their powers to the utmost, and it was more satisfactory, he thought, that the humble jog-trot of a summing-up should intervene between them and their verdict, than that they should come to their verdict with their minds necessarily disturbed by the very great ability which both learned counsel had shown yesterday. He said that it was, in this case, by no means a matter of course that they should keep their minds steadily on the evidence.

> A learned and very able counsel told you the other day that he hoped you would understand a good many things that I did not, and, so far as he is concerned, the whole thing has passed away from my mind. He was entitled to make that remark if he thought fit. But he also said he hoped you would understand a good many things that did not appear on the surface. Now, against that, gentlemen, I most emphatically protest. We have nothing to do with things that are not on the surface.

He then proceeded to make what the *Daily Chronicle* called 'a point by point answer' to Clarke's speech. He discussed the problem of gambling, whether it was wrong and sinful, but whether the jury thought so or not, it was no part of their duty to condemn their neighbours, that the actors in this case on both sides had a perfect right as long as they kept within the law – and from prince to peasant there was but one law, and prince and peasant alike had a right if they thought fit to spend their time in pursuits which might not suit the jurymen, or himself.

Rap one for Sir Edward who had hinted very plainly what the popular verdict on the sin of a prince playing baccarat with £100 in the bank might happen to be. Then came another slaughtering sentence. Sir Edward's ingenious attempt to explain what the Wilsons saw on the 8th and 9th on the psychological ground that they saw what they expected (possibly wished) to see, was set aside as quite inadequate to explain the detailed, cumulative story. . . . (*Daily Graphic*)

Now then, what is the charge? The charge is that on two nights – the 8th and 9th September last – the plaintiff at Tranby Croft, the house of Mr Arthur Wilson, cheated at cards. Removing for the present the question of abstracting the counters from the stakes, of which we have heard so much and on which, it seems to me, so little turns, substantially the cheating was all of one kind. It consisted of adding to the stakes after it was safe to do so . . . Did he in truth add to his stakes several times on the 8th and several times on the 9th?

He pointed out that it was upon the defendants that 'the proof of the affirmative' was thrown, and that if they did not make out the affirmative, whatever they might think, whatever they might suspect, Sir William Gordon-Cumming was entitled to the verdict. The defendants had put the justification of truth, and if it was true, they had a right to say it. In fact, since the allegation was that Gordon-Cumming had cheated at cards which is a criminal offence, 'the proof of the affirmative' meant proving the charge beyond reasonable doubt and the Lord Chief Justice should have directed the jury accordingly.

Lord Coleridge followed this up with long extracts from the evidence of Arthur Stanley Wilson and the young subaltern Berkeley Levett, reading, with emphasis, those points which were most deadly to Sir William Gordon-Cumming. (*Echo*)

A point was made, and not a bad point at all, that on the first night there would be a difficulty in being sure of any act of cheating in consequence of the colour of the cover on the table. This was an extemporary table made of three whist tables, the centre one being rather higher than the others. I could not quite make out whether they were all covered with a large tapestry cover or each separately, but at all events they were all covered with what they call tapestry covering –

that is to say, a covering with a pattern upon it, which would make it of a uniform sort of brown colour. Thus they say that the counters would not be so conspicuous as if they had been put on white paper and that, inasmuch as Sir William Gordon-Cumming had his counters on white paper, cheating in his case would have been much more easily detected, and that if he had intended to cheat he would not have used white paper. That is to be borne in mind on the first night. On the second it was a green baize cloth with a white chalk mark round it. In cross-examination reference was made to a system of playing baccarat which sounded like *coup d'état*. Of course, it could not be *coup d'état*, but it was some French term used to describe a certain way of playing.

CLARKE : *Coup de trois*, my lord. It consists of playing three coups in succession according to a certain rule.

COLERIDGE : At any rate, the effect of it would be that, if £5 were staked originally, there would be three counters of £5 each on the table.

RUSSELL : There would be six counters, my lord.

CLARKE : If he won the first two coups there would be six counters.

This was a curious little interlude, for nobody at that stage of the trial could possibly have really mistaken the expression *coup de trois* which had been repeated and explained again and again. Coleridge was merely discrediting Clarke's argument – which should have been put fairly to the jury – that Gordon-Cumming's system of play was mistaken for cheating by his inexperienced accusers : he was indicating to the jury that *coup de trois* was a French expression that the judge didn't understand, therefore it was not necessary that they should.

As to the *coup de trois,* Lord Coleridge, in spite of an interjected explanation of Sir Edward, professed not to understand it. Perhaps it was a little judicial affectation – judges are fond of shamming stupidity – at all events Sir Edward seemed hurt that his little lesson in baccarat had found so slow a pupil on the bench. (*Daily Graphic*)

We come to the next morning when they discussed this matter. There was one expression which I wished the Solicitor-General had not used. I admire his speech very much and wish he had not called Lord Coventry 'a false friend.' I do not see that he did anything to deserve it.

CLARKE : My lord, your observation gives me an opportunity which I should like to take advantage of. It is the only sentence in my speech which I unfeignedly regret. I did not mean to impute to Lord Coventry

and General Williams that they were false friends in the sense that
would be carried by those words.

Lord Coleridge expressed the pleasure he felt that the explanation had
been given, and went on with the review of the story. He impressed upon
the jury in the most emphatic terms that every one of the defendants was
positive about what he or she saw – ab-so-lute-ly certain, to use the
syllabic pronunciation given to it by both young Wilson and Mr Green.
Then, he asked, what did Sir William Gordon-Cumming say in his
examination? Why, the whole of the explanation he had was, 'I did
nothing of the kind. I played a perfectly honourable game all through.'
(*Echo*)

Then followed a gentle, quietly spoken, but very firm, rehabilitation of all
the defendants. Mr Jack Wilson, most dramatic of Johnnies; young Mr
Levett, mildest of Guardsmen, the Master of the Hounds, and all the
others at whom Sir Edward had poked his wicked fun or lifted the finger
of scorn. They had had their little laugh, said the judge rather cruelly,
now they must think and talk seriously. A deadly stroke that. And again
the examination of the defendants went on. As it proceeded the last hopes
of the plaintiff must have been ebbing fast. But there was no sign – save
perhaps a gentle flicker of the eyelids and a gathering cloud on Lord
Middleton's proud face – that Sir William and his friend and backer were
conscious of the approach of fate in the person of this silver-voiced judge
with his paternal manner and his chatty speech. 'He takes it well,' was the
whispered comment. (*Daily Graphic*)

Lord Coventry is an honourable man; he gave his evidence, and
General Williams was a friend too; and he was the friend of the Prince
of Wales. One of them gave a very good reason. They said that these
five persons told them they had seen cheating, and they were certain of
it, and therefore before they did anything more they must tell the
Prince of Wales. The plaintiff was there as the Prince of Wales's friend.
His Royal Highness has told us that he had known him twenty years;
for ten years he was entitled to say he was his friend. Here are two men,
the one a peer, the other a general in the army, and both of them men of
unspotted honour and character, and they say, 'We did not think it was
right that the Prince of Wales should go on extending his friendship
and favour to this man without being told what these people say
against him.' The Prince sends for the three gentlemen . . . Mr Lycett
Green is the chief. Let me say of him what I think the Solicitor-General
forgot, that whatever else he is, whether he is Master of Hounds and
hunts four days a week, whether he is wise or foolish, Mr Lycett Green,
by the account of everybody in this case, was a man who did not want

the thing burked. He was the man who was brought reluctantly to sign the paper, and who from the beginning to the end said, 'Confront me with him. Let us have it out now.' Over and over again he said, 'I don't like this delay; I don't like these proceedings. I saw it; and I'm prepared to say I saw it. Confront me with him and let's have it out now.' At all events, this must be said for Mr Lycett Green, above all witnesses in the case, from beginning to end he manifested the strongest belief in his opinion; he was very reluctant to have it settled except by direct conflict or meeting with Sir William Gordon-Cumming. That Mr Lycett Green had perfect confidence in his own truth, and was firmly persuaded of what he said, no one can doubt.

It must have surprised Lycett Green to learn how anxious he had been to have a direct personal conflict with Gordon-Cumming after all the trouble he had taken to avoid it, running round trying to get somebody else to take the initiative, from his mother-in-law to the Somersets, to Lord Coventry, until at last he got General Owen Williams to act for him and be the bearer of his ultimatum – the contemptible threat to Gordon-Cumming that unless he immediately signed an undertaking that would be a protection to Lycett Green he would be publicly accused on Doncaster Racecourse in the morning.

Mr Lycett Green has been flown at. He is a Master of Hounds. Well, Masters of Hounds are rather proud of writing MFH after their names. It is not as great as KG, of course, but it is something. Certainly in the box he gave his evidence like a man, but it pleased the learned counsel to fly at him because his father was an engineer. As a sensible man he would not wish to help that, and, of course, he could not; but I cannot see why a man's father should be thrown in his face because he is an engineer, sits for a great place in Parliament, and has had rank given to him by the Queen. I cannot understand. . . .
CLARKE : I did not throw it in his face, my lord.
COLERIDGE : If you did not, Mr. Gill did.
CLARKE : I don't think so, my lord.

Coleridge was wrong, but he went on stubbornly :

I do not see why he should be laughed at because his father was an engineer. . . .

Another rebuke followed for Mr Gill because he had spoken of Mr Lycett

Green's father as 'an engineer', and this afforded a favourable opportunity for the introduction of another most damaging point to Sir William Gordon-Cumming. And it was delivered with every intention that it should find its billet. By whom were the allegations made? By no less than five persons who swore – and there was no reason to disbelieve their evidence – that they saw this cheating! The immediately succeeding points were dead against Sir William. He did not request to be confronted with his accusers. He did not go before his Commander-in-Chief. No; he did nothing to establish his innocence. (*Echo*)

Mrs Lycett Green very distinctly said she was absolutely certain she saw an act of cheating. She shows how he did it; there is no question about it at all. You have heard her. You cannot doubt she spoke in the strongest possible way of having seen cheating. Mrs Wilson says the same thing . . . Mrs Wilson's dislike to being mixed up in this matter was carried to a very unusual degree, and affected her memory to an extent which one would be very glad if in unpleasant circumstances one's memory might always be affected. She did not tell her husband on the 8th because it was too late, and next morning she forgot all about it, and after she had been told that the baccarat table had been altered she totally forgot all about the cheating. It is certainly very strange – one is obliged to strain one's courtesy to think she is not a little overstating these occasions. If it be so, the question is whether she did not see what she says she saw.

Mr Arthur Stanley Wilson has been a good deal laughed at. He went to Magdalene College, which, I fancy, enjoys the reputation of not being the slowest college at Cambridge. After spending a little time there, his father thought he was not doing very much good, and took him away, and he lives at home where, as a young man, no doubt, he was exceedingly glad to live. But why should he be attacked for that?

. . . Mr Berkeley Levett was excessively annoyed at being dragged into the case, and he said as little as he could. He has been made fun of, and all this has been turned into ridicule. You are asked to say one of two things : either that he did not see what he says he did see, or that he must be conspiring with these people to bring a most infamous charge against a man with whom he had no quarrel.

He said there were some people he would not believe guilty of a thing even if he saw it, or at least, in the case of a man whose heart and head he had known, unless he had seen the act beyond all possible doubt. But he didn't apply this to Lord Coventry and General Owen Williams who had believed at once in the guilt of the man whose head and heart they had known, even although they had seen nothing wrong.

> They said, 'We must go to the Prince and tell him that we have come
> to the conclusion that he is guilty; we must judge of what defence he
> has to make, for we cannot – although we have a very strong impression
> against him – we cannot be certain of what we ought to do until we
> see him.'

This reconstruction was directly contrary to the evidence which showed
conclusively that they had determined what to do before they saw
Gordon-Cumming.

He went on to maintain that Gordon-Cumming's explanation that he
was surprised into signing the paper, that he had yielded to influences he
ought not have yielded to, was not valid.

> Sir William Gordon-Cumming has had it said in his favour, and with
> perfect truth, that he was a gallant officer, who had stood up under
> fire, who had served his country bravely, who had been of great use to
> the Queen and people of England, who had lived all his life amongst
> people of the highest society; and he says that he was so taken aback, so
> overcome by circumstances, that he signed the document when, to use
> his own strong and graphic expression, he had 'lost his head'. General
> Williams and Lord Coventry both said he had not; and both said he
> showed no outward signs of it. He discussed the matter carefully, took
> time to consider, he argued with them, and eventually signed . . . I
> should have thought a man of honour, if he were innocent, apart from
> the consideration to which I would draw your attention presently,
> would have said, 'What, I, Sir William Gordon-Cumming, sign a
> document which is to write me down as a card-sharper? If there were
> twenty persons who have said I have done it, I, in my own mind, am
> perfectly certain that I did nothing of the kind.' It is said that before
> that, he had shown by his conduct that he was maintaining his
> innocence. I think there is evidence that he was told that Mr Lycett
> Green was only anxious to be confronted with him. . . .

Clarke rose and protested:

> That is not so, my lord!
> RUSSELL: Three witnesses have sworn it.
> CLARKE: I do not think this is so. Lord Coventry put it exactly when
> he said he told him the names of his accusers, and that nothing was
> said at the first interview about confronting him with Mr Lycett Green.

RUSSELL : General Williams has said that he told Sir William Gordon-Cumming that Mr Lycett Green desired to be confronted with him; and Lord Coventry said he believed he told Sir William Gordon-Cumming so. He also said that Sir William Gordon-Cumming never expressed a desire to be confronted with his accusers.

COLERIDGE : Mr Lycett Green objected to the arrangement, and it was excessively likely that something was said about being confronted with him.

Thus, through a moment's inattention to one of General Williams's answers, Clarke lost this very important point. He could easily have dealt with it at the time, the answer having been so obviously untrue that one can only suppose that the general misunderstood the question. To have conveyed a 'challenge' from Lycett Green to Gordon-Cumming would have provoked a row that would have precipitated the scandal that he was so desperately trying to avoid. To act thus would have been to run counter to everything else he did on that evening. He obviously did not tell Gordon-Cumming that Lycett Green wished to be confronted with him – and it would not have been true. We have to bear in mind also the general's answer to another question in which he made it quite clear that when Lycett Green said he wanted to have the matter out at once he did not mean by a confrontation, but to have the accusation brought out on Doncaster Racecourse. The whole 'asking to be confronted' business was merely verbal juggling.

Was there any basis for it? We know from a document in the Royal Archives, Captain Somerset's statement, that late on the evening of the 10th, when the Prince was asking all concerned to add their signatures to the undertaking he remarked that Gordon-Cumming denied the charges, whereupon Lycett Green flared up at once with, 'Oh, does he sir? Then have him here and I'll tell him to his face that he's a cheat and a liar.' He was perfectly safe in saying this, for he knew by then to what lengths the courtiers would go to prevent this happening. Naturally, so far from conveying this 'challenge', they immediately soothed him and assured him that the signed undertaking would be sufficient protection for him. No doubt the other vague references to Lycett Green wanting a confrontation can be traced to this incident, and it was certainly not conveyed to Gordon-Cumming because none of them saw him again before he left.[1]

Lord Coleridge saw nothing suspicious, or malicious, or overacted, or even unchivalrous in the defendants' conduct. The reference to the Prince, the leaving of the table, the watching on the second night, all seemed natural, inevitable, just what most people would have done. No doubt the Williams-Coventry syndicate wanted to keep things quiet. With a censorious public – no subservient *plebs*, such as that of Stuart or Tudor days, but a watchful, much-judging voting demon outside – these friends of the Prince were right in trying to keep the monarchy out of a card scandal. But was it credible, was it natural, that Sir William Gordon-Cumming would strain his loyalty to such a point as to sacrifice to it his honour, which men, especially in his profession, set before all else, preferring death itself to its loss?

And then came a fine rendering of the exquisitely appropriate apt quotation from *Henry V* 'I am not covetous for gold, nor care I who doth feed upon my cost; but if it be a sin to covet honour, I am the most offending soul alive.' What Shakespeare said, that greater classic of all Englishmen, their Bible, said too : 'Let us die, but let us not stain our honour.' And yet the plaintiff's counsel would have them believe that he preferred to that precious thing the obligation to keep the world knowing that the Prince of Wales had been playing baccarat for a couple of nights at a friend's house – the innocent game of baccarat. It might not be the best method of spending one's time; but was there very much harm in it, or much risk to royalty in the disclosure of such a thing? (*Daily Graphic*)

It has been suggested, and more than suggested, nay, it has been pressed upon you, that Lord Coventry and General Williams treated the plaintiff harshly, and behaved to him as two gentlemen who had known him so long ought not to behave. If it were so, I don't know that it would have much to do with single important, and very melancholy issue you have to try . . . They were sensible men, and they saw that neither in his desire to be confronted with his accusers nor in his desire to go to the Commander-in-Chief did he really persevere, and the conclusion they came to was undoubtedly hostile to the plaintiff . . . The Prince of Wales, who came as a witness, and who swore to speak the truth, he also, it is clear, was of the same opinion. . . .

Hum-hm-hm went on the Judge's voice in a musical murmur. Every now and then there was a moment of relief, as when the Judge, commenting on Mr Levett's remark, 'Good God, Lieutenant-Colonel Sir William Gordon-Cumming, Baronet, caught cheating at cards,' and finding it very natural, suggested as a parallel, 'My God, here is the Lord Bishop of Nova Scotia, Prelate of the Order of the Sun, found swindling !' (*Daily Graphic*)

The question of whether or not military regulations had been broken, Coleridge brushed aside as having nothing to do with the jury. He proceeded to explain to them that the *précis*, strictly speaking, was not evidence in the case at all : that it was incorrect in several particulars, about the agreement to watch and so on, But the whole thing was profoundly indifferent and the errors not important. He thus disposed of Clarke's important, and legitimate point that the Prince, Lord Coventry and General Williams had originally decided that Gordon-Cumming was guilty because of statements made to them by the Wilsons, some of which they had now withdrawn. He also brushed aside Clarke's contention that the agreement to watch had been proved 'against their oaths' because the words of the *précis* had been confirmed in the witness-box.

He mentioned that Gordon-Cumming had kept his winnings, and asked the jury if, under the circumstances, they would have done so : 'I pass no opinion, I merely ask the question.' But he left the jury in no doubt as to his opinion. This was most unfair. Obviously if Gordon-Cumming had returned the money, his opponents would have said, and with greater reason, that he was ashamed to keep it.

He referred to Clarke's contention that Lord Coventry and General Williams would not have continued to address Gordon-Cumming in so friendly a style if they had believed him guilty – but the General had explained in the witness-box that he did not think it would have been kind to change the style of his letters, and so had continued to address him as 'My Dear Bill' as he had always done. Whether General Owen Williams would stand the worse with them for having done this was for them to consider, but that that question had much to do with the case he could not say. He agreed that it was perfectly natural for Gordon-Cumming to attempt through Berkeley Levett to get the Wilsons to withdraw their accusations; it would have been a complete answer and a happy end to the whole affair.

Those are all the circumstances and all the facts of the case that I need say anything about, except one, and of that I must say something. Sir Edward Clarke, in the course of his able speech distinguished between his position as Solicitor-General and as an advocate. I do not.

He thus associated himself with the views of the Prince's friends that it was Clarke's business as an officer of the crown to defend the Prince, not to attack him.

In the course of his speech he said the true solution, or nine-tenths of it, was to save the Prince of Wales. He said royalty is great. He said royalty has been the parent of the beautiful feeling called loyalty, and loyalty has led people to sacrifice everything for their king and for their queen, and people lay down their lives for kings and princes, and thus Sir William Gordon-Cumming came to sign this document to save the

Prince of Wales. He put it much better than that, but that is what he meant . . . Do you believe that an innocent man, a perfectly innocent man, would write his name on a dishonouring document, a document which, in fact, stated that he had cheated and taken money out of the pocket of the Prince of Wales by craft and sharping, simply that it might not be made known that the Prince of Wales had played baccarat for very moderate stakes? Is not the consequence too great for the cause? Is it not attributing far too much to this spirit, a good spirit in its way, a noble spirit, I frankly admit : is it not putting an incredible weight upon it to suppose that any gentleman would allow himself, not to die but to be called a card-sharper and a cheat for the rest of his life, for fear it should be known that the Prince of Wales had done something of which many people would disapprove? I could quite understand a man giving up his all except his honour, but I cannot understand a man doing as this man did. I can understand a man giving away life, but I cannot understand a man giving away all that life is valuable for and without which it is not worth while to live. You must judge of these acts and of all that he has done exactly as you would judge the acts of any person either in the middle or in the lower class of society. And now I send you to your duty. You have a very grave and a very important duty. You have sworn to perform it, as God shall help you, according to the truth. You must not, and you will not, I am sure, perform it in any other sense than the single, simple, unalloyed desire that truth and justice should prevail. You must remember that the consequences are not yours, but the duty is, and I send you to do your duty in the noble words of a great man many years gone : I divert them from his purpose to adapt them to this case. When you pass your judgement upon Sir William Gordon-Cumming's honour, I pray you recollect your own.

The jury retired at twenty-five minutes past three.

Five – ten minutes passed, and they did not return. By a single impulse every eye was fixed on the man whose social life hung in the balance. He bore the ordeal well. He clasped his gloved hands on his stick, and with composed features waited. His counsel's face flushed with excitement, even Sir Charles Russell, assured as he must have been of his laurels, looked moved. But the figure in black, crowned by the still handsome face, sat as if of stone, unmoved as the judge now reclining easily in his chair, his pretty wife by his side. In the next moment there was a movement to the right. The jury were coming back – a sure sign of doom. The cold grey eyes turned in their direction, and there rested. The calling of the names made an intolerable interval of suspense. (*Daily Graphic*)

The jury had been absent only thirteen minutes. The Associate asked, 'Gentlemen, are you agreed upon your verdict?'

THE FOREMAN : (He had a nervous tremor in his voice) We are.
THE ASSOCIATE : Do you find for the plaintiff or for the defendants?

The Foreman almost whispered, 'We find for the defendants.' This was greeted by prolonged booing and hissing from the public and the junior Bar. Mrs Wilson seized a telegraph form that was lying ready before her on the table and had the joyful news despatched at once to the Prince. Coleridge remained smiling beatifically through his gold-rimmed spectacles.

RUSSELL : Your lordship will give judgement in accordance with the findings of the jury?
COLERIDGE : Yes.

A request by the Foreman for extra pay for the jury was the signal for hissing to break out again, and it was renewed when they left their box.

There had been stealthy hissing all over the Court when the verdict was announced, the judge wisely taking no notice. It was repeated as the jury rose to leave the box – a strange, unprecedented act. Lord Coleridge turned to chat with the ladies, the audience rose, there was a deep breath – the tension was over. Still the figure of stone sat on – perhaps dazed for the moment with the shock of the stupendous doom which those dreadful words had conveyed; and then, without a word, without a tremor, walked squarely to the well of the court and disappeared into the world that will know him no more.

P.S. It was not a popular verdict. The defendants, who had the grace not to smile and who behaved with perfect dignity, were so fiercely mobbed that they had to take refuge under Mr Lewis's sheltering wing in Mr Justice North's court, and then get quietly away. (*Daily Graphic*)

'I was not a little indignant,' Clarke wrote, 'when after the trial, the sketch-book was brought to me with a request that I would put my signature to the sketch of myself which was inserted between the signed likenesses of Sir Charles Russell and Mr Asquith.'[2]

The demonstration outside the Lord Chief Justice's Court when the Wilsons emerged after the verdict was given was of a remarkable nature. Mr and Mrs Wilson and her family with Mr George Lewis came out of the court by a side door and retired to a quiet corner of the corridor. They stayed there for a few moments. Mrs Wilson taking the arm of Mr George Lewis walked out into the corridor, the members of the Wilson family following. Immediately a great crowd gathered round them. They hissed and hooted and jeered in the most excited fashion. They followed the party from one corridor to another, completely choking the narrow passages, and at one time there were fears for the safety of the party. (*Reynolds News*)

The defendants in the company of Mr George Lewis, their solicitor, passed out of the court, they were loudly hissed by the spectators in the corridor. Some attempt was made to hustle them. As the crowd became more menacing, the defendants sought refuge in Mr Justice North's Court. Here they remained for some little time while the people crowded round the doors and waited for them to leave. (*Standard*)

Finally they climbed over the bench and escaped by the judge's private entrance under the protection of a number of attendants.

It is fortunate, (says the *Birmingham Post's* London Correspondent) that the heir-apparent was at Ascot yesterday instead of being seated on the Bench next the presiding judge, as he had hitherto been throughout the hearing; for it was evident from the temper displayed by the majority of those in court after the verdict that he was thus spared the possibility of personal humiliation. The depth of popular feeling may be judged from the scene which followed when Mrs Wilson and the Tranby Croft party, escorted by their solicitor, Mr Lewis, went through the corridor and, being hissed and even hooted by the well-dressed crowd, and saluted by the epithet, 'The Watching Brigade,' only escaped personal molestation by hurrying into Mr Justice North's Court, and thence escaping by a private staircase. (*St James's Gazette*)

Meanwhile the usual large crowd had flocked to the Ascot Races. *The Times* reported :

It was only a few minutes past one o'clock when, with the sun just beginning to dispel the gloomy pall which had hung over the heath all the morning, the Servants of the Royal Hunt, with Lord Coventry, Master of the Buckhounds, in the centre, were seen coming up the course, a few yards in front of the five carriages which conveyed the Prince of Wales and the other memebers of the Royal family who were at Ascot yesterday ... The Prince and Princess of Wales, who were very respectfully greeted as they drove up the course, at once took their seats in the Queen's Stand, the lawn of which soon began to present a very animated appearance. ... (*The Times*)

But the drive up the course had been attended also by boos and catcalls mingling with the cheers, and cries of 'Oh! Baccarat!' and 'Have you brought your counters?' 'There's ten pounds more to pay here, sir,' and 'If you can't back a horse you can baccarat!' and similar witticisms. 'A most unpleasant ordeal,' according to Princess Mary of Teck, who was in one of the carriages.[3]

> Everyone tries to be in his place before the royal procession arrives at one o'clock. The rich scarlet and gold of the liveries of the royal servants can be seen afar off, glittering in the green landscape, long before the carriages sweep up the centre of the course. Lord Coventry trots solemnly in the front on a big bay, looking not unlike a respectable family coachman in the green livery coat and top boots of the Master of the Buckhounds. No cheer greets him. There was even a little groaning among the stern moralists of the turf. Nor have the royal party any ovation. Never has it been received with such coldness ... The Prince of Wales, however, looked sufficiently well pleased with himself in his dark grey frock coat and had apparently determined to banish from his mind all recollection of his recent appearances on Lord Coleridge's bench. (*Pall Mall Gazette*)

He had been kept well informed of the progress of the trial and in the course of the afternoon he was able to assure Captain Somerset that the summing-up was going well. He was heard to remark to a friend, as if he were mentioning an interesting fact in natural history, 'George Lewis tells me that the Solicitor-General's speech will give the Radicals 100,000 votes at the general election.'

CHAPTER TWELVE

A Chorus of Condemnation

The verdict in this famous case appears to be quite unjustified. Clarke always maintained that Gordon-Cumming was innocent : there is little doubt that he was right. If we put this question : would a man who was cheating, or who was intending to cheat, deliberately put the counters he was staking on a sheet of white paper where they were clearly visible, instead of putting them, as the other players were doing, on the tapestry cloth of all sorts of colours which, as Captain Somerset stated, 'made it very difficult to see the chips on the table?' There seems to be no alternative but to accept that for a man to act in this way, or for us to believe that he would act in this way, would be contrary to sense. He would not have made his stakes as conspicuous as possible. This entails :

(1)   That Stanley Wilson was mistaken. We have to disallow his evidence about the first night's cheating, the only evidence in the whole trial against Gordon-Cumming that can be called unprejudiced or unpremeditated. On all other occasions witnesses saw only what they expected to see, or what they had been told they would see.

(2)   That Berkeley Levett's evidence must be eliminated altogether, that most conscientious of witnesses, leaving no reason whatsoever for judgement to be given in his favour against Gordon-Cumming, for his accusation related only to the first night's play.

When we accept that the evidence of the witnesses relating to the first night's play must have been mistaken, we immediately see that the evidence for cheating on the second night is even less convincing. It was probably not so well understood in those days, though Clarke explained it clearly enough, that under stress of emotion a suggestion tends to transform itself into a reality, as when we sometimes hear the door bell ring before it has done so when we are expecting a visitor. Mrs Wilson's evidence particularly reads like a case history from a text-book of suggestion and auto-suggestion : she forgets what she wants to forget and she sees what she expects to see as soon as it is suggested to her, though the others watching, and the more experienced players whose business it is to observe the stakes, don't see what she claims to have seen.

We must conclude, therefore, that Mrs Wilson, Stanley Wilson and

Ethel were quite pleasant, inexperienced and certainly talented people who were simply deluding themselves. 'There is nothing makes a man suspect much,' Bacon observed, 'more than to know little.' Having made their original accusations, they found it impossible to go back on them : they would have been lost, as Mrs Wilson said, (socially, that is,) so they made a brave show of it, except poor Mr Lycett Green who had none of the talent of the Wilson family and had to fall back on almost total loss of memory – apart from the actual alleged instances of cheating which he was able to discuss with the rest of the family. From the descriptions of the newspaper representatives who were there, we can see that the Wilsons in the witness-box were not simply saying what they thought they had seen, they were giving perfectly rehearsed and polished theatrical performances.

What we cannot answer on Mrs Wilson's behalf, except by pleading that she was flustered by her responsibilities as a hostess on this exciting occasion, is her friend Lady Middleton's cry from the heart, 'Oh, Mrs Wilson if I had thought your son or husband was doing such a thing I should have warned him privately, for your sake.'

Lycett Green was in a different category. It can hardly be a co-incidence that the one man who was determined, scandal or no scandal, to bring down Lieutenant-Colonel Sir William Gordon-Cumming, Bart., arrogant man about town and notorious seducer of young wives, was the husband of the charming Ethel Wilson. All his actions and emotions indicate a deep personal motive. Russell's and Coleridge's descriptions of him as a sort of Mr Steadfast for Truth making his accusations rather in sorrow than in anger was ludicrously incorrect – he made his accusations in anger and with no sorrow at all. The most probable explanation is that, consciously or unconsciously, he feared Gordon-Cumming on Ethel's account. It was quite natural that he should. Clarke could not take this line without lowering his client's reputation in the eyes of the jury, Russell had no wish to question the motives of his principal witness, and neither of them could even mention such a possibility without throwing Ethel's reputation to the sensation-hungry reporters. Lord Coventry and General Williams should have thought of it and not taken Lycett Green's accusations at their face value without further investigation. But after their first panic at the prospect of a scandal involving both the Prince and themselves, and having allowed themselves to be the bearers of Lycett Green's ultimatum to Gordon-Cumming that he would be accused on Doncaster Racecourse in the morning unless he signed an undertaking implying that he had cheated at cards, they simply blundered on, trying to justify their behaviour by assuring everyone that he was guilty. The ultimatum was, of course a threat to the courtiers and to the Prince as well, all of whom had an interest in the scandal not being published, and Gordon-Cumming was expected to get them all out of trouble by merely signing the under-taking. No wonder they exercised 'extreme pressure'!

The Prince's answer to the juryman on the second day of the trial seems to have had little effect on the final verdict. After all, he was not saying that he believed Gordon-Cumming to be guilty then, but when he first heard the accusations from Lord Coventry and General Williams. Russell, following his brief, had already hammered in the point again and again that all three of them believed him guilty, so it was nothing new, but perhaps hearing it from the Prince's own lips had a certain effect, and jurymen might have been tempted to shuffle out of their responsibility by adopting the same view as the Prince.

This effect however, must have been largely dispelled by subsequent events and particularly by Clarke's final speech. The writer of *The Times'* leading article of 10th June does not mention the Prince's statement as one of the important factors influencing the jury's decision. They were, he says, the Wilsons' direct evidence, the belief of Gordon-Cumming's friends, his signing of the fatal document and his subsequent behaviour :

> Twist and turn how he would, Sir Edward Clarke could not get over this cumulative mass of evidence. The five witnesses might have been mistaken, they might have seen what they expected to see, but how were they to persuade those old friends of the accused, Lord Coventry and General Owen Williams, unless Sir William's own demeanour had supported the charge? (*The Times*)

It is interesting to note that the writer of this leading article believed Gordon-Cumming's friends judged him guilty from his demeanour, whereas in fact they judged him guilty without seeing him and therefore could have told nothing from his demeanour. It is a tribute to the skill with which Russell and Coleridge succeeded in whitewashing these two men who had caused so much havoc, that the writer unconsciously invented a respectable motive for their behaviour. The *Pall Mall Gazette* listed the same four factors as having been decisive for the jury.

And what are we to think of a judge who states in his address to the jury, 'We have nothing to do with things that are not on the surface'? Surely to-day he would be ridiculed. But of course he only said it to damage the plaintiff's case, Clarke having drawn attention to some important factors beneath the surface that condition super-ficial behaviour – the suggestibility of the human mind, the distortion which, it is sufficiently well known, may be caused by the workings of suspicion that can re-arrange impressions in the memory.

After Clarke's final speech had been enthusiastically received, a verdict in favour of Gordon-Cumming might have been expected with confidence, but then Coleridge exercised all his ingenuity to sway the jury against him, answering and belittling Clarke's case point by point, and echoing Russell's words in a milder but more deadly form exactly as if he too were working from Mr George Lewis's brief. Misrepresentation of facts on the part of a counsel in an attempt to win a case for his client may be accepted as part of the game, but it is the duty of the judge not to incline to either side : he must remain upright, hold the balance even, and put the case for both sides fairly to the jury. This Coleridge most certainly did not do.

It was a very interesting situation : while Coleridge was proclaiming that it was beyond his comprehension that a man should sacrifice his honour to serve the Prince, was not he doing precisely this himself, for what could be more dishonourable than an unjust Lord Chief Justice? And what other motive could he have had for his injustice than to serve the Prince? Friendship for Russell and dislike of Clarke, don't seem to be strong enough motives for so serious an offence. If Gordon-Cumming had secured a favourable verdict, the Prince would have been blamed for having tried to prevent an innocent man from getting a fair hearing, instead of a guilty one. It was from this that Coleridge saved him.

How are we to explain the almost unprecedented demonstration against the jury? Coleridge had drummed it into their heads for four hours that Gordon-Cumming was guilty, and had ended – most unkindest cut of all – by implying that it was their duty as honourable men to give their verdict against him; reminding them also that the Prince, who had been so very much in evidence all through the trial, also thought him guilty. Who were they to dispute it? Well, they were a jury. They could not have helped noticing, as representatives of the Press did, that the judge was biased. This put them in a situation of particular responsibility, for one of their main functions was to prevent a biased judgement being delivered. So they were faced with a very difficult problem, and not one that could be resolved in thirteen minutes. Did they weigh, discuss and consider the validity of the many points that the judge had put to them in four hours of meticulous argument? Not a single one of them – it would have been impossible in the time. It was a jury with a singularly inadequate conception of its duty. Clarke had entrusted to them the honour of a British officer – but Russell knew them better. They had earned their extra money, and they wanted to go home. It was probably their precipitancy as much as their unpopular verdict that provoked, and deserved, the hostility of the spectators, which, according to the *National Observer*, 'reflected a considerable body of public opinion out-of-doors.' This paper called Coleridge's summing-up 'a melancholy and flagrant violation of the best traditions of the English bench.'

The *Birmingham Express* had doubts about the verdict. The *Star* said, 'I wish the jury could have given their verdict the other way,' is what everyone feels at the Baccarat Trial. The *Birmingham Gazette*: 'We could have wished his condemnation rested on surer proof of his guilt.' The *Daily Chronicle* was more emphatic :

> Yesterday the baccarat case, which may perhaps have as malign an influence on the career of the Prince of Wales as the affair of 'The Diamond Necklace' had on the fate of Marie Antoinette came to an end. The jury, to the amazement of all cool critics of the evidence, found a verdict for the defendants.

This means, the article continues, that Gordon-Cumming, after playing cards for twenty years without provoking the least suspicion, had suddenly plunged into an orgy of cheating, using a trick which must have taken him long toilsome years of practice to acquire, in order to win a few pounds that he didn't need from the Prince of Wales upon whose good will and patronage his future depended.

> Sir Charles never seemed to put his heart into his address. On the other hand his clients had the inestimable advantage of the impassioned advocacy of the Lord Chief Justice of England, and they must therefore draw their own conclusions from the fact that even he was unable to suggest a theory rationally accounting for the plaintiff's sudden lapse into crime. All the probabilities of the case were against the story told by the Wilson family. (*Daily Chronicle*)

Truth was equally scornful of the verdict : it was edited by a Member of Parliament, Labouchere, who made a specialty of exposing gambling swindles. He wrote :

> I say as an expert that never is cheating done in this fashion. The cheat places, not one counter as his stake, but a handful of counters or coins, and to these adds several, the object of the handful being that neither the banker nor any of the players should perceive the addition. I cannot conceive the most dishonest of human beings staking one large, bright-coloured counter and then adding two to it; nor can I conceive this palpable manoeuvre being performed several times without the banker and several of the punters perceiving it. . . .
> Which is more probable? That Sir William cheated in this obvious

fashion, and that no one who had not been told that he had cheated on a previous occasion saw him, or that those in the secret were so convinced that he was a cheat, that they took every movement made by him as confirmation of a foregone conclusion. Let a man suspect that another will do something, and his evidence as to his doing it is comparatively worthless. The condition of the minds of those in the secret is shown by the conduct of Lieutenant Levett. He was exactly opposite Sir William. Yet, during the whole evening, he says that he did not look at him. Why? Because he was convinced that his brother officer would cheat, and he did not wish to witness so painful a sight. Men and women in this frame of mind would only have to look, in order to perceive what they expected to see . . . On evidence such as that of these five witnesses I would not hang a dog, much less consign a distinguished officer to a living death.

I confess I attach very little importance to Sir William having signed a document which was tantamount to an admission of the truth of the charge. What had happened? The lads and ladies, still keeping everything secret from the sensible owner of the house in which all these pranks were being performed, took Lord Coventry and General Williams into their confidence. It would seem by the *précis* that these two wiseacres drew up, that they had a very vague idea themselves as to what the exact allegations against Sir William were. They, however, picked up in a general way, that certain persons accused him of cheating, and having done so, they agreed, before asking him what he had to reply to the charge, that he ought to sign an admission of guilt. Suddenly they burst in upon him while he was dressing for dinner. He denied the charge indignantly. They used 'the utmost pressure' to force him to sign. They told him that there were five witnesses against him, and that, in the face of this, his denial was worthless. They gave him to understand that, if only he would sign, the whole business would remain a secret for ever. If he did not, he was to be publicly denounced as a swindler. the next day on the Doncaster Racecourse. 'What shall I do?' he despairingly asked. 'You are my old friends; advise me.' 'Sign,' was the answer.

The scene reminds me of what must often have occurred in the dungeons of the Inquisition. 'Recant, or –' And often the victim did recant.

Sir William, it is urged, might have asked to be confronted with his accusers, but he did not. I am not surprised at this, since accusers and accused were to meet before two judges who had drawn up the sentence before they had interrogated the accused . . . So he signed, protesting that he was innocent, and preferring that a dozen persons should account him a cheat, than that he should be publicly denounced as on evidence against which the old friends told him his denial would count for nothing. This was foolish, but it was not inconsistent with innocence. I have known many charges of cheating, and charges proved on far more substantial grounds than this one. Yet I never knew of one in which the guilty person signed his own condemnation. The more hardened the cheat, the stronger the evidence against him, the more did they deny the charge.

And why did the old friends give him this strange counsel? Why did they urge him to sign the document? Lord Coventry tells us. It stands recorded in his diary :– 'To keep the name of the Prince of Wales out of it, and in consideration of their host and hostess who were suffering from domestic affliction.' Host indeed! they had not condescended even to let their host know what had occurred.

The *Pall Mall Budget* of 12th June illustrated Lebouchere's article by a take-off of a picture by the Hon. J. Colier, entitled 'Waiting for the Accused'. The Prince of Wales as the Grand Inquisitor is shown seated at a table with Lord Coventry and General O. Williams on either side, the Prince of Wales's Feathers and 'Ich Deal' prominently displayed on the canopy behind him. To one side Stanley Wilson and Berkeley Levett are heating up the instruments of torture and saying, 'This is too hot, old chappy.'

The *Christian World* in a leader on 'Our Prince's Amusement', wrote :

The throne rests on a foundation of public opinion only, and a few more scandals like that of Tranby Croft will destroy the foundation, and Edward VII will never be crowned . . . Royalty in these iconoclastic days has many growing prejudices to combat, and it cannot afford to outrage the public conscience, and fly in the face of all the Churches of a religious people . . . While the Church that prays for the Prince of Wales at its every service, the church of which he will one day be the head, unites with every nonconformist body in condemning gambling as a sin and a public danger, and appeals to him to use his incalculable influence as the leader of English society to discourage it, the Heir to the Throne, it appears, carries with him baccarat counters from house to house. . . .

The social reformer, W. T. Stead, in his *Review of Reviews*, estimated the number of millions of times the Prince had been prayed for in the churches, and asked what was the result – 'the baccarat scandal!' The Fifth Form at Rugby School sent in the following topical quotation :

> If that a Prince useth hasarderie
> He is by common opinion
> Yhold the lesse in reputation.
> > *The Pardoner's Tale: Chaucer.*

The *Methodist Times* said :

This trial has once more illustrated the folly and rottenness of the ethical code which rules so-called 'society' . . . It is an awful calamity that the immense social authority of the Prince of Wales should be employed to encourage and extend gambling ! Sycophants and flatterers, among whom it is very painful to be obliged to include Sir Charles Russell, are already trying to pooh-pooh the significance of these disclosures, and it is to be feared that His Royal Highness is surrounded by many persons who will mislead him . . . No one can doubt what the late Prince Consort would have said if he had been among us.

The Times suggested that the Prince too should sign an undertaking never to touch a card again, and this was endorsed by resolutions passed at conferences of the various Non-conformist Churches. The Bishop of Carlisle and the Bishop of Durham preached indignantly against the Prince's way of life, and so did Dr Furze at Westminster Abbey. The Rev Dr Parker, preaching at the City Temple, said, 'Long live the *Queen* !' Political and Trade Union meetings registered protests. Comments in the dominions were equally severe.

The *Manchester Guardian* said that decent people throughout the country had followed the reports of that miserable case day by day with growing shame and indignation, the *Nottingham Express* that the British Empire was humiliated, the *Liverpool Courier* that the whole affair was disgraceful and reflected dishonour and shame on everyone concerned, and so it went on, column after column of violent indignation filled the newspapers for days after the verdict. There was even a ridiculous rumour credited to Skittles, the courtesan, that the Prince had played baccarat behind the scenes during the hearing of the case – which would have been impossible considering the hours we know he spent in Court and the public engagements he fulfilled.

On the side of the Prince, there was another long article in the *Pall Mall Gazette* in the unmistakable style of Mr Lewis, justifying his clients. The *Observer*, reversing the order of events in a rather laughable way, commented, 'The verdict may be said to have been endorsed by the presiding judge . . .' and added, concerning the Prince's part in the negotiations, 'At all events the error in judgement, if error there was, was due to the kindliness of heart which has rendered the Prince so popular amongst his countrymen. . . .'

The *Daily Telegraph* praised 'the nobly comprehensive and eloquent summing-up of the Lord Chief Justice . . . He fulfilled his duty perfectly, displaying nothing but impartial desire for the truth. . . .'

Among the many letters to the press from ex-officers and others, protesting against the encouragement given to gambling, or criticising or defending the Prince, was this one of a different kind :

To the Editor, Pall Mall Gazette. – There is one point which doesn't seem to have been investigated, but it is of importance. I hope you will admit a few lines on the subject. General Williams wrote to Sir William Gordon-Cumming that he was at liberty to state that great pressure had been brought to bear on him to induce him to sign the celebrated paper. It came out in evidence that this pressure was a threat to denounce Sir William as a cheat on Doncaster Racecourse. Nothing more serious than this could happen to a man whether innocent or guilty. It is not to be wondered at that Sir William's mind was powerfully influenced by it. The point I wish to draw attention to is that no one asked whose intention it was to denounce Sir William in this manner. That the Wilson family could have meant to treat their guest in this manner seems absolutely incredible, and one is thus driven to think that this terrible threat must have originated with General Williams, and been used by him in order to bring the greatest possible pressure to bear. General Williams is, as we all know, the Prince of Wales's man body and soul, and it was clearly his instinct and, indeed, his duty, to shield the heir to the throne whoever else might suffer. The Lord Chief Justice endeavoured to minimise the scandal which must attach to His Royal Highness, but nothing more serious than has actually occurred could have been anticipated, and certainly, from General Williams's point of view no sacrifice of himself or of his old friend would have been too great to avoid the lamentable exposure which has produced such a deep impression on the public. I am, yours obediently – June 12th

So much had been said and written about the case, and Russell and Coleridge had so surrounded the Wilsons with the aura of righteousness, that to the writer of this letter, and no doubt to many others, it now seemed 'absolutely incredible' that the Wilsons were going to denounce their guest on Doncaster Racecourse, but with Mr Lewis's brief before us we cannot escape from the fact that that was their intention. After all, Lycett Green had already denounced Gordon-Cumming to seven people, within a few hours; we cannot believe that he would have stopped doing so if there had been no compact of secrecy. It was not for this reason that the public turned against the Wilsons, but because of the unjust summing-up leading to an unpopular verdict in their favour, and because of their plan to watch their guest's play. The *Scotsman* said about them, 'Probably there are few country houses in Great Britain where the family would think it proper to watch one of their guests in a game of cards, or to talk of what had been done.' *The Times* commented, 'With or without their will, the family have been the cause of the social death of a distinguished man. When a man dies physically those who have to do with him remain in seclusion for a time. Those can hardly do less who are indirectly responsible for this far more tragic calamity, the ruin of a fine career.'

The *National Observer* put the matter more bluntly :

> As to the singular collection of persons generally spoken of as the Wilsons, they have passed, we hope, from the pages of contemporary history as suddenly as they appeared upon it, and if they never re-emerge from their native obscurity no one will regret it. Themselves least of all, if their brief occupation of the thoughts and tongues of ladies and gentlemen has taught them anything of the feelings with which such persons as they, and such doings as theirs, are generally regarded.

General Owen Williams, like the Wilsons, could not go back on anything, could not give an inch, or admit in the slightest degree that he had been wrong. Preserving his complete self-approval to the last, he wrote to Lycett Green, 'I cannot see that any of the Tranby Croft party can *in any way* reproach themselves, with the exception of the cheat,' and he continued,

> It was clear as anything could possibly be that Cumming had cheated in a barefaced and systematic manner, and this being the fact, his offence could not be condoned and we were as lenient as possible under the circumstances . . . The truth is he is a real bad one, and he instanced the old adage of the pitcher too often to the well. Now that his crime has been found out, there are 50 people to give instances of his cheating elsewhere.'[1]

Which simply shows what happens when you give a dog a bad name – and shows also very aptly the same process at work that went on in the Wilsons minds once they had been told he was cheating. An interesting American view appeared in The *Albany Law Journal* :

> The Cumming trial, now going on in England, reveals a state of English society which is almost incomprehensible to American gentlemen. It shows that the unlawful practice of gaming, and for large stakes, is tolerated among English gentlemen of the upper class, and that the heir-apparent to the throne of the British empire will condescend to act as 'banker' on occasion . . . Then the trial reveals the fact of an English gentleman of high rank capable, or thought to be capable, of cheating his friends and associates at gaming, in the presence of his prospective sovereign. Then it reveals a conspiracy of his fellow-gamblers to disgrace him without giving him the benefit of a public denial. And it reveals the willingness of the heir-apparent to promote the conspiracy without giving the accused a fair opportunity to vindicate himself; – it amounts to this : if five of the Prince's boon companions agree to stigmatize a sixth, it is all up with the unfortunate man in the prince's estimation; he turns his back on him as coolly as Prince Hal turns his back on poor Jack, after he has become King in the play. Then the trial reveals the English notion of justice in that

the Prince is praised for obeying a subpoena. And it reveals the extraordinary reverence of the English bar in the tenderness with which the Prince was treated on the witness stand, and the homage with which he was accorded a seat by the side of the judge. All this seems strange to democrats . . . Whatever the merits or the result, there will be very little sympathy in America with Sir William. He must abide the verdict of the company he trains in. It may very well be that the whole party were not in a condition to know exactly what the facts were, and it would be rather to their credit if it were so.

Of Sir Edward Clarke, who was unwell for several days after the trial and had to return his brief for the Wiedemann-Walpole breach of promise case, the *Evening Post* of New York wrote,

Sir Edward Clarke's attack on the Prince of Wales was something unprecedented in the legal and political annals of England, and it will be interesting to see whether Lord Salisbury keeps him in office after so bold a departure from the established forensic usage.

It was rumoured in London that he had done for himself by his plain speaking, but the London Correspondent of the ultra-Tory *Sheffield Telegraph* wrote that for the sake of the Prince he was sorry to say that Clarke's speech represented pretty accurately the majority of ministerial opinion. On this situation the *Albany Law Journal* commented :

Out of all this unwholesome mess there emerges one redeeming possibility. Is it true, or was it only the suggestion of some subtle transatlantic humorist, that Sir Edward Clarke is threatened with social ostracism and political ruin for the admirable way in which he conducted his client's cause? What a spectacle it would be for the democratic masses the world over; what a theme for the satirist of royalty and snobbery, if this able lawyer, the solicitor-general of England, should be expelled from the London clubs, dismissed from his high office, 'disciplined' (Heaven save the mark !) by the Queen – for what? For 'disloyalty' in having, in the course of his argument in court, referred temporately but 'disrespectfully' to the royal gambler whose folly had brought the whole sad business into court ! We sincerely believe that the London clubs and London society and their Royal Highnesses would be capable of this contemptible exhibition of spite and snobbery, but it is almost too good to expect. Sir Edward will probably be obliged to get his advertising in some other way.

There was a great deal of speculation about who had betrayed the secret, the general opinion, the general belief rather, being that the Prince had told Lady Brooke and that she had spread the story. Labouchere commented, 'I should rather ask who did not betray it. Mr Green had no secrets from his wife. May not each of those entrusted with the secret have had someone from whom they had no secrets?' The London correspondent of the *Birmingham Post* wrote :

> The Prince of Wales, I have the best reason for stating, feels keenly certain of the criticisms which were passed by the press on Wednesday about his connection with the Tranby Croft baccarat scandal. One comment, in particular, appears to His Royal Highness and his immediate friends to be unduly harsh and uncalled for, and that is the one which suggested that as he alone of the signatories of the by now historic paper was not asked in the witness-box whether he had betrayed the secret, it was either he who had done so, or that one of the others had committed perjury. His Royal Highness, without, of course, accepting the second alternative, absolutely denies the first; and it can only be regretted, therefore, that the question was not put to him, because the name of one moving in the highest society – a name that was not once mentioned in the course of the trial – is being very freely given by rumours here as that of the person who first talked. . . .

Gordon-Cumming when he lost the case immediately resigned from all his clubs. As *The Times* put it :

> He is, in fact, condemned by the verdict of the jury to social extinction. His brilliant record is wiped out and he must, so to speak, begin life again. Such is the inexorable social rule. A man who defrauds a friend whom he meets at the card table has forfeited his honour. He has committed a mortal offence. Society can know him no more.

On leaving the Law Courts he went to Florence Garner who was staying with Lord and Lady Thurlow. He told her all that had happened, and again suggested that their engagement should be broken off. But, being in love, she refused to give him up in spite of all that her friends and family could do.

> It was announced yesterday that Miss Florence Josephine Garner in company with another lady have applied for and obtained at the Bishop of London's registry a special marriage licence for herself and Sir William Gordon-Cumming. (*Pall Mall Gazette*)

Thus on 10th June, the day following the verdict, at a few minutes before eleven, Gordon-Cumming was sitting with his best man, Major Vesey Dawson of the Coldstream Guards, in the front pew of Holy Trinity Church, Sloane Street, Chelsea, listening to an army of workmen installing a new organ with loud hammering. The only other occupant of the large

tomb-like building was a lady journalist from the *Nottingham Express*.
This is her description of the scene :

> Sir William was, of course, faultlessly attired in a frock coat and pearl-grey
> gloves . . . he looked fatigued and worn, and appeared to be in a far from
> cheerful frame of mind. Presently a carriage and pair drove up to the
> church from which there alighted Miss Garner, Lord and Lady Middleton,
> and a young lady who was understood to be the bride's sister. After a
> momentary hesitation, as though not quite knowing what to do next in
> the absence of a master of ceremonies, the party walked up the path to the
> church door where they were received by the verger and conducted up
> the aisle.

The bride was a tiny slim figure, exceedingly vivacious and very dark :
she wore a dove-grey walking dress with very wide sleeves and a black
straw hat. She carried her gloves in her hand. There were no bridesmaids.
The ceremony was performed by the Rev Mr Walker, Senior Curate of
Holy Trinity.

> As she walked smilingly up the aisle, while the bridegroom advanced to
> meet her, she seemed bubbling over with gaiety and good spirits – a strong
> contrast to Sir William's evident gloom. As the ceremony proceeded Sir
> William seemed to lose the nervousness and to throw off the melancholy
> which had marked him upon his arrival. The bride was given away by
> Lord Thurlow, and placed her hand in that of the bridegroom with a
> winning smile that was very pleasant to see.

Upon leaving the church, the bridal party drove to Lord Middleton's
house for the wedding breakfast. Then Sir William and Lady Gordon-
Cumming went by train to Nottingham and drove to Wollaton Hall
which the Middletons had lent them for the honeymoon. On their arrival
he declined a request for an interview, but sent a courteous reply in writing
to the *Nottingham Express*, in which he said, 'My own sentiments were
fully expressed in Sir E. Clarke's speech on Monday, and I am of opinion
that, but for the gross partiality shown by the judge in his summing-up
the case would have gone very differently.'

A representative of the Press Association had an interview with a
gentleman whom he described as an intimate friend of Gordon-
Cumming's who had stuck by him through thick and thin. They discussed
the gossip concerning Lady Brooke. . . .

> In high places the name of a lady of title and rank has been freely
> mentioned in society as having been one of the factors in the case, and
> also the betrayer of the secret. The correspondent was assured by Sir

William Gordon-Cumming's friend that the baronet positively declared that there was not a scintilla of truth in the widespread allegations made against the lady in question. The party really altogether responsible was a lady whose name is well known, not only to Sir William Gordon-Cumming, but also to a large section of the general public.

And then the friend gave Gordon-Cumming's views about the case in greater detail:

Sir William, he said, is still smarting under what he considers to be a great wrong, and is not sparing in his condemnation of the Lord Chief Justice. The plaintiff in the action went into court in quite a friendly frame of mind, with not the slightest animus against any of the defendants, several of whom he still wished to regard as his personal friends. The case, he states, was opened under the natural impression that, having heard a full and ample explanation, the defendants would have come forward and withdrawn all imputations, admitting that an unfortunate mistake had been made. To the surprise of Sir William, they did not adopt this course, and then the Solicitor-General, to use Sir William's expressive language, 'took off the gloves' and prepared to contest the battle in as determined a fashion as Sir Charles Russell evidently intended to do.

Although Sir Edward Clarke is on the losing side, his client is full of praise and very grateful for the 'extraordinarily powerful' address delivered by him. Sir William felt that it had swept away many a doubt, and that it had exercised a great influence upon the jury. He cannot see how the jury can possibly have made up their minds against him prior to the summing-up. Almost from the first words the Lord Chief Justice spoke, it was seen by Sir William that the summing-up was not going to be in his favour. He is of opinion that nothing could be more biassed from start to finish than what was said in the course of the tedious summary of the case. The judge proceeded, in the eyes of Sir William and his friends, to pick everything the Solicitor-General had said to pieces. Sir William had not the slightest doubt in his own mind that the summing-up of the judge influenced the jury very strongly.

Asked about the signing of the agreement, the friend said in an unmistakable tone of despondency that Sir William felt that it was an extraordinary act of folly – an act which he should never cease to regret. He did it under the strongest pressure and fully thinking that his secret would be kept. It was too much to expect that such a number of people could keep such a secret. Sir William heard nothing about it having been divulged until the month of January, but he now knew for a fact that a great many people knew about the scandal within a week after the pledge of secrecy. . . . There was, he also contended, practically no necessity why the Prince should have been consulted; but it seemed right and proper to the Wilsons that the Prince should be mixed up in the affair. Sir William, said his friend, preferred to say nothing about the parties in the case, now that it was all over. 'Of Mrs Wilson's conduct,' he had said, 'the public must judge.'

A few weeks later, however, Gordon-Cumming wrote to Clarke, thanking him for his efforts, but added 'Should we have been wiser to have fought out the case on a more *vicious* system?'

The *Daily News*, Saturday, 13th June. Removal of Sir William Gordon-Cumming from the army. The following notice appears in last night's *Gazette*. 'War Office, Pall Mall, 12th June, 1891. Scots Guards. Major and Lieutenant-Colonel Sir William Gordon-Cumming, Bart., is removed from the army, Her Majesty having no further occasion for his services. Dated 10th June, 1891.'

The following notice appeared in *The Times*, 13th June 1891 :

A Dalziel telegram states that the New York Herald has been requested by a member of the Garner family, whose action has the approval of the whole family connexion, to print the following statement :– 'Several papers have, by mistake, stated that one of the sisters of Miss Florence Garner, now Lady Gordon-Cumming, was present at her marriage. Her elder sister, Mme. la Marquise de Breteuil, is at present in New York with her husband. Her younger sister, Miss Edith Garner, is Vienna with her aunt Mrs Lawrence. The family wish to rectify this mistake; also to state that not one of Miss Garner's relations were present at her marriage. It is needless to add that, being of age, she took the step against the wishes of her entire family.

On the evening of 13th June, Sir William and Lady Gordon-Cumming arrived at Grantham at eight o'clock, dined at the Angel Hotel and left by the Great Northern express train for Forres, the nearest station to Altyre, his beautiful Scottish estate. The people there had worked all night to prepare a reception for them, and when they arrived the station was decorated with flags and bunting and there was a crowd to welcome them. The whole of the Town Council were drawn up in the square outside where Provost Watson in his gold chain and robes of office presented an illuminated address. Gordon-Cumming made a suitable reply, saying how much he appreciated their kind and cordial welcome. Everyone wanted to shake hands with him. When he handed his bride into the waiting landau, the people unyoked the horses and dragged it for half a mile through the streets, the town band leading the way.

That the Prince and society considered him a social outcast mattered not at all to his own people. The Gordon-Cummings in the North were a symbol for all that was brave and chivalrous – he could not have been guilty of what the despised Southerners accused him. 'Fortunate Sir William!' wrote the *Albany Law Journal*, 'Heroic American Girl! What need you care for the London Clubs or the army register or for 'society'. Have you not all these and more on that Scotch estate?' And it commented further,

> We do not believe that when his Royal Highness was 'banking' on his wealthy friends, the Wilsons, he accidentally gambled away his royal mother's throne. He is no fool, is this long-deferred heir-apparent, but a shrewd, clear-headed man of the world, with an eye to the main chance, who does the functions that pertain to his vice-presidential office with consummate tact and invariable success, whose vices are the vices of an English gentleman and are not unnecessarily paraded before the public, and who is tremendously popular with all classes of the English people. He gambles, of course, and the Dissenters are shocked and pass resolutions expressing their sentiments, beautifully engrossed copies of which they send him by first mail; he shows that he is capable of sacrificing the reputation of an old and honoured friend, and then of violating the regulations of the army of which he is the head in order to keep secret the scandalous affair in which he finds himself entangled, and we intimate that he is no gentleman – according to American standards – and our Anglomaniacs tremble for the monarchy. Have no fear, gentle friends! That venerable support of American society will never fall through the indiscretions of Albert Edward. He will die a king, if he lives long enough. . . .
>
> No, if the American people 'dearly love a lord,' as they are accused of doing, the English people still bend the knee to royalty, with much the homage of their fathers. And while we are unable to agree with our lurid contemporary, the *Sun*, in the opinion that the Prince's conduct in this affair has been manly, discreet and in every way commendable, and that it will have the effect of increasing his hold on the popular affections, but are convinced that his conduct has been immoral, unmanly and despicable – he nevertheless acted like a prince (*noblesse oblige*) and we do not believe that the affair will seriously prejudice him at home. Probably he doesn't care very much what is thought of him over here. We wouldn't if we were in his place.
>
> It must be said that the verdict of the jury in the Cumming trial hasn't helped matters much. It was expected to find a verdict for the defendants, and, like a good English jury, did as it was expected. Probably Sir William was guilty, but we have our doubts. The letter and confession are damaging, but not conclusive. Is not Sir William also an Englishman? and was it not necessary to save the Prince? We democrats don't know what that means, but the pressure must have been more than a loyal subject of the Queen could bear. . . .

The Prince of Wales had written on 10th June to Prince George who was serving with the Royal Navy in the West Indies :

The Cumming trial came to a close yesterday with the unanimous verdict for the defendants. This has been a great relief to my mind after the spiteful way in which the Solicitor-General (Sir E. Clarke) attacked me. The newspapers in their articles, many of them, have been very unpleasant and spiteful, but I must grin and bear it as I may. I have the implicit conviction that I have acted perfectly straightforwardly and honourably in the matter, thank God! The army and society are well rid of such a damned blackguard. The crowning point of his infamy is that he this morning married an American young lady, Miss Garner, sister of Madame de Breteuil, with money![2]

And on 14th June he wrote to his sister, the Princess Royal:

Thank God that detestable trial reached its determination on the day you wrote and the verdict was for the defendants which was a great relief to my mind as any difference of opinion on the part of the jury would have been fatal. I have had a most disagreeable and painful time of it on account of the personal remarks that have been made about me. The press has also been very severe and cruel (because they know I cannot defend myself.) . . . Fancy that dreadful man married an American lady, a Miss Garner, the day after the verdict, and yesterday when the newspapers announced that he was cashiered from the army, he was received in Scotland with an address of welcome from the provost with a grand reception. This certainly passes all comprehension.[3]

The Prince's friends shared his indignation against Sir Edward Clarke. Sir Francis Knollys wrote to McDonnell, Secretary to the Prime Minister, that the Cabinet 'who must know what sort of man their Solicitor-General is . . . ought to have taken steps to protect him from the public insults of one of the law officers of the crown.' McDonell replied that any attempt to restrain Clarke might have been exceedingly dangerous, to which Knollys retorted, 'HRH remembers that, in 1869, when he was called as a witness in the Mordaunt Trial, Mr Gladstone, who was then Prime Minister, took all the *indirect* means in his power (and successfully) to prevent anything being brought out in the course of the Trial that would be injurious to the Prince, or the Crown.[4]

Captain Somerset took a very personal view of the case. He wrote:

I heard Sir Edward Clarke's speech – a more magnificent forensic address never was made. But though I could not help admiring it in a way, it was a disgraceful speech to be made by Her Majesty's Solicitor-General, a law officer of the crown, as he was at the time. Sir William's explanation of having signed the paper was that he had sacrificed himself to save the scandal on account of the Prince, and all through the case his Counsel were hinting at this, and in his final peroration Sir Edward Clarke spoke as follows : 'Instances have been known in the history of the world of men, aye, and women too, who have been known to sacrifice themselves to support a tottering throne, or prop a falling dynasty.' This struck me as so appalling and shocking as coming from a law officer of the crown, that I have never forgotten it.[5]

Clarke, however, did not say this; nothing about a tottering throne or a falling dynasty – so Captain Somerset's statement is yet another instance of how emotion can distort the truth and make of it something different which the deluded person firmly believes he has heard or seen, and indeed is prepared to swear he has.

Queen Victoria was angry with everyone concerned in the case, and particularly with General Williams for dragging the Prince into it. She had objected to his appointment as Equerry on the Indian Tour and now, with bitter memories of the Lady Aylesford affair, she decided that the Williams's were a bad family.[6] Continuing her series of letters to her eldest daughter, she said that the feeling about the Prince's gambling was tremendous, that it must do him harm, and that it was the light that had been thrown on his habits which alarmed and shocked people so much, and that the monarchy almost was in danger if he was lowered and despised.[7]

Against the advice of Lord Salisbury, the Prime Minister, she tried to get the Prince to write a letter to the Archbishop of Canterbury for publication, condemning gambling as a social evil. He objected, and put it off, but at last, unhappily, complied : he wrote that he had a horror of gambling but that he considered that playing for money was not gambling so long as you could afford it. In an interview with the Archbishop of Canterbury, he emphatically denied what Mrs Wilson had asserted in the witness-box – that he had been told that Mr Arthur Wilson objected to baccarat being played in his house.[8]

There still remained to be settled the awkward question of why, when Gordon-Cumming had told the Prince and General Williams that he wished the matter to be placed in the hands of his commanding officer or the Commander-in-Chief, they had objected and dissuaded him. This was the regulation in question :

Every commissioned officer of her Majesty's service whose character or conduct as an officer and gentleman has been publicly impugned must submit the case within a reasonable time to his commanding officer or other competent military authority.

Gordon-Cumming had complied with this – if the Prince, who was a field marshal and the second highest ranking officer in the British Army, and General Williams were competent military authorities.

Certain Opposition Members of Parliament announced that they would draw the attention of the House to the scandals attaching to three officers of the army resulting from the baccarat case, and move the reduction of the Army Estimates by a field marshal's and a major-general's pay.

The Prince of Wales and General Williams knowingly and deliberately broke the army regulation which requires any such offence as cheating at cards to be reported to the officer commanding the offender's regiment, and for that wilful breach of discipline they ought to be called to account and punished. They have proved themselves unfit for the retention of their commissions. But fancy the Duke of Cambridge dismissing the Prince and the general ! It is too much to expect. The matter will doubtless be passed over. (*Glasgow Mail*)

It wasn't easy to pass over. Clarke had maintained that, as cheating at cards was a statutory offence, they could not have believed that Gordon-Cumming was guilty or they would not have conspired to cover it up – which also was an offence. Now they had both said in the witness-box that they did believe him to be guilty – and therefore they were liable to prosecution.

Upon the question being asked in Parliament, the Secretary for War, Mr Edward Stanhope, answered on behalf of the Prince that he admitted an error of judgement had been made, and regretted it : his attention had not been drawn to the regulation in question. Stanhope went on to point out that the man most to blame for not reporting the matter to his commanding officer was Gordon-Cumming himself. This answer was well received, except by a few members of the Opposition.

The *Globe* commented that Berkeley Levett had most properly expressed his deep regret for his grave mistake and that his youth and inexperience afforded some excuse for his having lent himself to a conspiracy of silence, but that no acknowledgement had come from General Williams who had left the army on half-pay and was therefore no longer amenable to the military code : 'Surely General Williams will not take advantage of being beyond the reach of military authority to set public opinion at defiance.'

It was particularly the military aspect of the question that excited the greatest interest on the Continent. The Vienna Correspondent of *The Times* wrote :

The Prince of Wales, besides being a field marshal in the British army, is the colonel-proprietor of an Austrian regiment. It is thought most strange that a field marshal and a general in the British army should condone an act on the part of a colonel in the Queen's Guards, and should make themselves privy to an arrangement by which this officer was to retain his commission and his membership of various respected clubs. Leaving the Prince of Wales altogether out of the matter, and referring only to General Owen Williams, it must be said that if any Austrian General would have acted as this general has done, he would have found himself embroiled in a deadly quarrel not only with the regiment, but with all the clubs to which the offending officer belonged, and he would have had to throw up his commission to avoid a court-martial.

. . . that His Royal Highness should have sat down to gamble with youngsters, one of whom was a mere lieutenant in the army, seems most surprising. According to all the codes of Continental military etiquette, senior officers are bound to discountenance gambling among subalterns, and it is simply unimaginable that a German, Austrian or French field marshal should sit down to win money from, or lose money to, a mere lieutenant who, if he gambles, must be paying away his father's money or prematurely squandering his inheritance.

Truth said it had learned that the German Emperor had thought fit to express his sentiments respecting the baccarat case in a letter to the Queen . . . 'Of course, under ordinary circumstances his letter to the Queen would be regarded as an impertinent meddling in matters in which he has no sort of concern, but unluckily His Majesty finds an excellent excuse for censuring sharply the Prince's strange method of dealing with an alleged offence against military honour in the fact that His Royal Highness is Colonel of the Prussian Regiment of the Bluecher Hussars. The Emperor's severe dissertation however, will be very bitterly resented, and especially as he takes, as usual, a God Almighty to a black beetle tone which is exceedingly exasperating.'

Many newspapers printed translations of Continental comments on the baccarat case :

French papers have it in large type, and long columns in the best position. In Germany the *feuilletons* have room for nothing but the 'Baccarat Skandal Prozes'. The Italians have comic illustrations on the subject, Scandinavian papers, to which all things English are welcome, are just finding out that something extraordinary is happening in London Society, something *Tilldragarsic.* . . .

La Justice in a long article on *Baccara Princier*, says 'It cannot be pleasant for the heir apparent of England to have been for such a long period the friend of a man who is accused of having cheated at cards . . .

The Prince of Wales, who is already the hero of a certain number of *aventures gaittardes*, would probably have given a respectable number of banknotes in order to avoid the publicity now given to what is called by telegrams from London, *Le Baccara-Scandale*. (*Pall Mall Gazette*)

Another leading article said that the Tranby Croft Affair was the kind at which *La Pudique Albion* might well hang her head – but the Prince was popular in Paris, and comment was not all unfavourable. There was sympathy for Gordon-Cumming also : one paper suggested that the reason why he signed the undertaking was that he feared Miss Garner would hear of the accusations. Two papers, *Figaro* and the *Gaulois*, published telegrams from London and Berlin to the effect that it was rumoured in court and official circles that the Prince of Wales would abdicate his right to the throne in favour of his eldest son, and that he would also resign his posts in the army and at Court. An enterprising journal announced that the Prince of Wales had celebrated the occasion by inaugurating a new costume for men which, it assured its readers, was now the rage and nothing else was worn by the Prince's Set : the hat was grey, the vest was grey, the trousers were blue, the overcoat nut-brown, the gloves were yellow – it was called, 'The Baccarat Scandal-Suit.'

In London the trial was a great occasion for the exercise of Cockney humour : for Rosa Lewis, the famous cook patronised by the Prince, and who had also cooked for Lycett Green's father, the family were the 'Slice-it Greens', and Berkeley Levett 'Baccarat Leveret.' A tobacconist of Leeds whose name happened also to be Wilson, sent sandwichmen through the streets bearing placards : 'Where do you get your baccar – at? Why, Wilsons, of course !'

The *Globe* published the following verses,

THE GREAT SCANDAL
(Being a Letter from a Son of Toil in London, to a
friend in the country.)

Of all the interesting things I ever read in my life,
The excitingest is certingly the late Affair in High Life.
All them what loves an intellectual talk have been in clover
In droring-room and barber's shop, a week and two days over.

When HRH appeared in Court to give his private version
Of what occurred at Tranby Croft, just like a common person,
And tell us whether or not he saw Sir William into sin fall,
Then every neck in Court was stretched – you might have heard a pin fall.

He stated how the sad affair was brought to his attention,
And how they said the horrid facts they'd never, never mention,
If the Bart. would set his name to an unfortunate agreement
To confine the awful secret to the breasts of two or three meant.

'You'd better sign this here,' they said, 'and so prevent a scandal.'
'What, no more shilling points !' say he – 'the game's not worth the candle.'
'Think what the *Star* will say,' they urged, 'and what the *Weekly Sky-sign.*'
'But you'll suppose that I've confessed,' the Bart objects, 'if I sign.'

'It can't be helped,' the Prince replied, 'there's five to one agin you,
And if the Duke of Cambridge hears of this, my lad, he'll skin you.
You woldn't like the thing made known to common Jacks and Tommies.'
Says Cumming then, 'Give me the pen,' and so signs the promise.

Then Master Arthur Wilson, who had been to Cambridge College
(A place where nobles go, I'm told, to get a taste of knowledge),
Explained his share in this affair before the excited Court,
With histrionic chick and wurve (they call him Jack for short).

He saw Sir Gordon-Cumming's game, and scarcely could believe it.
'Good Gawd !' says he, 'this here's too hot.' 'As how?' says Mr Levett.
'The chap next me's a cheating, see !' Says t'other most emphatic,
'Im-possible !' 'Look for yourself,' says Jack. ('twas quite dramatic !)

After that they said no more and went no further for the present,
For there and then to have a quarrel wouldn't have been pleasant :
For this happened in the parlour, and the Prince was in the said room,
So later on they talked the matter over in the bedroom.

Then, says Mr L., exhausted with these intellectual labours,
'Sir Gordon-Cumming, Baronight, caught cheating of his neighbours?
It makes me feel quite faint.' says he, 'to think such public woes of.'
So down he plumps upon the bed – he hadn't took his clothes off.

Then Mr Green and Mrs Green, and other folks of quality,
Give evidence to prove Sir Gordon-Cumming's immorality;
Told how they watched him nightly, their suspicions growing stronger,
Until at last they simply couldn't stand it any longer.

And Mr Levett stated how he met the Bart. in London,
Who said 'If you'll retract them words, this trouble may be undone,
'Why are you?' says the Baronight, 'Why are you so *acharny*?'
(These chaps talk French, then; fancy that !) Says Levett, 'That's all
   blarney.'

But doubtless you have read the tale, so full of solemn warning,
Since the papers told it all, most circumstantial every morning.
For sure they gave it so complete, 'twere useless to refine on 'em –
Ten columns in the *Telegraft* ! I read 'em, every line on 'em.

I blush for our aristocracks, their utter depravation;
They inspires the British workman with a honest indignation.
Their morals are the dickens, though their manners may be polished,
And their hautiness and wealth is such they ought to be abolished.

P.S.
We went to Temple Bar, to see the nobs come out;
We was nearly squashed to jelly – there was never such a rout.
But we didn't mind, we saw them; Sal observed that Mrs Wilson
Had a splendid satting costume, with a quantity of frills, on.

CHAPTER THIRTEEN

An Outcast from Society

As if one scandal on the scale of the Tranby Croft affair were not enough, another had been looming up and was approaching a climax. The Prince had first become involved in it by trying, chivalrously enough, to help a lady in distress – his friend, Lady Brooke : she was impetuous, hard-riding, extremely emotional and, according to all accounts, one of the most fascinating women of her time. She had sent a highly indiscreet letter to her lover, one of the Prince's closest friends, Lord Charles Beresford, an officer in the Royal Navy, forgetting that he had rejoined his ship. Lady Beresford opened it, and her indignation was so intense that she sent it to Mr George Lewis with the object of using it to destroy her hated rival's social position.

At Lady Brooke's earnest entreaty, the Prince went to Mr Lewis to see what could be done about getting the letter back. Mr Lewis allowed him to read it, and then locked it up in his safe again. The Prince then called upon Lady Beresford and asked for the letter : she refused to give it up. He tried a second time, with the same result. He had to go back to Lady Brooke and confess failure – but he found other ways to console her, and he crossed Lady Beresford off the list of guests who might be invited to Marlborough House. His friends, naturally, dropped her likewise.

Lord Beresford then re-appeared. He was very angry with the Prince, not so much because Lady Brooke had deserted him as because his wife had been ostracised by society. He made a nasty scene, threatened the Prince with violence and went off again, this time to the Mediterranean to take command of the cruiser *Undaunted*. In July 1891 he wrote a letter threatening to make the whole affair public if his wife were not reinstated in society. He sent this letter to Lady Beresford, instructing her to deliver it to Marlborough House on receipt of a telegram from him, and in the meantime to show it to the Prime Minister. She did so : he strongly advised her not to deliver the letter.

Lady Beresford therefore consulted Sir Edward Clarke, hoping to find in him a champion who would not be overawed by the Prince. She began by asking him if Mr Lewis could be prosecuted for showing him Lady Brooke's letter : he replied that a solicitor could not be criminally prosecuted in such circumstances, but a civil action could be brought against him.

But the main point about which she wished to consult him was whether or not she should deliver her husband's letter to Marlborough House. This was Clarke's opinion :

I have carefully considered the narrative which was sent me this afternoon . . . and I have, of course, reconsidered the letter which Lord Beresford has sent home for delivery to the Prince of Wales. I repeat my earnest hope that that letter will never be delivered. For I have a clear and strong opinion upon three points.

(1)   The Prince of Wales acted rightly in going to the solicitor as a friend of the lady and asking to see the letter. Any gentleman might and ought to act for a lady who in such circumstances applied to him for advice and help. I do not think the solicitor committed any breach of duty or of trust in showing the letter.

(2)   I think Lord Beresford would be generally and rightly condemned if for whatever reason he were to make public the fact that Lady Brooke was formerly his mistress. You or some friends of yours may interfere but your husband appears to me to be the one person who is bound to silence.

(3)   The threat which Lord Beresford made to the Prince of Wales was not justified by the circumstances and necessarily prevented the Prince from receiving you at Marlborough House. No gentleman could receive a lady at his house under a threat from her husband that he would be denounced if he did not. I should be extremely sorry if Lord Beresford were to destroy his public career by bringing about a great social scandal with no possible advantage to you. I am firmly persuaded that the public judgement would be in favour of the Prince of Wales and against Lord Beresford.

You will, I am sure, understand that I speak very plainly because I look upon the matter as extremely serious. I cannot undertake to advise further : if you act at all it should be through some relative, not your husband, who could make a strong but quiet protest about the way you have been treated.[1]

This was not the counsel the angry lady had expected, but moderation prevailed. The Prime Minister persuaded the Prince to write her a half-hearted letter of apology saying that he hadn't intended to hurt her feelings, and in March 1892 the indiscreet letter was returned to Lady Brooke to be consigned to the fire. Thus a public scandal was avoided :

it could have had serious effects, coming so soon after Tranby Croft. Lord Beresford went on to make a brilliant career for himself in the Royal Navy. The Prince and Lady Brooke remained devoted lovers for several years : their friendship lasted even when, as Countess of Warwick, she became imbued with radical ideas and tried to create the welfare state a generation or two before it actually came about : for this, added to her other extravagancies, even her large income and vast store of energy proved insufficient. Mr George Lewis was knighted two years after the Tranby Croft affair. When he retired and handed over the business to his son, he destroyed all documents that could have been a source of embarrassment to anyone – and let it be known that he had done so.

The Prince made no change in his way of life, except that he gave up baccarat and took to whist, and yet he gradually won back his popularity. By rebelling against the ideas hammered into him in his youth he had become the first truly English member of the royal family : his home life at Sandringham, on his rare holidays, was that of an English country gentleman, shooting over his estate and breeding pigs and horses. He was constantly before the public at official ceremonies at which he presided always with punctilious courtesy, and the people were pleased by his regular appearances at the important race meetings where all classes shared in the excitement – all men being equal, as the saying goes, on the turf or under it. In 1893 he had the beautiful racing yacht *Britannia* built on the Clyde : her victories over all her rivals during the next four years were hailed with delight. Then, in 1896, came the crowning triumph of his racing career – his horses *Persimmon*, won the Derby by a nose amid scenes of wild excitement. He had never been more popular.

Gordon-Cumming's ostracism by his brother officers and society was complete. 'Among a host of acquaintances,' he told his daughter, 'I thought I had perhaps twenty friends. Not one of them ever spoke to me of his racing career – his horse *Persimmon*, won the Derby by a nose again.' His handwriting which had been firm and legible now became sprawling and difficult to read. He had beautiful Altyre, he had the gloomy ancestral castle of Gordonstoun, he had a loving wife, he was surrounded by friendly people – another man might have been happy, but he longed always for the society from which he had been excluded and for the regiment from which he had been ignominiously dismissed. It was perhaps mainly as a soldier that his life had had a purpose : now it had none, except the rapidly fading hope that he might even yet be able to clear his name. When that was gone, he was as empty of purpose as the corner towers of his castle which were hollow inside with pale green daylight filtering in through slits of windows choked with ivy. At first he filled the house with people, there were great and continuous house parties which Florence did not enjoy : she had looked forward to an ideal love, she wanted to do everything for her husband, she neither needed nor wanted all these people; but he couldn't be without them.

Soon there came a slight rift. When they had been married only a few months she came running to him and demanded indignantly that one of the guests who had tried to make love to her should be turned out of the house. He replied, 'My dear child, don't be so silly. You must learn to take care of yourself.' Her sister Lita once said that both Florence and herself, owing to fastidious prejudices over which they had no control, were totally unfitted to the *milieu* in which they lived.

Florence was now alone. She had been left an orphan at the age of four, and neither of her two sisters was permitted to acknowledge her existence. She put up with the guests and tried in every way to be part of her husband's life, to join in with everything he liked to do. She even learned to shoot – an unusual accomplishment for a woman in those days. It was customary for women to dress in heavy tweeds and thick boots, join the men for a picnic lunch on the moors, and then go home again.

The next disappointment was the birth of a girl, christened Elma, when both of them had confidently expected a son and heir, but in the following year they did have a son, Alastair, who became the darling of his mother's heart, and then two more boys and another girl. They were all taught to ride so young that they never remembered having to learn, the boys were shooting rabbits at four and deer at six, professionals were engaged to teach them to play cricket, and they were brought up to play cards almost from the time they could hold them. There were no other standards of excellence except at sports and shooting things : Elma, liking neither, was banished to the schoolroom in charge of a puritanical German governess. The winters were spent at Altyre, the summers at Gordonstoun, one lovelier than most places in the world, the other more strange.

What happens to a man whose heart is in the army and in society, and who is dismissed from one and exiled from the other? And what effect does he have on his family? Fortunately there was a keen observer among them – Elma. She grew up to be a talented authoress. Here is her description of Altyre and Gordonstoun as she remembered them from her childhood :

Although the two places are only seventeen miles apart, it would be difficult to imagine a greater contrast. Climate, architecture, scenery, atmosphere, all were different. Gordonstoun is old and grey and full of evil. Huge trees surround the house, and from the flat roof one can see into the rooks' nests, rooks that blacken the sky at sunset as though cruel memories revisited the place that has known so much pain. But beyond the shelter of the trees the country is bare and bleak, a chessboard of turnip and cornfields divided by straight roads and defended here and there by windbreaks of close-grown fir trees, facing gales that blow out of Norway. A grass road without a curve in it runs for a mile and a quarter from the front door to the sea. There the cliffs are cut into smugglers' staircases and riddled with caves.

Altyre, on the other hand, is soft and well-fed, almost smug in its beauty. Beeches and limes shadow the mossy lawns; rhododendrons carpet the pine woods; where there is a clearing lilac and laburnum spring from heather and broom. Trees spread for miles in every direction till you fight free of them on moors that are not even bleak, and from these look out on the mountains of seven counties with a strip of blue Firth among them. . . .

There were about thirty indoor servants at Altrye, and outside there were gardeners, grooms, chauffeurs, ghillies,. foresters, keepers and roadmen. Sometimes the family went abroad, avoiding the fashionable places where her father would have been recognised. After one trip to the Mediterranean, he brought two girls to stay at Gordonstoun during the summer holidays. It happened at a time when Elma was beginning to notice things :

> Nothing was ever said, no word of criticism ever uttered in my presence. But I knew that Mother deeply resented these women; and I think that from this time she realised clearly that Papa never was, or had been, or could be, faithful as she interpreted faith. In marrying him she had sacrificed friends, family, youth, social position. She had expected in return complete possession, perpetual gratitude. Papa was incapable of understanding that she wanted more than he could give. There was a difference of twenty-two years in age between my parents, but ever since I can remember Mother looked, and indeed was, the elder.

Once during a family holiday in Algiers they witnessed the public degradation of a French officer on a vast parade ground. While a gaping crowd was held back by ropes, he put his men through their evolutions for the last time, standing alone with a white expressionless face. When he had given his last command his sword was taken from him and he was led away to prison. 'I wonder,' Elma commented,

> when he took us to see that condemned officer, whether he thought of his own military career, forcibly ended, not for a crime, nor for a racial blunder, but for a social one. We didn't know then about 'the Case.' We were too young to be told . . . I did not know that he too had been condemned, not to prison but to freedom; to boredom everlasting; an endless filling in of time.

Finding that her marriage was not working out as she had expected, Florence turned her attention to refurbishing the estates. She rebuilt most of the house at Altyre and redecorated it : there was a new dining-room with parquet floors, red walls and a white scrolled stucco ceiling, new gunrooms and nurseries and schoolroom, mosaic floors in the bathrooms and corridors. She added immense stables. 'Years afterwards,' Elma writes, 'I understood the bricks and mortar had been as drugs to Mother, soothing an unhappiness I didn't dream of.'

> Mother built a school and a church, turning the people very temporarily into Episcopalians; introduced games; gave school treats and Christmas trees. At Christmas each maid received two dress lengths, one of print and one of black serge; and each man a pair of boots. She knew everyone on the estate personally; helped the women to have their babies; replaced hovels by model cottages. And everybody had to behave exactly as she wanted them to. Employees had to go to church, marry their mistresses, keep sober. When they were ill the deserving poor got soup and blankets, but their lives were interfered with and their wages were small. It was a form of slavery run on philanthropic lines; a remainder of the feudal system. It so happens that Mother was exceptionally benevolent, but I don't think that made it a good system.

On Gordonstoun itself, the wings of which were said to be 800 years old – they were connected by seventeenth century staterooms – she had less of an impact : bathrooms and electric light did little to change the atmosphere of gloom and mystery, of dungeons and oubliettes, of secret rooms and hidden staircases in walls that in places were thirty feet thick – the ghosts still wandered as before, particularly that of an ancestor reputed to have been a wizard. She laid out an Italian garden, put panelling, a reredos and painted windows in the chapel.

She started a home in Elgin for children who had been ill-treated : after a few years it was discovered that the matron had run up huge bills for champagne and *pâté de foie gras* – booked as quaker oats and soap – to entertain her lover. The home was closed, and the children who could not be placed in other orphanages were brought to a cottage at Altyre. Meanwhile Papa went salmon fishing, or curling, not because he liked these occupations, but because they were expected of him. For the same reason he went to church where his manners put the family to shame :

> He would enter last of the family, alone, making his effect; breathe for thirty seconds into hat before placing it under the seat. He never knelt down; and during hymn or psalm-singing swung round to observe the congregation, staring at every pretty female if such could be found, and

waving his book with no pretence that it was open at the right place. Through the sermon he would ostentatiously open his watch every five minutes.

Art and music were never discussed : Papa had no interest in them, and Mother disapproved of anything that might arouse the children's emotions and lead them to make the same mistake that, she now believed, she had done. Their newspapers were the *Morning Post* and the *Bystander*, giving news of the people he had known, and the sporting weeklies describing the race meetings he could never attend.

Once His Royal Highness expressed a desire to see the children – he was lunching in Paris with their Aunt Lita, Madame de Breteuil, and learned they were in the house. Aunt Lita replied that as he had persecuted their parents with so much hatred he could not now inspect them as though they were specimens in an aquarium. Monsieur de Breteuil was one of his closest friends and most valued contacts in Paris. The Prince's love for France had never varied. When the empire of Napoleon III ended in the Franco-Prussian War, and revolution, he had welcomed the imperial family kindly when they sought refuge in England, but he continued to visit France, and made a friend of Gambetta, the Republican leader. He used his authority and skill as a diplomat to improve relations between the two countries, and he actively fostered *L'Entente Cordiale* – with the object of restraining German aggression.

From the time of the Tranby Croft scandal his popularity steadily increased, and when he came to the throne and reigned for nine years as Edward VII he was universally respected. People were able to identify themselves with his problems, his feelings, and his successes, as if they were their own : they understood him, and liked him, and sympathised with him. The days of personal autocratic rule were over. He presented in its place the image of a popular monarchy which, though still above the recriminations of party politics, no one felt as a threat or as a restraint on his personal liberty. It had become a tradition in which all shared, and it was an element of stability in the troubled years that followed. No doubt the fact that he had had to obey a summons to appear as a witness in the baccarat case like any other citizen, and that he had behaved in Court with unruffled dignity and good humour, contributed to that image.

Fifteen years after Florence's unconventional marriage, the American money failed to arrive. After an interval it started again at only half its former rate. They let Altyre with its excellent shooting 'for immense sums' Elma tells us, and went to live at Dawlish in Devon with only a few servants. The move had a bad effect on the family relationships. 'Papa shrank' with the leaving of Altyre, and his views and opinions were pushed more and more into the background. Mama gave up struggling not to be fat, and let herself go altogether. At thirty-six she talked of herself as being an old woman, and behaved as one. She got involved in local church activities and brought worthy women home to tea : Papa shocked them by his language, and drove them out again. Still, she made pathetic efforts to engage his interest such as cutting down a fine tree to make room for a croquet lawn, hoping that he would amuse himself there instead of straying to other pastures.

Mother must have known that all this Church talk and dowdiness was the surest means of cutting herself off from Papa, and yet as the years passed she seemed to set herself more and more deliberately against his way of being and living. It was as though she had given up trying . . . Then had come somewhere, somewhen – as in so many marriages -- the parting of the ways; the divergence of interests; the struggle to draw away the children. Mother had never really wanted a social or worldly existence; Papa had never in his heart cared for the estate or the tenants' welfare, had never been remotely 'churchy'. When he would not meet her ten per cent of the way, she decided not to meet him at all.

When he discovered that Elma, at eighteen, was in the throes of an innocent but intensely serious love affair with a married man he was highly indignant although he, at the same time, was pursuing someone else's daughter of exactly the same age in a manner that was far from innocent. Her mother took the affair even more seriously. She was so incensed when she learned that her daughter had been kissed and that her love letters had been filched and read by the servants, that Elma in desperation married the first eligible male that came along, with unhappy results. When her marriage was announced, the baccarat case became news again, and wherever she travelled she heard echoes of it, and people wanted to know what had really happened, and she couldn't tell them. One journal published her photograph describing her as 'the daughter of Lieutenant-Colonel Sir William Gordon-Cumming of Tranby Croft, which was surely the biggest gaff of the year.

Mother was fearful of sending us out into the world with the burden of scandal on our backs. When there was a question of Roly going into the navy, Aunt Lita asked the Queen whether King Edward was likely to vent his animosity on the younger generation. Her majesty replied doubtfully : 'You know, Bertie never forgives.'

In the event Roly, that is, the second son, Roualeyn, went to Osborne in the same term as 'Bertie's' grandson, and like him served in the Battle of Jutland which he found 'as exciting as a grouse shoot.' The third son, Michael, also joined the Navy, and all three survived the First World War. The eldest, Major Alastair Gordon-Cumming of the Queen's Own Cameron Highlanders, was awarded the Military Cross.

In 1922 Florence died, 'a very old woman,' at the age of fifty-two. She was buried at the Gordon-Cumming burying place near Gordonstoun. 'None of Mother's own family was present. She had come to Scotland alone, as an alien; and now, still alone, was committed to foreign soil.'

> No one ever understood Mother. Only as I grow older I come inevitably nearer to comprehension; am filled with sympathy. Worry and ill-health and disappointment make sad bedfellows with insomnia. It has been said that we all suffer equally in this world . . . I consider this theory as so much nonsense. How, for instance, can we – whose sons have merely died in battle – compare our petty hurts with those of Poles and Czechs and Jews who have seen their children starved and tortured. We have no right to a tear . . . Mother told me that she had had a very unhappy life, and probably it is true, but less by fact than by her thinking it so. She never had the big sorrows that I have had to face, who make no claim to an unusual share of slings and arrows. She never experienced the death of a child, nor, I believe, of any specially loved person. But if she thought she was unhappy, well then she was, and my heart goes out to her.

Elma's father died eight years later, at the age of eighty-one, after nearly forty years in exile.

> He never, not even when he was eighty, lost the touch of swagger in his walk, the hint of scorn for lesser mortals, the suggestion that he was irresistible. He had worn it for so long that neither trouble nor disgrace nor old age could change his habit . . . we had not supposed he was seriously ill, as indeed he was not. Only on that same Tuesday morning had Alastair suggested sending for a doctor, and Papa had said, 'I'm not going to croak, am I?' Half an hour later he was dead.

For two days he lay in state in the big hall at Altyre, and his people filed through to pay their respects.

> The tenantry at Altyre are convinced that his death will be followed by the public vindication of his honour, but so far no documents or messages have been found which in any way throw light on the unhappy incident. (*Daily Mail*)

> The death of Sir William Gordon-Cumming, after having lived 'outside society' for forty years as the result of a card scandal, is the end of a story

which reads like reopening the pages of a dusty three-volume novel. The man himself was tall, very handsome and strong. A friend who had served with him in the Egyptian campaign described him as like a hero in one of Ouida's novels. No luxury was too great for him at home, and no hardship too great for him in war. He was always high-spirited and much liked by his men. What happens when a man is 'cut by society'? In Gordon-Cumming's case it meant that he departed for ever from London life and the racecourses; hunting and fashionable Continental places saw him no more. He lived on his estate in Scotland, where his tenants and many of his neighbours disbelieved the whole Tranby Croft story that he had cheated at baccarat, and resented, with true clan spirit, the verdict of the south. (*Manchester Guardian*)

Perhaps because of the general dissatisfaction with the summing-up and the verdict, mystery still hangs about the case. Gordon-Cumming is felt to have been unjustly treated, and the legend began, and persists, that he was a scapegoat for – the Prince, of course, who else? It is frequently said that it was actually the Prince who had cheated – but this was never suggested at the time, nor is there the slightest foundation for it. It was not on account of any cheating by the Prince, but in the hope of avoiding a scandal in which he would be involved, that Gordon-Cumming can truly be said to have been made a scapegoat.

The rumour also persists that the Prince told the secret to Lady Brooke and that she let it out. She became known, therefore, as 'The Babbling Brooke' – but even if he did tell her, there is no reason to believe that she abused his confidence. Captain Somerset has pointed out that there were other guests at Tranby Croft, who had not signed any undertaking: they could not have failed to notice that something had happened. He thought it most likely that one of these guessed the truth and that one of the signatories, seeing that he appeared to know all about it, gave him the information.

Another story has filtered down to us through Gordon-Cumming's wife who related it to Elma; the suggestion that he was framed by the Prince 'for having cut out His Royal Highness with a certain lady' – and it is implied that this was Lady Brooke – 'and that somebody else,' Elma continues, 'a nobleman known to dislike my father, had been asked to stage the game and had indignantly refused.' What can be said about this? It is not surprising that in the long bitterness of his exile the possibility should have occurred to him that he had been the victim of a plot, but no further evidence about this has come to light. We can take it as a reminder that people's actual motives, conscious and unconscious, do not necessarily come to the surface in an affair of this kind.

Lady Brooke's feelings for him were expressed as follows in her autobiography : 'Sir William Gordon-Cumming, the smartest of men about town, was a constant friend, but he cut us all off in his retirement, and I often had sad thoughts of him, and always kept a warm corner in my heart for him.'

With Elma's own explanation we feel on surer ground : 'It didn't take the Baccarat Case to make enemies for my father. He had made them for himself long before; he had cuckolded so many husbands; been witty at the expense of so many fools . . . He was spoiled and he was arrogant, and it seemed that the world was at his feet. When the lion crashed, what wonder that the jackals fell upon him. It was the tragedy of my mother's life, its explanation, that in spite of all that she was able to give and do for him, he never ceased to hanker for that fashionable existence among the 'smart set' from which he had been driven forth.'

Sir Edward Clarke believed passionately in his innocence. 'The result of the case,' he says in *The Story of my Life*, 'greatly disappointed me. . . .'

> I thought it possible that when Sir William's evidence had been given the defendants would say they accepted his denial and would withdraw the idea of their justification. That course would not have saved my client from social ostracism. He had made many enemies, and society, with the leader of society at its head, would have refused to receive him. But it might have saved him, and the loyal and devoted lady who in the hour of his distress became his wife, and the innocent children of his marriage, from the shameful cruelty with which in later years they were pursued.
>
> Any counsel of experience distrusts his own judgement upon the merits of a case in which he has himself been advocate. But so many years have passed since the Baccarat case was tried that I think I am able now to form an unbiased opinion, and I think I ought to leave that opinion on record.
>
> I believe the verdict was wrong, and that Sir William Gordon-Cumming was innocent of the offence charged against him.

Elma, however, was not conscious of any cruelty She didn't know in her youth that the people who visited their house were not 'the right people', neither would she have cared. She had been taught early not to depend on fine friends in time of trouble.

Before he died, Sir Edward Clarke sent for Mrs Cecily Mure, Gordon-Cumming's youngest daughter, and assured her that her father was innocent. Careful consideration of the evidence has brought us to the same conclusion.

APPENDICES

I   The Forensic Flaws and Fables in the Baccarat Case

by Edward Grayson

During the seven years between 1970 and 1977, when Michael Havers and I were assessing, discussing, evaluating, researching, writing and rewriting the legal hard-core issues involved in this saga of Victorian High Society, in precious time snatched from our working lives as practising barristers, one issue alone required a compromise on professional attitudes. To what extent should and could we explain to non-legal readers the complex documentary machinery inherent in many civil lawsuits, and particularly slander actions?

In the end, in the best traditions of the camaraderie of the Bar, we merged our differences amicably with the explanation given at page 72 of the main text:

'Clarke had to make his opening speech in defence of his client without knowing what his opponents would say against him.'

As Junior Counsel I summarised the position a month after publication in November 1977, in an article entitled 'The Fascinating Forensic and Legal Issues in the Baccarat Case' *(Guardian Gazette, 21 December 1977)*. There I cited for practitioners the legal source of the hard-core pre-trial legal skirmishing reported formally in and as *Gordon-Cumming v Green and others* (1890-1), Vol. 7: *Times Law Reports, p.408.*

The preliminary judicial rulings denied to Gordon-Cumming's legal team full particulars of the Defendants' lawyers' plea of justification for the slander alleged against them. It was ruled that

as the charges stated by the plaintiff were specific as to time and place and also in character, it was unnecessary for the defendants to enter into any more detail than to say that they were true.

The minutiae of the allegations, crucial to proving the accusation, were to be undisclosed until trial of the action.

That non-disclosure was the first forensic flaw. It led to the second: how to deal with the undoubted fact that cheating at cards was — and still is — a criminal offence under section 17 of the Gaming Act 1845. Ordinarily the accusers would be required to testify prior to an accused person's evidence (if advised to give any) to establish guilt and thus rebut a plea of innocence. Thus, as p.196 of the text describes, Clarke

explained to the jury that he might have put the Wilsons in the witness-box first, in order to know all they had to say before calling upon Gordon-Cumming to answer; but he considered that when a man came into Court to defend his honour, his place was to stand in the witness box as soon as possible, there to meet any suggestion or accusation that might be raised against him, and there by prompt conduct, and the prompt denial of a gentleman, to clear himself from the accusation made against him.

Accordingly, the normal criminal trial procedure was reversed, within the framework of a civil claim for slander. The cheating charges were admitted, but pleaded to be justified. This did not undermine or diminish in any way at all the Wilsons' need to satisfy the high level of legal proof *beyond reasonable doubt* demanded in a criminal trial; and that led to the third legal flaw.

That level of criminal legal proof was never formulated by the judge's summing-up. Yet when all three were linked to the fourth legal flaw, the wrongfully allowed juryman's question to, and the equally wrongfully allowed answer of, the Prince of Wales, they led inexorably to but one conclusion. It was not surprising that the jury took only 13 minutes to deliver its verdict adverse to Gordon-Cumming.

On reflection it is arguable that the tactical decision to allow Gordon-Cumming to testify without knowing the details of the charges against him might have worked:

1   without the wrongfully permitted dialogue between the juryman and the Prince, and

2   with a fairer summing-up.

Linked to the departure from the usual sequence of testimonies in proving guilt and denying innocence, the flaws became fatal.

With hindsight, from the wrong end of a telescope after nearly a century's perspective, there was another legal route which might have achieved Gordon-Cumming's desired result to clear his name. For the signature under pressure opened up avenues for challenging the document in the High Court before a Chancery judge without a jury, under traditional legal categories which today are identified in the criminal law as evidence obtained by oppression; in the Queen's Bench Division common law courts as actions committed under duress; and in the equity courts as undue influence. Clarke in particular would have been familiar with the last-named form of relief. Four years earlier, during 1886, in the celebrated precedent still cited today of *Allcard v Skinner (1887) 36, Ch D. 145,* he had achieved a judgement under that head, for the purpose of setting aside certain disputed transactions.

If that route had been followed the action would have been heard before a Chancery judge with extensive documentary preparation. The burden of proof would have been argued in the restrained atmosphere of the equity courts without the emotional and non-responsive climate which faces counsel who have to try and persuade an impassively faced tribunal of 12 laypersons, guided or, as in the Baccarat Case, misguided, by the trial judge on issues of law.

Indeed, while the manuscript was being prepared for the first edition of this book, its working title was *Undue Influence*. Later, consideration was given to *Conduct Unbecoming* — which, certainly, much of the activity on each night at Tranby Croft appeared to be. That title, however, was pre-empted by a celebrated play and film under the direction of Mr Val May who, at the time of writing in late 1987, was preparing the dramatised version of *The Royal Baccarat Scandal* by Royce Ryton, based upon the book's text.

The flaws which led to the jury's verdict have doubtless contributed to the fables which it has spawned. They are illustrated by traceable sources, eminent in their own spheres, but without the pooled experiences which have led to practitioners' conclusions in 1977 confirming those of Sir Edward Clarke cited on p.270 of this text.

Sir Philip Magnus's judgement on Gordon-Cumming in his biography *King Edward the Seventh,* that 'he was guilty, predatory and mean', so far as the jury's verdict is concerned, is a classic example of a leading historian straying beyond his boundaries into a territory outside his province and sphere of knowledge. His *Author's Note* does not identify any legal source who was consulted.

Another commentary claimed, 'There was no law in the case — it was a straight issue of fact. Did Gordon-Cumming cheat?' As an issue that was correct. As a statement of law it was wrong, as this Appendix indicates.

Curiously, that error directs attention to yet another flaw, one of practice and preparation for trial rather than legal analysis. It was raised by one of Gordon-Cumming's kinsmen, who has achieved high judicial office during our own time, while addressing young practitioners and students at a celebratory dinner of the Hardwicke Society in Middle Temple Hall, when the manuscript of this book was in its earliest drafts. Sir Roualeyn Cumming-Bruce, as Lord Justice Cumming-Bruce, alluded to the book's preparation with the comment: 'If any of you young people contemplates calling the Prince of Wales as a witness, do make certain that you have a proof of evidence, so that you know what he will say in the witness-box.'

II Playing the Game, and Betting at Baccarat

by Edward Grayson

Baccarat, as played at Tranby Croft or elsewhere, is a variation of many other card games: Blackjack, *Chemin de Fer,* Pontoon, *Vingt-et-un* — in the same way that Association Football is linked historically with Rugby Football and its different permutations of Rugby Union and professional and amateur Rugby League. Furthermore, consistent with football's worldwide appeal, Baccarat is described in the standard work on indoor games, *Hoyle's Games Modernised* (first published in 1742), in its twentieth edition in 1950, as 'the most popular of all card games'.

It is also, however, a game of chance. In his opening address to the jury, Sir Edward Clarke commented: 'It seems to me to be about the most unintelligent mode of losing your own money, or getting somebody else's, I ever heard of' (See p.73 of main text.) This is echoed on p.148 of the twentieth edition of *Hoyle*:

Although from a bare description it may sound stupid and uninteresting, it needs but a single experiment in actual play to prove its charm and fascination — that is of course from a gambling point of view.

That charm and fascination was synthesised in 1955 by the Senior Steward-elect of the Jockey Club, Lord Willoughby de Broke, MC – AFC, in a Foreword to *The Hill Story* — an account of the William Hill organisation — when he wrote:

> One of the strongest characteristics of the British is the love of wagering, and of 'backing one's fancy'. This is not entirely due, as the anti-gamblers would have it, to a desire to get 'easy money' without working for it, but rather to a wish to support one's opinion about a particular sport in a practical manner, and to pit one's wits and judgement against those of other people.

Unlike racing and all other sports, Baccarat has no universal governing body, or even rules of the game. Played privately or in casinos throughout the world, its form has varied in detail dependent upon the particular country or gaming house in which it has flourished. Nevertheless, there is a principle common to the version played at Tranby Croft and its associated card games.

The players are opposed to an appointed banker, and the object of the game itself is for the player to beat the banker's card-holding without exceeding a specific number. Thus, twenty-one is the figure for Pontoon; nine is the number for Baccarat.

As played at Tranby Croft, four packs of fifty-two cards each, comprising 208, are shuffled and placed in front of the banker, in that case the Prince of Wales. The players flank the banker, an equal number on each side. The numbers vary, but at Tranby Croft, there were only two cardholders and players. The remainder of the players hold no cards, but simply bet on those held by the players on either side of the banker.

The scoring method of Baccarat has always been as far as possible to meet the number nine, with tens and court cards not registering. Thus $5 + 4 = 9$; or $5 + 3 = 8$. Further details are explained on p.27 of the main text.

The key issue, of course, in the Baccarat case, was the staking or betting *system*. All bets must be placed on the table before the cards are dealt. Gordon-Cumming's method of play was the *coup de trois*. That, too, is explained on p.27, and also in Gordon-Cumming's evidence cited on p.78:

> 'When I stake a £5 counter and win, that would represent £10, and I should then add a third counter in front of me, which would represent a second coup of £15.'

At the heart of the case was whether or not Gordon-Cumming added to his stake after the cards were called. Americans call this 'sugaring the bet'. When an intended cheat wins, he reaches out to count how many chips or counters he has placed, but the real purpose is to deposit an additional counter on top of his original bet *(How to Cheat at Cards,* A D. Livingston, 1973).

This was rejected emphatically by the proprietor of *Truth*, Labouchère, as we have seen in the citation on pp.241-3, shortly after the trial in June 1891. His anger at the verdict fired his instructions for the savage cartoon for the Christmas edition which has inspired the cover for this new edition. Indeed, when one considers his own judgement:

I say as an expert that never is cheating done in this fashion. . . I cannot conceive the most dishonest of human beings staking one large bright coloured counter and then adding two to it; nor can I conceive this palpable manoeuvre being performed several times without the banker and several of the punters perceiving it . . .

two final thoughts are inevitable.

If Labouchère or any other card-playing expert had been called as a witness to testify for Gordon-Cumming, would the jury, mesmerised by the Prince of Wales' presence, and seduced by Coleridge's blatantly biased summing-up, have arrived at a different verdict than it did? And was this the most fatal forensic flaw of them all?

Source Notes

The extracts from the accounts of eye-witnesses in the chapters covering the hearing of the case are from the *Pall Mall Gazette, Pall Mall Budget, Star Daily News,* the *Morning Advertisers, Globe, Standard, Reynold's News, Daily Chronicle, Illustrated London News, Graphic, St. James's Gazette* etc. Those who wish to read the details will find them fully set out in the newspapers of the first week in June 1891.

Chapter One : The Wilsons of Hull
1 *Pall Mall Budget,* 4th June 1881.
2 Ibid
3 Princess Marie Louise : *My Memories of Six Reigns,* pp. 140-1.
4 Frances Countess of Warwick : *Afterthoughts.*
5 Osbert Sitwell : *Left Hand, Right Hand,* p. 224

Chapter Two : A Game of Baccarat
1 *Echo :* 2nd June 1891
2 *Doncaster Gazette* : 12th September, 1890
3 Bulmer : *History and Directory of East Yorkshire.*
4. Christopher Sykes : *Four Studies in Loyalty.*

Chapter Three : An Appeal to the Royal Courts of Justice.
1,2,3, Royal Archives Y 182/27.
4 Royal Archives Y 182/28.
5,6,7 Royal Archives Y 182/27.
8 Royal Archives Y 182/5.
9 Royal Archives Y 182/8.
10 Royal Archives Y 182/22.
11 Royal Archives Y 182/5.
12 Royal Archives Y 182/28.
13 Royal Archives Y 182/27.

Chapter Four : Behind the Scenes.
1 *Strand Magazine,* Vol. VI 645ff.
2 C.P.L. Du Cann in the *Star,* 28th January 1959.
3 Frances Countess of Warwick : *Life's Ebb and Flow,* p. 195
4 R. Barry O'Brien : *Lord Russell of Kilowen,* p. 128.
5, 6 Royal Archives Y 182/27

7 Royal Archives Y 182/4.

8 Royal Archives Y 182/5.

9, 10 Royal Archives Y 182/27.

11 Royal Archives Add. MSS A. 12/1752.

12 Royal Archives Y 182/10.

13 *Pall Mall Gazette*, 17th February 1891.

14 Royal Archives Y 182/10.

15 Royal Archives Add. MSS A 12/1752.

16 Royal Archives Add. MSS A 12/1755.

17 Royal Archives Y 182/22.

18 Royal Archives Y 182/18.

19 Royal Archives Add. MSS A/12.

20 *New York Times*, 8th February 1881.

21 Royal Archives Y 182/27.

22 *Pall Mall Gazette*, 17th February 1891.

23, 24 Royal Archives Add. MSS U. 32.

25 *Echo*, 17th March 1891.

26 *The Life of Sir Edward Clarke* by Walker-Smith and Clarke, p. 54.

27 R. Barry O'Brien : *Lord Russell of Killowen*, p. 33.

28 Edward Abinger : *Forty Years at the Bar*, p. 75.

29 R. Barry O'Brien, *Lord Russell of Killowen*, p. 101.

30 Fordham : *Notable Cross-examinations,* p. 194.

Chapter Five : Standing Room Only.

1 Royal Archives Add. MSS A/12.

Chapter Six : The Prince in the Witness-box.

1 Frank Harris : *My Life and Loves.*

Chapter Nine. A Star Performer.

1 Royal Archives Add. MSS A/4.

2, 3 Royal Archives Add. MSS U 32.

Chapter Ten : 'This is not a Theatre !'

1 Heber Hart : *Reminiscences and Reflections*, p. 23.

2 Heber Hart : *Reminiscences and Reflections*, p. 24.

3 Sir Edward Clarke : *The Story of my Life*, p. 297.

Chapter Eleven : A Question of Honour.

1 Royal Archives Y 182/28.

2 Sir Edward Clarke : *The Story of my Life*, p. 296.

3 Royal Archives Y 182/27.

Chapter Twelve : A Chorus of Condemnation.

1 Quoted by H. Montgomery Hyde, in *Their Good Names*, p. 166.

2 Royal Archives Geo V AA 19/10.

3 Royal Archives Add. MSS A/4.
4 Magnus : *King Edward the Seventh*, p. 229.
5 Royal Archives Y 182/28.
6 Quoted by Anita Leslie in *Edwardians in Love*, p. 88.
7 Royal Archives Add. MSS U. 32.
8 E. F. Benson : *As We Were*, p. 216.

Chapter Thirteen : An Outcast from Society.
1 Walker-Smith and Clarke : *The Life of Sir Edward Clarke* 227-30.
For references to Sir William and Lady Gordon-Cumming, see Elma Napier's *Youth is a Blunder* and *Winter is in July*.

Select Bibliography

Abinger, Edward : *Forty Years at the Bar.* N.D.
Anonymous : *Uncensored Recollections*, 1924.
More Uncensored Recollections, 1926.
Benson, E.F. *As We Were*, 1930.
King Edward VII, 1933.
Final Edition, 1940.
Birkenhead, The Right Hon. the Earl of : *Contemporary Personalities*, 1924.
Blyth, Henry : *Skittles*, 1970.
Bowker, A.E. *A Lifetime with the Law*, 1961.
Bulmer : *History and Directory of East Yorkshire*, 1892.
Clarke, Sir Edward, K.C. *The Story of my Life*, 1918.
Coleridge, Ernest Hartley : *The Life and Correspondence of John Duke Coleridge, Lord Chief Justice of England*, 1904.
Cowles, Virginia : *Edward VII and his Circle*, 1956.
Escott, T.H.S. *King Edward and his Court*, 1903.
Fordham, E.W. *Notable Cross examinations*, 1951.
Fulford, Roger : *The Prince Consort*, 1949.
Graham, Evelyn : *Fifty Famous Judges*, N.D.
Fielding, Daphne : *The Duches of Jermyn Street.*
Girouard, Mark : *Victorian Country Houses*, 1971.
Harris, Frank : *My Life and Loves*, 1964.
Hart, Heber, L. *Reminiscences and Reflections*, 1939.
Hastings, Sir Patrick : *Famous and Infamous Cases*, 1950.
Hyde, H. Montgomery : *Their Good Names*, 1970.
Lee, Sir Sidney : *King Edward VII*, 1925-7.
Leslie, Anita : *Edwardians in Love*, 1972.
Jennie, 1964.
Magnus, Philip : *King Edward the Seventh*, 1964.
Marie Louis, Princess : *My Memories of Six Reigns*, 1956.
Maurois, André : *King Edward and His Times*, Trans. Miles, 1933.
Napier, Elma : *Youth is a Blunder*, 1948.
Winter is in July, 1949.
O'Brien, R. Barry : *The Life of Lord Russell of Killowen*, 1901.
Pearson, John : *Edward the Rake*, 1975.
Ponsonby, Arthur : *Henry Ponsonby, His Life from His Letters*, 1942.
Ponsonby, F. *Recollections of Three Reigns*, 1951.
Portland, the Duke of : *Men, Women and Things*, 1937.

Roby, Kinley : *The King, the Press and the People*, 1975.

Shore, W. Teignmouth (Ed) : *The Baccarat Case* : *Gordon-Cumming v. Wilson and Others*, 1932.

Sitwell, Osbert : *Left Hand, Right Hand*, 1945.

Sykes, Christopher : *Four Studies in Loyalty*, 1946.

Tingston, H. *Victoria and the Victorians*, Trans Grey, 1972.

Walker-Smith and Clarke : *The Life of Sir Edward Clarke*, 1939.

Warwick, Frances Countess of :   *Life's Ebb and Flow*, c 1929.
                                    Afterthoughts N.D.

Welcome, John : *Cheating at Cards*, 1963.

Wyndham, Horace : *The Mayfair Calender*, N.D.

Wortham, H.E. *The Delightful Profession*, 1931.

Index